Fairbairn, Then and Now

W. R. D. Fairbairn, Ph.D. in his consulting room
in Edinburgh, Scotland, about 1955
(photograph by his son Nicholas)

Fairbairn, Then and Now

RELATIONAL PERSPECTIVES BOOK SERIES

STEPHEN A. MITCHELL AND LEWIS ARON
Series Editors

Fairbairn

THEN AND NOW

edited by

Neil J. Skolnick ◆ David E. Scharff

THE ANALYTIC PRESS

1998   Hillsdale, NJ   London

Published by
The Analytic Press, Inc.
     Editorial Offices:
     101 West Street
     Hillsdale, New Jersey 07642

Index by Leonard S. Rosenbaum

Library of Congress Cataloging-in-Publication Data

Fairbairn, then and now / edited by Neil J. Skolnick, David E. Scharff.
        p.   cm — (Relational perspectives book series : v. 10)
     Proceedings of a conference held Oct. 4–6, 1996, at the New York
Academy of Medicine.
     Includes bibliographical references and index.
     ISBN 0-88163-262-7
     1. Object relations (Psychoanalysis)   2. Psychoanalysis.   3. Fairbairn, W.
Ronald D. (William Ronald Dodds).   I. Skolnick, Neil J.   II. Scharff,
David E., 1941–   .   III. Series.
     [DNLM: 1. Psychoanalytic Theory—congresses.
WM 460 F163 1998]
BF 175.5.024F37   1998
150. 19'5—dc21
DNLM/DLC
for Library of Congress   97-47789
                                                                                    CIP

Printed in the United States of America

10   9   8   7   6   5   4   3   2   1

Contents

Part 1   Historical Connections

Part 2   Theoretical Connections: To the Past

Part 3 Theoretical Connections: To the Future

Part 4 Artistic Connections

Part 5 Clinical Connections

Contributors

Hilary J. Beattie, Ph.D. is Assistant Clinical Professor of Medical Psychology, Department of Psychiatry, Columbia University; Faculty, Columbia University Center for Psychoanalytic Training and Research.

Ellinor Fairbairn Birtles, B.A. (Hons.) provides supervision for volunteers working on the Great Ormond Street Hospital section of the National Child Death Helpline (U.K.); Co-Editor, *From Instinct to Self: Selected Papers of W. R. D. Fairbairn.*

David P. Celani, Ph.D. is Author, *The Treatment of the Borderline Patient: Applying Fairbairn's Object Relations Theory in the Clinical Setting* and *The Illusion of Love: Why the Battered Woman Returns to Her Abuser.*

Jody Messler Davies, Ph.D. is Supervising Analyst and Co-Chair, Relational Track, New York University Postdoctoral Program in Psychoanalysis and Psychotherapy; Associate Editor, *Psychoanalytic Dialogues: A Journal of Relational Perspectives.*

James S. Grotstein, M.D. is Clinical Professor of Psychiatry, UCLA School of Medicine; Training and Supervising Analyst, Los Angeles Psychoanalytic Society/Institute.

J. Alan Harrow, R.N. is Director and Training Analyst, Scottish Institute of Human Relations.

Otto F. Kernberg, M.D. is Professor of Psychiatry, Cornell University Medical College; Supervising and Training Analyst, Columbia University Center for Psychoanalytic Training and Research.

Steven Z. Levine, Ph.D. is Leslie Clark Professor in the Humanities, Department of History of Art, Bryn Mawr College, PA; Author, *Monet, Narcissus, and Self-Reflection: The Modernist Myth of the Self.*

Stephen A. Mitchell, Ph.D. is Editor, *Psychoanalytic Dialogues: A Journal of Relational Perspectives;* Author, *Influence and Autonomy in Psychoanalysis* (The Analytic Press, 1997).

Richard L. Rubens, Ph.D. is Faculty and Supervisor, William Alanson White Institute; Adjunct Professor, Clinical Psychology Doctoral Program, Teachers College, Columbia University.

David E. Scharff, M.D. (ed.) is Clinical Professor of Psychiatry, Georgetown University; Co-Director, International Institute of Object Relations Theory.

Jill Savege Scharff, M.D. is Co-Director, International Institute of Object Relations Theory; Editor, *The Autonomous Self: The Work of John D. Sutherland.*

Jeffrey Seinfeld, D.S.W. is Professor, New York University School of Social Work; Private Consultant, Jewish Board of Family and Children's Services.

Neil J. Skolnick, Ph.D. (ed.) is Associate Professor, Ferkauf Graduate School of Psychology, Yeshiva University, NY; Faculty and Supervisor, New York University Postdoctoral Program in Psychoanalysis and Psychotherapy.

Introduction

David E. Scharff and Neil J. Skolnick

In 1952, Ernest Jones wrote in his introduction to Fairbairn's *Psychoanalytic Studies of the Personality*:

> Instead of starting, as Freud did, from stimulation of the nervous system proceeding from excitation of various erotogenous zones and internal tension arising from gonadic activity, Dr. Fairbairn starts at the centre of the personality, the ego, and depicts its strivings and difficulties in its endeavor to reach an object where it may find support. . . . All this constitutes a fresh approach in psycho-analysis which should lead to much fruitful discussion [p. v].

W. R. D. Fairbairn brought an original voice and formulation to psychoanalysis. His theoretical contributions have guided the revolution in psychoanalysis during the past 25 years although they have often done so without specific recognition or attribution (Greenberg and Mitchell, 1983; Sutherland, 1989; Scharff and Birtles, 1994). They have contributed to the widespread application of analysis to the study of the self, trauma and multiple personality, infant development, marriage and the family, religion and pastoral care, as well as to the understanding of groups, institutions, and society, to a psychology of the arts, and to an evolution in the philosophical understanding of human experience. Fairbairn's ideas have passed from being little known to being general assumptions without ever being widely and distinctly acknowledged.

The conference that occasioned the writing of the papers published in this volume was our attempt to recognize Fairbairn's importance and to explore the implications of his seminal contributions for psychoanalysis, psychotherapy, the arts, and the philosophy of science.

Fairbairn's Object Relations Theory of the Personality

Fairbairn worked in relative isolation in Edinburgh, Scotland. Despite periodic contacts with many of the major figures in British analysis during the 1940s and 1950s, his geographical separation from London and the British, European, and American analytic worlds may have kept his ideas from achieving greater recognition, although, paradoxically, it may have also helped preserve his independence in theory building.

Early on, the heart of Fairbairn's work became an intrinsic, accepted core of the thinking of the Independent Group of British analysts whose prominent members included Balint, Winnicott, Sutherland, and Bowlby. His work was of immediate interest to Melanie Klein (1946) and her followers, as was hers to him. But, whereas Klein remained always dedicated to Freud's drive theories, Fairbairn altered his orientation fundamentally to a relational perspective, beginning with his 1940 paper on schizoid phenomena and doing so completely with his 1944 paper on endopsychic structure. His shift from Freud's topographical, impulse, and structural models to a psychology based on the need for and internalization of relationships gave a theoretical basis to the centrality of the therapeutic relationship and therefore helped lead to the Kleinian school's introduction of countertransference as a central tool in analysis (Heimann, 1950; Joseph 1989) and to the modern literature on the use of the therapist's subjective experience and of countertransference (Jacobs, 1991; Scharff and Scharff, 1998). Fairbairn's understanding of the importance of the relationship with the mother and family in infant and child development preceded Winnicott's and Bowlby's expansion of ideas in this realm and largely set the climate in which those writers developed their contributions. Fairbairn brought to his own writing a careful study of Freud's major contributions and a dedication to logical thought that had grown out of his own philosophical training—a history that Ellinor Fairbairn Birtles's paper in this volume elaborates.

Fairbairn's early writing and teaching were unpublished until 1994 (Scharff and Birtles, 1994). In the years from 1928 to 1930, he explored Freud's contribution focusing on psychic structure, instinct theory, and the nature of repression. In his studies of psychic structure, Fairbairn (1928) identified logical inconsistencies inherent in Freud's postulates. It was logically inconsistent, Fairbairn wrote, to say that the ego grows out of the id but is in fundamental opposition to it, as it was to assert a similar opposition of the superego to the ego. In his lecture notes on the superego, Fairbairn (1929a) explored Freud's (1923) account of the relationship between the three structures. Fairbairn's argument hinges on the primitive nature of the Freudian superego and its functioning as both a conscious and an unconscious phenomenon and as both agent and subject of repression. His own clinical experience demonstrated that Freud had mistaken psychic functions and phenomena for structures. Instead, he followed Freud's account of the development of the superego as analogous to a process of object identification, but he added that this development is associated with "sentiment formation," a first step along the path of locating the central role of affects in object relations. It was in these lectures that Fairbairn first used the term organized self instead of the term ego, an initial step on the road to personalizing endopsychic structure, in which Guntrip (1969) later took the lead. In his study of the relationship between repression and dissociation, Fairbairn (1929b) wrote that repression was a special instance of the general process of dissociation, being specifically the dissociation of unpleasant experience.

Fairbairn's Object Relations Theory

Between 1940 and 1944, Fairbairn wrote the series of papers that form the heart of the only book he published in his lifetime, *Psychoanalytic Studies of the Personality* (1952). In the first of the papers, "Schizoid Factors in the Personality" (1940), he described splitting in the personality. That paper was followed by "A Revised Psychopathology of the Psychoses and Psychoneuroses" (1941), in which he based the framework of psychopathology on the vicissitudes of dependence. He thought that the total dependence of the newborn takes a gradual path to the mature dependence of the adult personality. An individual is necessarily dependent on relationships with others for this process to occur. Each person begins with dependence on the parents, which gradually extends to a wider support group and eventually to the dependence we all have on culture and society. Fairbairn (1941) described mature dependence as "a capacity on the part of the differentiated individual for cooperative relationships with differentiated objects" (p. 145). In this paper, Fairbairn went on to describe various syndromes—hysteria, phobias, obsessive disorder, and paranoia—as varying techniques for handling internal object relationships during the transition from infantile dependence to mature dependence.

The third paper of the collection, "The Repression and Return of Bad Objects (with Special Reference to the 'War Neuroses')" (1943) described the dedication of the ego to painful object relationships lest it lose part of itself. These painful part-object relations are split off and repressed, but they continue to press for a return to consciousness. Fairbairn explained that children persistently blame themselves for bad experiences so that they can maintain the object as good and maximize the chance of being loved. If the object is seen as bad, then nothing the child can do, not even atonement for badness, will secure love—a condition he termed "unconditional badness." But, if the child sees itself as bad and the object as good, there is a chance for being loved if only the child can right himself—"conditional badness."

By 1944, Fairbairn was able to formulate his object relations theory almost completely. In "Endopsychic Structure Considered in Terms of Object-Relationships" (1944), he wrote that the infant is born with an initially integral but undifferentiated self or ego. In the face of inevitable dissatisfactions with the mother's handling, the infant incorporates the object as a first defense to deal with the pain of frustration. Now faced with the problem of having a painfully rejecting object inside, however, the central part of the ego—or Central Ego—splits off and represses those aspects of the object still felt to be intolerably painful. Fairbairn added that a part of the ego itself is always split off in conjunction with these part-objects and that this constellation of ego and object is characterized by the affective tone of the problematic relationship, which cannot be borne in consciousness. He described the fate of ego and object constellations organized around persecution and rejection, which he termed a relationship between the Internal Saboteur (the ego component) and the Rejecting Object. (He later called these the Antilibidinal Ego and the Rejecting Object.) The other class of painful object relationship is that between the Libidinal Ego and Libidinal Object—described as a relationship built around the excessive excitement of need, that is, the part of the mother felt to taunt with false promise, hover anxiously, or act seductively. The Central Ego itself acts to repress both the rejecting object constellation and the libidinal object constellation, because they are too painful to be borne in consciousness.

Later Fairbairn (1954) supplemented his model by adding that there was a parallel relationship between Central Ego and an Ideal Object—that aspect of the object not subject to repression. In the case of the hysteric, the Ideal Object is shorn of sexuality and aggression and is left a neutralized and rather barren object. The complete endopsychic structure is, therefore, made up of six subparts that are in dynamic relation to each other through repression and mutual influence. Fairbairn (1944) further noted that even the object parts of the self are actually ego structures and therefore are capable of initiating psychic action

(p. 132), a situation illustrated when patients act in identification with the way they felt as children when treated unsatisfactorily by their parents.

Figure 1 provides a synopsis of Fairbairn's six-part structure of the personality.

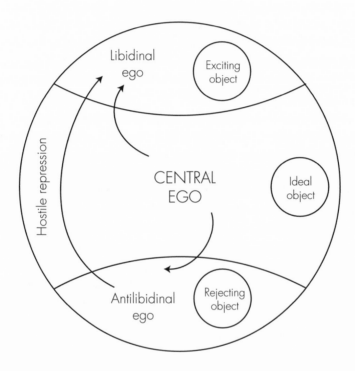

Fig. 1. Fairbairn's Object Relations Theory of Personality. From D. E. Scharff, *The Sexual Relationship*. London: Routledge, 1982.

Finally, Fairbairn described the way the internal ego and object structures exert dynamic influence on each other. The situation he described specifically involved what he called Secondary Repression of Libidinal Ego and Libidinal Object by the Antilibidinal Ego. This situation, indicated by an arrow in Figure l, exists in patients who use anger to cover up the unrequited longing of the libidinal object constellation and are more comfortable taking an angry stance toward objects than they are with painfully unsatisfied longing.

Although Fairbairn did not describe the parallel situation, we can see that the libidinal ego can also secondarily repress the antilibidinal relationship, as represented in a patient who shows an exaggerated sense of love and hope in order to mask resentful anger, which is even more painful to him. Fairbairn led us to see that all internal structures are in constant dynamic interaction with each other, a dynamic that is more fluid in health than in pathology, where it tends to become fixed or frozen in one or another pattern.

In "Endopsychic Structure" (1944) and later in his paper "On the Nature of Hysterical States" (1954), Fairbairn also redefined the oedipal situation: It is not dependent, he thought, on a castration complex or on the possession or lack of a penis, or even on active or passive sexual characteristics. Instead, the oedipal problem is based on the original deprivation of the baby abandoned on the hillside (1954, pp. 27–29), a deprivation associated with parental neglect and the child's frustration. Sexual development depends not on childhood fantasies, but on the child's understanding of the dependence relationship as involving exciting and rejecting objects projected into sexual parts of the body. Gender and sexual orientation depend on both identification and object seeking. Maturity for Fairbairn is not the result of a sexual genitality that infuses the personality, but is the ability of a mature individual to relate to another whole person who is understood to have genitals. It is the parents' mature responsiveness to the child's needs that predisposes that child to future mental health, rather than a relatively isolated aspect of sexual development.

Fairbairn believed that the genetic and constitutional makeup of an individual is important, but for him such development combines with actual experience. The biological aspects of personality—the drives—achieve meaning only within the structure of relationships. Therefore personality is the outcome of continuous encounters between constitutional factors and external reality.

Fairbairn took as his beginning point an ego—which we might now call an unformed inherent potential to become a self (Sutherland, 1994)—that is intrinsically structured from the beginning to seek relationships with important sustaining figures. Within the sustenance of these relationships, the infant and growing child takes into its psyche experiences that are painfully frustrating and those that are satisfying. As the child does this, its psyche is organized by this introjection of objects and by a splitting of the ego or self into units of relational structures. In the process, the child constructs an internal reality that mirrors external reality. The mind is thus made up of structures that contain prior relational experience, although these structures are heavily modified by the intrinsic process of the structuring itself—by the limitations of the child's capacity to understand at the time experience is taken in and by the distortions and modifications introduced by developmental issues and the biases of prior experience. Once inner reality is thus established, it monitors and influences external reality and relationships in a never-ending cycle in which it also continues to be modified by these external relationships.

In his only paper on the meaning of object relations theory for the clinical situation, Fairbairn (1958) noted the fixity that occurs when patients attempt to maintain internal patterns as defensive, closed systems, attempting to bar continual interaction with and feedback from others. In other words, patients try to keep their inner worlds as closed systems. This attempt presents to the therapist as resistance, which Fairbairn thought emanated not from internal conflict between mental structures or from an attempt to make the unconscious conscious. He thought that resistance stemmed from patients' reluctance to show parts of their internal reality to the therapist, an unwillingness to give up parts of their internally organized selves:

> I have now come to regard . . . *the greatest of all sources of resistance [to be] the maintenance of the patient's internal world as a closed*

*system. . . . [I]t becomes still another aim of psychoanalytical treatment
to effect breaches of the closed system which constitutes the patient's
inner world, and thus to make this world accessible to the influence of
outer reality* [p. 84].

Under these circumstances, the patient feels that psychoanalysis is an assault on the closed system of the inner world
and turns his resistance toward the person of the analyst, who
he feels is responsible for the assault.

Fairbairn (1958) came to realize that it is the relationship
between patient and therapist that is the really decisive factor for
growth and change, not, as others had considered, the isolated
factors of exact interpretation, genetic reconstruction, transference interpretation, or any particular technical recommendations
separated from the relationship between patient and therapist.

> In my own opinion, the really decisive factor is the relationship
> of the patient to the analyst, and it is upon this relationship
> that the other factors . . . . depend not only for their effective-
> ness, but for their very existence, since in the absence of a ther-
> apeutic relationship with the analyst, they simply do not occur
> [pp. 82–83].

This theoretical shift has now moved even further in contemporary psychoanalysis to emphasize the person of the analyst
and the use of the analyst's subjective experience as a fundamental therapeutic tool (Joseph, 1989; Jacobs, 1991). Before
Fairbairn, analysts thought they should be impersonal projection screens, striving to be technically correct and uninvolved.
Fairbairn's focus on relatedness showed that relationships are at
the center of psychoanalytic theory and practice.

The chapters that form this book elaborate on Fairbairn's
contribution in many ways. Part 1 introduces the reader to a
historical and philosophical context within which to place
Fairbairn's contributions. J. Alan Harrow provides an illuminat-
ing account of the historical connection from Suttie to Fairbairn
to Sutherland. He offers a sense of the uniquely Scottish philosophical climate that gave context to their ground breaking

theories. He distills the issues connecting Fairbairn's ideas to those of Suttie before him and Sutherland after. We see in Suttie's thinking the origins of Fairbairn's placing a striving for human connection as primary and not as derivative of sexuality. Furthermore we find in Suttie the beginnings of Fairbairn's emphasis on environmental failures as the underpinning of psychopathology. Moving forward in time, we find Sutherland (who was an analysand, disciple, and friend of Fairbairn's) extending Fairbairn's emphasis on the inherent wholeness of the self to the societal level. For Sutherland, individuals, in order to promote the integrity of the self, not only seek relationships with singular others but seek to create relatedness with progressive levels of organizations (e.g., with family, group, and community). Like Fairbairn, Sutherland stresses the open nature of the system between the self and the environment as each influences and changes the nature of the other while also maintaining continuity.

In a discussion with David Scharff, Otto Kernberg describes the influence of Fairbairn's thought on his own. He was made aware of Fairbairn's work through contact with Sutherland at the Menninger Clinic and found that Fairbairn, like Edith Jacobson, put the relational capacity of individuals at the center of psychoanalytic theory. This interview demonstrates the range of Kernberg's knowledge and highlights those elements of Fairbairn's contribution which he has found most useful. The interview is also notable for Kernberg's personal style.

Ellinor Fairbairn Birtles, Fairbairn's daughter and a student of the history of ideas, describes how Fairbairn's contribution forms a connection among scientific, philosophical, and psychoanalytic ideas "and above all [provides] a model which fulfills the criteria required by modern versions of these three disciplines" (Birtles, this volume). Noting the dedication to logical thought that he brought to his theorizing and that was honed during his training in philosophy, she focuses on several of his pivotal concepts, their philosophical heritage, and their complementarity with modern paradigmatic systems of thought. She clearly distinguishes between Freud's philosophical heritage in the mind–body dualism of the Platonic tradition and Fairbairn's Aristotelian roots in the dialectic account of human nature, within which the individual is seen as striving for integration and reciprocity. Hegel presented a 19th-century derivative of Aristotle, especially emphasizing the dialectic exchange between self and other in the development of man's capability for language and thought. Birtles focuses on the antecedents of Fairbairn's ideas in the psychological accounts of Hegel. Fairbairn's switch in emphasis from Freud's motivational theory based on drive gratification to one based on a primary need for love and the acceptance of love, his stress on infantile dependence, and his descriptions of ego splitting can all be traced to counterparts in Hegelian thought. Birtles also describes Fairbairn's theory as an outgrowth of 20th-century models of science as they have been influenced by Einstein, Heisenberg, Planck, and others. These models are built on the interchangeability of matter and energy, and content and structure. They conceptualize truth as relative, as existing in the relationship between the observed and the observer. Here we may find the roots of Fairbairn's paradigmatic shift to a consideration of psychological structure in dynamic relationship with matters of content and energy, thereby doing away with the artificial distinction between id and ego.

Psychoanalytic theories, particularly when presenting radical alternatives, typically pay respectful homage to their theoretical forebears. Part 2 of this volume provides a consideration of some of the primary psychoanalytic antecedents of Fairbairn's thought and suggest interesting possibilities for an integration of his thinking with those he seemingly opposed. In a particularly stunning fashion, Jody Messler Davies, collapsing a century of psychoanalytic history, reminds us that contemporary models of the mind that focus on the ongoing dialectic between integration and dissociation, between fragmentation and renegotiation of psychic structure and meaning, obtain their theoretical heritage in pre-Freudian, preanalytic theories of mental structure, particularly as put forth in the work of Pierre Janet. Furthermore, she credits Fairbairn with providing, in his concept of endopsychic structure, a "significant nodal linchpin" uniting preanalytic psychologies with contemporary relational and constructivist models of the mind. We can discern in Fairbairn's concept of endopsychic structure, with its dynamic interplay of split-off self and object interactions, the influence of Janet's emphasis on the tendency of dissociative processes to result in split-off aspects of personality that operate as autonomous centers of awareness and initiative.

An implicit goal in much of relational theorizing today is to provide an integration of the work of theorists who come from different theoretical heritages but who emphasize the primacy of relational issues in their work. The intersecting points of agreement are brought to the forefront. The irreconcilable aspects of the theories are typically relegated to the background, or, as James Grotstein (1994) attempts to do in his dual-track theory, are constructed as a dialectical tension between opposing theoretical propositions. In his contribution to this volume, Grotstein invokes arguments concerning the conceptualization, ontology, and phenomenology of the internal world of self and objects so as to demonstrate that the endopsychic structure model of Fairbairn is not only suitable for, but also compatible with and complimentary to, Klein's concept of the internal world. Tracing their mutual departure from Freud's concept of primary narcissism in favor of primary object relatedness, he explicates their subsequent divergence. He focuses on Klein's adherence to a one-person model emphasizing unconscious psychic determinism (phantasy) and Fairbairn's two-person model emphasizing reality perception that relegates unconscious phantasy to a subservient position. Invoking the principle of "autochthony," a variant of infantile omnipotence, which accounts for infants' belief that they have created themselves and their own objects, Grotstein argues that infants can be conceived of as being paradoxically the author of their experience as well as its victim. He arrives at an integration of Fairbairn's and Klein's conceptions of infantile neurosis that is ensconced in a dialectic between a realistic trauma (Fairbairn) and an autochthonously (omnipotently) created one (Klein). An appreciation of this dialectic, he maintains, can further potentiate an appreciation of the clinical situation.

Jeffrey Seinfeld, also taking a dialectical approach to theory integration, illustrates the usefulness of such a tack for the understanding of clinical case material. Starting from similarities between the philosophical interests and theoretical approaches of Fairbairn and Bion, he continues by explicating basic points of agreement and departure in their theories and focuses on the processes of splitting, projection, and introjection. We discover that they shared a philosophical interest in the Greek classicists, as well as the German Idealist tradition of Kant and Hegel. They are most complementary in their view of splitting as an active process undertaken by the self in the face of frustration. Each viewed frustration as arising from different sources—Bion from instinctual frustration and Fairbairn from object frustration. In a masterful stroke Seinfeld describes points of intersection between their conceptualizations of the object world. In essence, he posits that the earliest knowledge of objects—Bion's notion of innate preconceptions, which is his version of Klein's a priori knowledge of the world—can be realized and shaped through actual, Fairbairnian interactions with real-object experience. He encapsulates this integration in a dialectic tension between Bion's notion that the infant creates its world largely through the process of projective identification and Fairbairn's idea that the infant relies primarily on the process of introjective identification. The tension between these two processes is clearly and thoughtfully explicated in a clinical case example.

The chapters in Part 3 posit potentially fruitful directions for further elaboration and extension of Fairbairn's ideas. In a way, these chapters travel back in time to some of Fairbairn's seminal ideas, then move forward reconsidering their impact within the contemporary context of the paradigmatic shifts that have taken place since he wrote, many of which he foretold but did not have the opportunity to observe. Thus, Mitchell presents us with a newly contextualized perspective on Fairbairn's thinking within the history of psychoanalytic ideas. Instead of a reading of Fairbairn that relies on more conventional psychoanalytic paradigms, he presents Fairbairn as struggling to move to a radically different theory of mind, one that takes as its starting point the idea that human nature is fundamentally social. Mitchell invokes references to comparative psychology and biological processes, such as breathing oxygen, to make his point that Fairbairn was challenging the most fundamental assumptions of the classical, one-person model of psychology. If we are to consider mind as embedded in a matrix by definition and not pulled into interaction by the drives, we need to reexamine some of the constructs of more traditional classical theory, such as impulses and guilt, and the problem of internalization, from relational perspectives. Mitchell presents compelling clinical vignettes demonstrating the advantages of Fairbairn's radical shift for both theoretical understanding and clinical application.

Fairbairn struggled throughout his project with the issue of the place for good objects in the endopsychic structure. Indeed, one of the most frequently cited criticisms of his opus is its lack of a consistent mechanism for the taking in of good-object experiences. Beginning with a review of the inconsistencies in Fairbairn's theory regarding introjection of good objects, Neil Skolnick's chapter draws on clinical and theoretical data to argue for a mechanism for the introjection, and *repression*, of good objects into the unconscious endopsychic structure. Invoking a contemporary understanding of ambivalence unavailable to Fairbairn at the time, he argues that while the dependency-related conflicts of Fairbairn's early oral period lead to the splitting processes of the schizoid position, these splitting processes need to be distinguished from the experience of ambivalence of the later oral period largely ignored by Fairbairn. It is the struggle to maintain whole-object relating under the pressure of intolerable ambivalence that fuels the repression of good-object relationships. Skolnick thus argues for a possible mechanism for the internalization of good objects without compromising the basic integrity and theoretical premises of Fairbairn's model of endopsychic structure.

Jill Savege Scharff provides a lucid summary of the evolution and extension of Fairbairn's ideas by one of his major proponents, John D. (Jock) Sutherland. Sutherland, Fairbairn's biographer and analysand, makes explicit the focus on self (as opposed to a narrower definition of ego) that some (e.g., Guntrip, 1969; Rubens, 1994) claim Fairbairn was implying. Placing the development of the dynamic self at the center of his theory, Sutherland offers a perspective that takes as its starting point Fairbairn's major premises about the genesis and maintainence of internal object relations and proactively attempts to account for their modifications both throughout the life cycle and within the context of the broader social structures of family, groups, and institutions. Eschewing structure for process, he invokes contemporary notions of open systems theory and holistic organizing principles to account for both the continuity of, and change to, the self as it exists in a constant state of flux and interaction with varying levels of organizations within the environment. Scharff makes the claim that Sutherland's focus on the autonomous self, a dynamic and continually evolving structure/process, is his most far-ranging contribution. She notes, in particular, that he rooted aggression in the interference with the aims of the autonomous self. In so doing, Sutherland takes Fairbairn's ideas about aggression into a biosocial explanatory realm.

Volumes have been written about the application of Freud's ideas to culture. By comparison, the number of scholarly contributions that address the confluence of cultural phenomena and the thinking of subsequent psychoanalytic giants, are few. Part 4 attempts to redress this lack. As the psychoanalytic ground shifts beneath us with the advent of relational models, it becomes increasingly rich for cross-disciplinary efforts that clarify the relevance of contemporary theories to the broader culture. In this section two authors wrestle with the integration of

Fairbairn's ideas with creativity and artistic endeavor. Steven Z. Levine, an art historian, weaves a fascinating connection between Fairbairn the theorist and Fairbairn the analyst and person, whose struggles with internal identifications can be viewed as the embodiment of Surrealist paranoia. Moving beyond Freud's understanding of art as primarily sublimation, Fairbairn conceived of art as primarily a process of restitution. Levine describes for us how he reached this conclusion by synthesizing the Hegelian notion of reconciliation of opposites with the Kleinian notion of the reparative processes involved in the integration of whole objects in the depressive position. Levine draws from Fairbairn's 1938 papers on art and aesthetics, papers he wrote before his seminal contributions of the 1940s. Like the exciting objects of his internal structures, these papers, while containing much that is uniquely Fairbairn, taunt us with the lost possibilities of further contributions he might have made had he written more on the subject after he had reformulated psychoanalytic theory. Levine, however, fills this gap by drawing on Fairbairn's lifetime struggle with urinary retention to depict how Fairbairn the person was not unlike Salvador Dali, a seeming opposite, in their surrealist transcendence of internal conflict.

Hilary Beattie, a psychologist—and, of no small interest, a Scot—presents a compelling argument for the deepening of understanding that can be obtained by a Fairbairnian reading of Robert Louis Stevenson's *The Strange Case of Dr. Jekyll and Mr. Hyde*. Her point of departure is to draw connections between the Scottish cultural heritage of both men and parallel patterns in their lives and families. She explores how the conflicts represented in *Jekyll and Hyde* have their origins in Stevenson's troubled childhood. Our understanding is enriched by viewing them through the complex prism of Fairbairn's theoretical perspective, particularly his tripartite split-ego structures and the repressed objects with which they interact. In a particularly creative coup, Beattie offers a fascinating explanation for the absence of female characters in the story, an explanation that draws both from Stevenson's life and from Fairbairn's ideas about repressed bad-object relationships.

Finally, in Part 5, we examine the relevance of Fairbairn's contributions to clinical practice and theory. As noted by Richard Rubens, Fairbairn had little to say about depression. Much of what he did say was influenced by Klein's thinking about the depressive position and then relegated to a place of secondary importance. Rubens takes a fresh look at depression from a Fairbairnian perspective. After reviewing what little Fairbairn did write on the subject, he creates a "virtual" Fairbairnian model of depression, one Fairbairn might have constructed. Agreeing with Fairbairn's focus on the primacy of the schizoid processes, Rubens argues that depression is better understood not as a separate developmental position, but rather as a technique for maintaining the closed nature of the endopsychic structure. Viewing depression as an attempt to deny or avoid the loss inherent in relinquishing the bad object ties of the internal world, he contrasts it with the experience of sadness, which involves the healthy recognition and acceptance of real object loss.

Fairbairn was greatly influenced by his work with abused children. It is particularly apt, then, that David Celani applies Fairbairn's ideas to a similar clinical population and especially one in contemporary focus—battered women. He presents us with a phenomenological and clinical mapping of their internal psychic world. In this application of Fairbairn's endopsychic structure to a specific clinical population, he provides a compelling understanding of battered women's choices and their tenacious maintenance of abusive relationships. He describes, again from a Fairbairnian perspective, the exquisite paradox created whereby the abused person maintains the integrity of her internal life by seeking brutally destructive ties that actually threaten her existence. He then describes, with vivid case material, the complex forms of the relational and self-resistances that face therapist and patient as they struggle to reorder the internal part-self and part-object relationships that provide the scaffolding of the battered woman's psychic existence. His focus is on the extreme cycling of great hope and great despair in the transference–countertransference matrix that must be endured as the patient enacts the intensity of her internal relationships with her therapist.

As we have noted, Fairbairn's student, Jock Sutherland, extended Fairbairn's theory into the dimension of time and considered the nature of growth and change of the human organism as it proceeds through a lifetime of changing environments. David Scharff, in whose work Sutherland and Fairbairn's influence is readily apparent, examines how insights gained from his own work with couples and families has informed his understanding of object relations theory. In particular, he notes that traditional psychoanalytic theorists place too much emphasis on the developmentally early introjection of objects, while subsequent mechanisms of introjection are ignored or underplayed. He notes that humans must take in objects at all stages of life in order to keep pace with the demands of continued growth and development. In the process, the self, its objects, and the mechanisms of introjection themselves become exceedingly complex. He examines some of these intricate mechanisms, including what he has classified as object construction, object sorting, and object exclusion and their importance in continued self definition and growth.

This book brings together the variety of contributions and contributors influenced by the richness of Fairbairn's thought and writing. We hope that the reader will be inspired, as these authors have been, to study, celebrate, and contribute to the evolution of object relations theory and practice that began with Fairbairn's work.

References

Fairbairn, W. R. D. (1928), The ego and the id. In: *From Instinct to Self, Vol. 2*, ed. D. E. Scharff & E. F. Birtles. Northvale, NJ: Aronson, 1994.

———— (1929a), The super-ego. In: *From Instinct to Self, Vol. 2*, ed. D. E. Scharff & E. F. Birtles. Northvale, NJ: Aronson, 1994.

——— (1929b), Dissociation and repression. In: *From Instinct to Self, Vol. 2*, ed. D. E. Scharff & E. F. Birtles. Northvale, NJ: Aronson, 1994.

——— (1940), Schizoid factors in the personality. In: *Psychoanalytic Studies of the Personality*. London: Routledge & Kegan Paul, 1952, pp. 3–27.

——— (1941), A revised psychopathology of the psychoses and psycho-neuroses. In: *Psychoanalytic Studies of the Personality*. London: Routledge & Kegan Paul, 1952, pp. 28–58.

——— (1943), The repression and return of bad objects (with special reference to the "war neuroses"). In: *Psychoanalytic Studies of the Personality*. London: Routledge & Kegan Paul, 1952, pp. 59–81.

——— (1944), Endopsychic structure considered in terms of object-relationships. In: *Psychoanalytic Studies of the Personality*. London: Routledge & Kegan Paul, 1952, pp. 82–136.

——— (1952), *Psychoanalytic Studies of the Personality*. London: Routledge & Kegan Paul.

——— (1954), The nature of hysterical states. In: *From Instinct to Self, Vol. 1*, ed. D. E. Scharff & E. F. Birtles. Northvale, NJ: Aronson, 1994, pp. 13–40.

——— (1958), On the nature and aims of psychoanalysis. In: *From Instinct to Self, Vol. 1*, ed. D. E. Scharff & E. F. Birtles. Northvale NJ: Aronson, 1994, pp. 74–92.

Freud, S. (1923), The ego and the id. *Standard Edition*, 19:12–66. London: Hogarth Press, 1961.

Greenberg, J. R. & Mitchell, S. A. (1983), *Object Relations in Psychoanalytic Theory*. Cambridge MA: Harvard University Press.

Grotstein, J. (1994), Notes on Fairbairn's metapsychology. In: *Fairbairn and the Origins of Object Relations*, ed. J. Grotstein & D. Rinsley. New York: Guilford, pp. 174–194.

Guntrip, H. (1969), *Schizoid Phenomena, Object Relations and the Self*. New York: International Universities Press.

Heimann, P. (1950), On countertransference. *Internat. J. Psycho-Anal.*, 31:81–84.

Jacobs, T. J. (1991), *The Use of the Self*. Madison, CT: International Universities Press.

Jones, E. (1952), Introduction. In: *Psychoanalytic Studies of the Personality*, by W. R. D. Fairbairn. London: Routledge & Kegan Paul.

Joseph, B. (1989), *Psychic Equilibrium and Psychic Change*, ed. E. B. Spillius & M. Feldman. London: Routledge.

Klein, M. (1946), Notes on some schizoid mechanisms. *Internat. J. Psycho-Anal.*, 27:99–110.

Rubens, R. L. (1994), Fairbairn's structural theory. In: *Fairbairn and the Origins of Object Relations*, ed. J. Grotstein & D. Rinsley. New York: Guilford.

Scharff, D. E. & Birtles, E. F. (1994), Introductory comments. In: *From Instinct to Self, Vols. 1 & 2*. Northvale, NJ: Aronson.

Scharff, J. S. & Scharff, D. E. (1998), *Object Relations Individual Therapy.* Northvale, NJ: Aronson.

Sutherland, J. D. (1989), *Fairbairn's Journey to the Interior.* London: Free Association Press.

———— (1994), *The Autonomous Self.* Northvale, NJ: Aronson.

◆ Part 1 ◆

Historical Connections

1

The Scottish Connection—
Suttie-Fairbairn-Sutherland

A Quiet Revolution

J. Alan Harrow

E. M. Forster (1973) said, "Only connect . . . only connect the prose and the passion and both will be exalted, and human love will be seen at its height" (pp. 183–184).

Connections, acknowledged or otherwise, in general are a crucial part of theory building and in particular have played an important role in developing and establishing a line of thought that is essentially Scottish in the work of Suttie, Fairbairn, and Sutherland. Just why this mold-breaking psychoanalytic perspective reflected in the theories of this trio of Scotsmen should have come about at all is not absolutely clear. Drummond Hunter (1995) offers an interesting philosophical clue to why the psychoanalytical theoretical development described here came about in Scotland. He says, "In the broadest sense (and its broad, philosophical background should never be forgotten) psychoanalysis was a child of the 18th century enlightenment and, in particular, perhaps of Schiller's (1982) great project, which was to realize the human in humanity" (p. 171). He continues, "It was no accident that the biographer of Schiller, Thomas Carlyle, who had introduced German philosophy and literature to Britain, may well have been the first British writer and thinker to rediscover the central (but now significantly enhanced) role of 'the self.'" This happened in a moment of insight when, in

3

1821, after three weeks of sleepless nights, he was walking down Leith Walk in Edinburgh. Carlyle (1897) describes the experience:

> To me the universe was all void of Life, of Purpose, of volition, even of hostility; it was one huge, dead immeasurable steam engine, rolling on in its dead indifference, to grind me limb from limb. . . . all at once there arose a Thought within me and I asked myself "What *art* thou afraid of?" . . . Behold thou art fatherless, outcast and the universe is mine (says the Devil) to which my whole *ME* now made answer: "I am not thine but Free and forever hate thee" [pp. 210–211].

Hunter (1995) describes how this reemergence of the self was accompanied, during and in the years after the Enlightenment, by a rediscovery both of the natural environment and of the brotherhood of man, that is, of the human community as an innate system of what the philosopher J. MacMurray (1970) (under whom Fairbairn and Sutherland had both studied at Edinburgh University) described as "persons-in-relation."

So, here, indeed, is a meaningful connection at a number of different levels which has helped me to set the scene for a somewhat condensed consideration of the theories of Suttie, Fairbairn, and Sutherland.

As my thesis is about the connections between three theorists of Scottish origin, I will try to briefly distill from Fairbairn's theories that which most obviously links him with Suttie before him and with Sutherland after.

Ian Suttie

It is now acknowledged that Suttie is a significant object relations theorist who anticipated ideas now more or less taken for granted.

As a way of briefly describing Suttie's line of thought, let me draw on two reviews of his book *Origins of Love and Hate* (Suttie,

1988) which are quoted in D. Heard's introduction. These reviews reflect both the positive and negative impact of his ideas. Suttie died at age 46, a few days before his book was published.

The review by Karan Stephen (1936) considered that it was stimulating for those steeped in a particular hypothesis to hear it vigorously attacked. For her, there was more to the book than criticism (of Freud). Suttie, she thought, had an original point of view to expound, and the originality lay in two concepts: First, that sociability, the craving for companionship (the infant's only way of self-preservation), the need to love and be loved, to exchange and to participate, are as primary as sexuality itself and are not derivatives of it; second, whenever this primary social love or tenderness fails to find the response it seeks, the frustration produces a kind of anxiety (separation anxiety), which is the starting point of neurotic maladjustment. Suttie was saying that behind the anxiety lay the dread of separation, the dread of being cut off from human sympathy and contact, represented in the first instance by the loss of the mother. Stephen regretted that the arguments put forward by Suttie took the form of a personal attack on Freud. Suttie, in effect, was replacing Freud's libido theory with the idea of an innate need for companionship, a love that is independent of genital appetite. In his review, Money-Kyrle (1936) commented that Suttie's book would be well received by all who wished to underestimate the extent of infantile sexuality and aggression. He admits, however, that Suttie's criticisms are near enough the mark to stimulate research. One suspects that Money-Kyrle may in particular have been responding to Suttie's bold summary of his ideas when he stated that "the most important aspect of mental development is the idea of others and of one's own relationship to them—Man (for Freud) he continued is a bundle of energies seeking to dissipate themselves but restrained by fear" (pp. 29–35). Against this idea Suttie says, "I regard expression not as an outpouring for its own sake, but as an overture demanding response from others. It is the absence of this response, I think, that is the source of all anxiety and rage" (pp. 29–35).

In contrast to Freud's emphasis on the instincts and his viewing of the infant as initially autoerotic, Suttie (1988) focused on issues of relatedness. He made his contrasting and challenging position clear when he stated that the child "wakes up to life with the germ of parenthood, the impulse to give and to respond already in it. The impulse with the need 'to get' attention and recognition, and so on motivates the free give-and-take of fellowship" (p. 58). Central to Suttie's thesis, and again in contrast to Freud (and Klein), was his belief that all aggressive and antipathetic feeling was evoked by a relationship to the social environment.

For Suttie, frustrated social love turns to anxiety and then hate if the frustration is sufficiently severe. It goes without saying that this line of thought had important implications for therapy. It involved a shift that emphasized the therapist's capacity to relate in what Suttie described as a "feeling interest relationship with the patient" (p. 212). He thought the approach helped establish "a fellowship of suffering" (p. 212) between patient and analyst. Suttie amplified the therapeutic importance of an empathetic response to the patient's suffering, which, in effect, can be seen to be linked with Suttie's belief in Ferenczi's dictum, "It is the physician's love that heals the patient" (p. 212). One detects, in both Ferenczi and Suttie, the importance of the subjective nature of suffering and emotional understanding between patient and analyst: Suttie had much to say about the taboo on tenderness in general and in therapeutic work, in particular: "that so harmless and amiable emotion (of tenderness), the very stuff of sociability" (p. 80). He thought a taboo on tenderness had become institutionalized in psychoanalysis. While the final paragraph of R. M. Rilke's (1934) eighth letter in *Letters to a Young Poet* speaks perhaps to all of us, I suspect that Suttie, and Ferenczi before him, would have been specially appreciative. Rilke said, "Do not believe that he who seeks to comfort you lives untroubled among the simple and quiet words that sometimes do you good. His life has much difficulty and sadness. Were it otherwise he would never have been able to find those words" (p. 72). Space does not allow an elaboration of the fact that Suttie's Christian beliefs were also a significant influence in his theorizing and therapeutic approach. I mention this partly because I think a religious or spiritual element is clearly discernible in the lives of all three men, although not openly expressed by either Fairbairn or Sutherland.

Suttie's focus on the idea that the infant is born to be companionable rather than to be just an id, until thwarted, and on the notion of an innate capacity for social relatedness is the most fundamental connection between his and Fairbairn's theories.

Ronald Fairbairn

Greenberg and Mitchell (1983) point out that, while Klein and Winnicott made their contributions to a thoroughgoing revision of Freud, Fairbairn was the only one who systematically scrutinized structure and only he openly challenged Freudian theory.

John Padel (1989) quotes Sutherland as saying (many years back), "You could count on the fingers of one hand all the British psychoanalysts who have read the whole of Fairbairn's published work; yet there is not much of it and it is so clear and comprehensive." While Padel must be acknowledged as a torch bearer, it is Sutherland who has given us the clearest account to date of Fairbairn's work. Sutherland (1994d, p. 339) considered the significance of Fairbairn's contribution to psychoanalysis to be that Fairbairn was the first to propose, in a systematic manner, the Copernican change involved in founding the psychoanalytic theory of human personality on the experience within social relationships, instead of on the discharge of instinctual tensions originating solely within the individual. In short, he replaced the closed-system standpoint of 19th-century science with the open-system concepts evolved by the middle of the present century to account for the development of living organisms in which the contribution of the environment is central.

All things considered, I think we have to see Fairbairn's partly self-enforced geographical isolation as a secondary factor in the hostility created by his radical challenge to Freudian theory. To underline the revolutionary nature of his theories, I will take just the first six points of Fairbairn's (1963) synopsis of an object relations theory of the personality:

> An Ego is present at birth.
> Libido is a function of the ego.
> There is no death instinct; and aggression is a reaction to frustration or deprivation, there is no such thing as an id.
> The ego and therefore libido, is fundamentally object seeking.
> The earliest and original form of anxiety experienced by the child is separation anxiety.

It was also his idea that structure and energy are inseparable, an idea that highlighted the theoretical cul-de-sac of Freud's psychic apparatus, which had led psychoanalysis into describing an unstructured id and a highly structured (but weak) ego (Yankelovich and Barrett, 1971, p. 163).

Fairbairn may have been prophetic in seeing the aspects of Freud's theories that had to go, for we now know that object relationship begins with birth, or, surprisingly, even before, if we follow Sir Thomas Browne, writing in *Religio Medici* in 1630, "in that obscure world the womb of our mother . . . it awaits the opportunity of objects" (McIntyre, 1996, private communication). We now know that his uncompromising alternative to drive-discharge theory was too radical and too difficult to be accepted and the fruitful discussion that Ernest Jones had predicted (Fairbairn, 1952) did not occur in Fairbairn's lifetime.

An obvious and clear connection between Suttie and Fairbairn is their view of environmental failure (or perhaps we should say interpersonal failure) as being the root of all pathological reactions. Fairbairn took a further theoretical step when he said all pathology is essentially a withdrawal from, which is to say a defense against, the trauma of not feeling intimately loved. He was referring to what he considered to be the mother's failure to convince her child that she herself loves him as a person. As a result, the child comes to feel that his own love for his mother is not really valued and accepted by her.

For Fairbairn the mother's personalized love for the child is crucial. Fairbairn thought that, from the child's point of view, when the child feels that his love has destroyed his mother's feeling for him, then we have the origin of the schizoid state, which is characterized by emotional withdrawal. Insofar as the child feels his hate has destroyed his mother's feeling for him, we have the origin of the depressive state. Fairbairn pointed out that the study of the person at the personal level, with all his or her subjectivity, has to be the essential focus. Concepts that reduced phenomena to impersonal processes were not acceptable to him. This philosophical stance was consistently sustained throughout his life and is reflected in his theorizing and therapeutic aims (see Sutherland, 1994d, p. 335).

Fairbairn's explanation for the universality of schizoid phenomena is that their fundamental determinant consists of splits in the initial whole ego or self, a process from which no one is entirely free. Psychoanalytic treatment, according to Fairbairn, attempts to unify the split psyche. He preferred to think in terms of a synthesis rather than an analysis for the integration of the split self. He believed that, through healing splits in the self, the patient is enabled to interact with, and be affected by, the open system of outer reality. According to Fairbairn, the patient's maintaining his inner world as a closed system, that is, significantly cut off from real relationships, has been partially determined by the sense of hopelessness in obtaining any satisfactions from objects or persons in external reality on whom he might allow himself to become dependent. From a treatment point of view, Fairbairn believed that analytic interpretation was not sufficient. He thought that it was the *actual relationship* between patient and analyst that was the crucial factor in psychoanalytical cure or change in the patient. By the actual relationship, Fairbairn meant not only the transference relationship but also the total relationship between patient and analyst as persons. Rather than aiming at the resolution of unconscious conflict over pleasure-seeking impulses, he strove to restore direct and full contact with real other human beings. Fairbairn said that the analyst's task is to force himself into the closed system of the patient. The patient opposes the analyst's efforts by using transference; that is, the analyst is transformed into figures in the patient's closed-system world. Fairbairn (1958) quotes the four factors involved in psychoanalytic "cure" first identified by Gitelson: insight, recall of infantile memories, catharsis, and the relationship with the analyst. Gitelson (1951) argued that cure was affected not by one factor, but by a synthesis of all four; and, while this view obviously appealed to Fairbairn, he believed that the decisive factor is the relationship with the analyst. Not only was it on this relationship that the other factors mentioned by Gitelson depended, but they could not exist without it. In other words, it is only through the relationship with the analyst that the other factors come into being at all.

Fairbairn put this therapeutic aim at the center of all his theoretical endeavors. Guntrip (1975) quoted him as saying, "You can go on analyzing forever and get nowhere. It is the personal relation that is therapeutic" (p. 145). The psychoanalytic interpretation for Fairbairn is not therapeutic per se but is so only insofar as it expresses a personal relationship of genuine understanding. This most crucial theoretical and therapeutic issue still arouses a mixture of skepticism and resistance to Fairbairn's point of view. Guntrip's comment that "to find a good object at the start is the basis of psychic health. In its lack, to find a genuine 'good object' in one's analyst is both a transference experience and a real life experience. In analysis, as in real life, all relationships have a subtly dual nature" (p. 156). In these words, we see a crucial connection not only between Guntrip and Fairbairn, but also between Guntrip and Sutherland.

Jock Sutherland

It was this framework of theory and practice that influenced Sutherland, who was in analysis with Fairbairn when he was formulating his new ideas. Sutherland (1994b, p. 53) acknowledges the prominent part Fairbairn played in his life and how this personal factor may have influenced his judgment regarding the development of psychoanalysis. He later goes on to say that Fairbairn's appeal for him rested, from the start, on his integrity as a good human being who never lost the primacy of his interest in the well-being of people and whose concern was never separated from his thinking about the nature and origin of psychological distress and how it might be alleviated. Fairbairn's additional interest in the wider dissemination of psychoanalytic knowledge is also reflected in Sutherland's view of him. Following Fairbairn, Sutherland emphasized that it was the quality of responsiveness and interaction between mother and infant that was crucial. This basic theoretical point reflects Sutherland's belief that a caring attitude is basic to the whole process of analysis. He saw such an attitude as a requirement dictated not by sentiment, but by the scientific facts of infant development.

The fundamental issue for Sutherland was that psychopathology in the individual is the result of a lack of a good early relationship. Like Fairbairn before him, Sutherland thought that the concept of drives as the single motivating force offered an inadequate picture of human nature. To understand his picture of human nature we have to take account of his interest in the theory of open, self-organizing systems. He was increasingly influenced in his latter years by modern biology. The main issue for him was that all living organisms start as wholes and create other wholes to survive. They cannot be made from the aggregation of parts. Living organisms are characterized by an open system in which there is constant exchange with the environment, which means there are constant transformations despite the fact that they maintain their own characteristic form by a process of self-regulation. It is this biological inclusion in Sutherland's vision of a theory of object relations that led him to begin to develop his ideas about the self. In fact, he wrote that the more you think of the self, the more you realize that object relations theory has acquired a misnomer that has given it a misleading status (Sutherland, 1994a, p. 381). It is really a theory of the self: the self makes the relationships, and the self is made by the relationships. The two interact, and the self is the agent of action. The integrity of the self is therefore seen as being fundamentally linked to the existence of meaningful social connectedness. Drawing on his (and others') clinical evidence from disorders of the self, he strongly suggests that effective development of the self rests on joyful empathic responsiveness from the mother. He thought that limited frustration can be tolerated by the baby if the overall feelings communicated by the mother, and later by the father, are those of a genuine joy in the baby as it is. When such a responsiveness is sustained, there is no pressure on the infant to match preconceived images that parents can sometimes force on it. Sutherland thought that interference to the steadily developing self elicits intense aggression. He thought that the joyous initial response was the essential aspect of good-enough mothering, which gives the first "layering" in the structuring of the self as a person. The infant needs to incorporate the mother in a personal way, that is, as having the significance of a whole object and not one confined to the feeding activity. He concluded (late in his own life) that for the eventual integration of the self the relationship between the parents and their joint attitudes toward the child are almost as critically important as that of each parent separately.

Following Fairbairn's theory of the closed inner-world system of the schizoid patient and of the development, through transference interpretation, of an increased ability to accommodate the world of real relationships, Sutherland used the theory of an open, self-organizing system to emphasize the way in which the self and the environment are engaged in a continuous interchange of information, promoting mutual growth and structural change. It is this interchange between self and environment that led Sutherland to argue that a "sense of self had evolved with the advent of homo sapiens and in response to the survival requirements of social connectedness." Another, not unconnected, concern that was with him all his working life as an analyst, was the social and cultural relevance of psycho-analysis. Sutherland described the self, family, group, organiza-tion and community as an interconnected whole, a progressive organization of relatedness. The future of psychoanalysis, he thought, involved both advancing a theory of the self and find-ing creative ways of making the psychoanalytic knowledge and insights based on this theory more widely available. He thought that psychoanalytic institutions should move toward a more flexible approach by combining psychoanalytic training with other human relation activities.

Following his return to Scotland in the late 60s, Sutherland paid particular attention to the Scottish caring-profession envi-ronment and decided that a narrowly based psychoanalytic insti-tution was neither in demand nor likely to be nurtured by a professional community desperate to acquire knowledge, and thereby support, in their attempts to raise the quality of psycho-logical health in Scotland. I always had a sense of, and belief in, Sutherland's sensitivity and in his capacity to listen to, and read, environmental conditions, but he was perhaps even more attuned to the importance, when it came to the business of creat-ing an institution like the Scottish Institute of Human Relations, of ensuring that such an institution was a welcome new arrival in the community. He put theory into practice when, at the beginning, he said, "What supports the carer is not encourage-ment in the conventional sense. . . . It is to be part of a learning system greater than himself" (Sutherland, 1994c, p. 277). Needless to say, he realized that the development of such an institution, whatever its huge potential, had all the difficulties inherent in an infant's relationship with mother, father, then family, and, finally, with the wider social context.

Conclusion

It seems to me that Suttie, Fairbairn, and Sutherland would, roughly speaking, fall within Symington's (1987) view that "it is emotional contact that an analysis is founded on, but interpretations are its boundaries" (p. 61). Implicit in their ideas about theory and practice (it's writ large in Fairbairn's thinking) is the influence of the person of the analyst on the analytic process. Fairbairn (1958) said, "If the patient did not make satisfactory progress then this could be due to some defect in the psychoanalytic method" (p. 379). Paula Heimann (1950), who emphasized the importance of countertransference as part of the psychoanalytic method, said that the analyst's skill is in the most intricate and complex ways conditioned by "his personality." I think Heimann's view is close to Fairbairn's notion of the patient's actual relationship with the analyst, which he regarded as "a therapeutic factor of prime importance." Klauber (1981) was following Heimann when he stated that "the analytic function cannot be conceptualised in isolation from the personality of the analyst who exercises it" (p. 138). In other words—and this notion is now well accepted—the personality of the analyst is his or her instrument in carrying out analytic work. Fairbairn made a proper theoretical place for the personal elements in the bond between patient and analyst and the centrality of emotional contact. One could argue that the growing interest in the compatibility or mismatch between patient and analyst and treatment outcome was anticipated by Fairbairn.

The Scottish theoretical perspective (which is what I have attempted to identify here) emphasizes the importance of using, as widely as possible, the psychoanalytic research findings that focus on "the self in society." It follows that the dynamic relationship between psychoanalytic institutions and the communities or social settings in which they exist is an integral part of this perspective.

Donald Schön (1971) said that "innovation, real innovation, moves quietly, unnoticed at first, from the periphery to the centre" (p. 177). It was this kind of quiet revolution that these three Scots "outsiders" initiated, and, as Freud slowly moves to the periphery, there is no doubt that object relations thinking (perhaps Fairbairn's in particular) is now beginning to move to the center.

References

Brown, Sir T. (1630), *Religio Medici*. London: Walter Scott.

Carlyle, T. (1897), *Sartor Resartus*. London: Adam & Charles Black.

Fairbairn, W. R. D. (1952), *Psychoanalytic Studies of the Personality*. London: Routledge & Kegan Paul.

—— (1958), Nature and aims of psychoanalytic treatment. *Internat. J. Psycho-Anal.*, 39:374–385.

—— (1963), Synopsis of an object relations theory of personality. *Internat. J. Psycho-Anal.*, 44:224–225.

Forster, E. M. (1973), *Howard's End*. London: Edward Arnold.

Gitelson, M. (1951), Psychoanalysis and dynamic psychiatry. *Arch. Neurol. & Psychiat.*, 66:280–288.

Greenberg, J. & Mitchell, S. (1983), *Object Relations in Psychoanalytic Theory*. Cambridge, MA: Harvard University Press.

Guntrip, H. (1975), Analysis with Fairbairn and Winnicott. In: *Personal Relations Therapy: Collected Papers of H. J. S. Guntrip*, ed. J. Hazell. Northvale, NJ: Aronson.

Heimann, P. (1950), On countertransference. *Internat. J. Psycho-Anal.*, 31:81–84.

Hunter, T. D. (1995), What Is Psychoanalysis For? SIHR Bulletin.

Klauber, J. (1981), The psychoanalyst as a person. In: *Difficulties in the Psychoanalytic Encounter*. Northvale, NJ: Aronson.

MacMurray, J. (1970), *Persons in Relation*. London: Faber & Faber.

Money-Kyrle, R. (1936), Review of Suttie *Origins of Love and Hate*. *Internat. J. Psycho-Anal.*, 17:137–138.

Padel, J. (1989), Fairbairn's thought on the relationship of inner and outer worlds. Fairbairn Centenary Conference, Edinburgh.

Rilke, R. M. (1934), *Letters to a Young Poet*. New York: Norton.

Schiller, F. (1967), *On the Aesthetic Education of Man*, ed. E. N. Wilkinson. Oxford: Clarendon Press (passim).

Schön, D. A. (1971), *Beyond the Stable State*. London: Temple Smith.

Stephen, K. (1936), Review of Suttie *Origins of Love and Hate*. *Brit. J. Med. Psychol.*, 16:149–151.

Sutherland, J. D. (1994a), On becoming a person. In: *The Autonomous Self*. Northvale, NJ: Aronson.

—— (1994b), Fairbairn's contribution. In: *The Autonomous Self*. Northvale, NJ: Aronson.

—— (1994c), A psychodynamic image of man. In: *The Autonomous Self*. Northvale, NJ: Aronson.

—— (1994d), Fairbairn and the self. In: *The Autonomous Self*. Northvale, NJ: Aronson.

Suttie, I. (1988), *Origins of Love and Hate*. London: Free Association Books.
Symington, N. (1987), *Illusion and Spontaneity in Psycho-Analysis*. London: Free Association Books.
Yankelovich, D. & Barrett, W. (1971), *Ego and Instinct*. New York: Vintage.

2

Fairbairn's Contribution
An Interview of Otto F. Kernberg

David E. Scharff

Owing to prior commitments, Otto Kernberg, M.D. was unable to attend the Fairbairn Conference in New York. He graciously agreed to this taped interview in order to contribute by video. The interview took place in November 1995 in his office in White Plains, New York. There, in the comfort of his office and surrounded by his library, we had the opportunity to reflect on Dr. Kernberg's interest in Fairbairn and the way he has applied and elaborated on Fairbairn's theory of object relations in his own work.

D.S.: Dr. Kernberg, I want to start by asking how you first became familiar with Fairbairn?

O.K.: Through Jock Sutherland,[1] whom I first met in Topeka, Kansas. I trained in Chile with Ignacio Matte-Blanco. He introduced the British schools to the Chilean Psychoanalytic Institute, but we were mostly under the influence of Kleinian thinking, on one hand, and ego psychology on the other. From the independents, only Winnicott was known a little. Let me remind you, I started my training in 1953 and graduated in 1960. Winnicott's work was not then well known outside Great Britain.

---

[1] Dr. John Sutherland was long-time Medical Director of the Tavistock Clinic, editor of *The International Journal of Psycho-Analysis*, and a yearly guest teacher and Board member of The Menninger Clinic.

D.S.: I don't think he was known much in the United States at that time.

O.K.: Although in Latin America there was relatively more contact with Europe than with the United States, as far as the British schools were concerned, the Independents and, of course, French psychoanalysis, were almost unknown here for many years. We had some contact, some information in Chile, but it was mostly with Kleinian analysts and those of Anna Freud's school, very little of the Independents, the middle group. Only through Sutherland did I become aware of the middle group. We also had some awareness of Balint, but very little Fairbairn. The only article of Fairbairn's that I studied as a candidate was his paper on the splitting of the personality, which was a wonderful paper. But I wasn't aware that it was part of a general theoretical formulation.

D.S.: Of course, that paper came first. I don't think he had the formulation when he wrote it.

O.K.: And his book had not yet come out. So, through Jock Sutherland, I became aware of Fairbairn and the importance that Fairbairn had in influencing Melanie Klein's thinking regarding the stages of development predating the depressive position. It was because of Fairbairn's work that she changed her designation of the paranoid position to the paranoid/schizoid position. I also, of course, became aware, after reading Henry Dicks, that he had used Fairbairn's framework, which made eminent sense, so I got very curious.

And then I had another experience that became important. The development of my own thinking regarding internalized object relations and object relations theory led me to the work of Margaret Mahler and Edith Jacobson. In Edith Jacobson's work I found a schema for the development of internal object relations that I found eminently practical and convincing in terms of my experience with borderline patients. And I found that Fairbairn independently had reached a theoretical schema remarkably similar to Edith Jacobson's. One of the things that I regret to this day is that I never asked Edith Jacobson whether she had read or been interested in Fairbairn. She doesn't quote Fairbairn, so I don't know why I didn't ask her that. We developed quite a close friendship in the last years of her life. We often talked about the importance of Fairbairn's work, and I made a strong point about it.

D.S.: So you don't know if it was independent discovery?

O.K.: My sense is that most probably Edith Jacobson and Fairbairn independently developed quite similar ways of thinking. There was one more person who interested me greatly, and that was Talcott Parsons. In 1959 and 1960 I had a Rockefeller Foundation Fellowship in this country, and I heard Talcott Parsons give a talk at the University of Maryland. He explained that, when we internalize a relationship, what we internalize is not the image of the other but the image of ourselves interacting with the other, the interrelation between the two—that all internalizations are dyadic internalizations. It struck me like a thunder bolt, and it stayed with me. And, of course, that is the basic idea in both Jacobson and Fairbairn. It is already contained to some extent in Erickson but he never developed it fully.

D.S.: No, I can't find it there either.

O.K.: It fits with Erickson's concept of introjection and identification, but, explicitly I think, Fairbairn and Jacobson are the two authors who introduced his concept of internalization into psychoanalytic theory. It is implicit also in Melanie Klein, but she never formulated it explicitly.

D.S.: She actually specifically avoided it in some ways.

O.K.: It's a fundamental concept on which my own theoretical development of psychoanalytic object relations theory rests, and so I'm deeply indebted to both Fairbairn and Edith Jacobson.

D.S.: You have really started with Edith Jacobson as your building block theoretically, as I understand it.

O.K.: Yes, and then Fairbairn naturally matched this theoretical thinking. It was Sutherland who alerted me to the importance of the affective link between self- and object representations, which he had developed in following Fairbairn's work. That really gave me a final push into that direction.

D.S.: It's not clear to me how much Fairbairn understood that the affect had to be emphasized as the link.

O.K.: That's right. That was implicit, but it fit naturally.

D.S.: Now, when did you first hear about that? I know that you discussed the paper that Jock Sutherland gave at the Menninger, which was published in 1963. Was that the point at which you got clear about that?

O.K.: Yes. I don't remember exactly when that discussion took place or when it was published,[2] but that day set the idea in my mind.

Incidentally, I heard a funny story about Jock if, you don't mind.

D.S.: By all means . . .

O.K.: There was a party where Jock was present. And several good friends of mine were there, although I was not. Somebody asked Jock, "Do you know Otto Kernberg?" Jock said, "What do you mean? Do I know Otto Kernberg? I *made* Otto Kernberg!" It sounded wonderful to me and made me feel very good.

D.S.: That does sound like Jock. Well, it seems to me that paper was the clearest and most concise explication of Fairbairn that existed at that time. In some ways it put him on the map. In that discussion you talked about the difference between projective identification and projection, I think. I wonder if you have changed your mind or if you still feel that projection is a more mature function than projective identification.

O.K.: I still think this way. Projection clinically, as I am defining it, is attributing to somebody else something that is deeply repressed in oneself. It is really a quite mature mechanism. As long as the person who projects stays away from

---

[2] J. D. Sutherland (1963), Object relations theory and the conceptual model of psychoanalysis. *British Journal of Medical Psychology*, 36:109–124. Discussion by O. Kernberg (1963), *British Journal of Medical Psychology*, 36:121–124.

being projected, the world is in order. Repression works, and projection complements it. In the case of projective identification, there is a primitive combination of projection, maintenance of empathy with what is projected, the need to control the object, and an unconscious tendency to induce that which is projected onto the other, or into the other, as a Kleinian would say. And that seems to me to indicate a lack of mature repression. It indicates the primitiveness of early mechanisms that have strong behavioral components to them. That's what one finds in the sicker patients, in the psychotic and borderline patients. Projection, as I defined it, is more typical of neurotic patients. For example, we can find a patient with a hysterical personality structure and severe sexual repression, who projects sexual impulses onto all others without regard to who they are. Such a patient thinks others have a kind of dirty mind, but as long as the patient stays away from such people he or she is OK. There is no awareness of the sexual feelings that are being projected. It's very different from projective identification, particularly of aggressive impulses, particularly in the typical paranoid patient who is afraid of being attacked but who knows very well how it feels when one is enraged and feels like attacking.

D.S.: What do you think about the difference about that way of thinking about it, and the way the modern Kleinians and the independent group in Britain would think of projective and introjective identification as a kind of all purpose mechanism for unconscious communication, starting with the mother and baby?

O.K.: I agree that it's a very pervasive and dominant mental mechanism. I think that all primitive defensive operations have both a growth potential and a defensive potential. But that's true for all of them. It's true for splitting, primitive idealization, denial, omnipotence, omnipotent control. Projective identification has the primary role, because it is connected, perhaps more directly than other primitive defensive operations, with affective communication. It operates through the inborn capacity to communicate affect and to read the affect communicated by the other person. I mean, we have an inborn capacity to read others' affects and to express our affects so that they are readable by others.

D.S.: Right from the beginning . . .

O.K.: From the beginning. I very much agree with Rainer Krause's proposal that affects are phylogenetically recent mechanisms of control that emerge in mammals and have the biological function of assuring the dependency link between infant and mother, given the prolonged early dependence of the mammalian infant on maternal and general parental care. That makes eminent sense to me. My concept of affects really combines the so-called central and peripheral theories. In other words, Magda Arnold's older view of affects as central subjective organizers of experience and motivators of behavior, with Sylvan Tompkins's view of affects as communicative expression and communicative link. I see affects as inborn psychophysiological structures, as instinctive components of the human being in contrast to drives. I maintain the Freudian position about drives, but I see drives as psychological motivators, the constituent components of which are instinctive components or building blocks, and I see affects in that role. And affects, in turn, are complex structures that contain a cognitive appraisal of good or bad, a subjective experience, psychomotor manifestations—particularly facial expressions—with a communicative function and neurovegetative discharge. It's a package view. Affects activate intense early object relations and then determine the internalization and the effect of such affectively invested object relations.

D.S.: They are organizers of the way object relations are internalized.

O.K.: Yes. This brings me back to Fairbairn, to what it is that has been most argued about in his drive or instinct theory. Here I'm partly in disagreement but also partly in agreement with Fairbairn, because he postulates that libido is really *object seeking* rather than pleasure seeking and considers aggression as secondary to the frustration of this need. I would modify this slightly. Libido is object seeking, which is pleasurable. Object seeking and pleasure and the reality principle originally are one.

D.S.: All the same thing.

O.K.: Yes. At the same time, I believe that aggression has an equally important role as a psychic motivator insofar as there are inborn dispositions to aggressive affect in the same way as there are inborn dispositions to libidinal affect. Therefore the inborn disposition to both is there.

D.S.: Right from the beginning.

O.K.: Right from the beginning. And, so, to say that aggression is secondary to frustration of libidinal needs downplays the fact that we are also constitutionally already wired to the two types.

D.S.: I think that, too. If they are both always there, why would you say that one precedes the other?

O.K.: And of course, clinically, Fairbairn talks about the internalization of aggression, in the form of internalized bad objects, and that is one of the strongest aspects of his contribution. For example, how patients are forced again and again to enact the relationship with bad internal objects in an effort to overcome the trauma, the frustration, by an externalization in which there is a secret hope that their good object relation will rescue them and the relationship from the bad object relation. He sees this as the source of the repetition compulsion. That's eminently reasonable. It's a very important aspect of the repetition compulsion. So, clinically, Fairbairn sees the internalization of both idealized and persecutory object relations, which is clinically very convincing. I'm 100% with him there, as well as with Melanie Klein. Of course, Guntrip and other disciples of Fairbairn have taken his theoretical position to categorically reject aggression as a drive. That is more Guntrip's position. Fairbairn is much less radical in this regard.

D.S.: It seems to me he had a philosophical reason for saying that aggression was secondary. But clinically he puts aggression and libidinal object seeking on a par, whereas Guntrip is much more dedicated to the priority of good object.

O.K.: Yes. What do you see as the philosophical reason?

D.S.: It had to do with his background in philosophy and the longing for the desired object as being the fundamental motivator. I understand that this idea comes from Hegel and German 19th-century philosophy. Since he then says that the only reason for internalizing objects is frustration, it seems that it's pretty important right from the beginning.

O.K.: I raised the question with you because he was a minister, wasn't he, before he became a psychoanalyst?

D.S.: He did philosophy as his first degree at Edinburgh University, so that his main background, the equivalent of undergraduate education, was philosophy. He continued to teach in the philosophy department in the department of mental philosophy, which is where psychology began as a discipline. I think it was fundamentally a philosophically rigorous background that he spoke from. But, he wasn't a minister. He did, however, say that what patients primarily want is salvation rather than cure.

O.K.: There is also religious acceptance of the principle of good and evil in Fairbairn. There is this curious, but wonderful, statement when he talks about the moral defense and how the internalized aggression from and toward the parents is transformed into morally good aggression because it is preferable to live in the world of a cruel God than to live in the world of the Devil. That has a kind of religious quality.

D.S.: Yes, it does. He had a feeling for religion. He was a church-going and very rigorous philosopher. I assume that he kept reading philosophy. The only published work I know about is his review of Berkeley's philosophy. But philosophy stayed as the background of the way he thought. He wanted to be philosophically rigorous throughout, although he thought about it as being scientifically rigorous and logical, too.

O.K.: I thought his concept of the moral defense was a very important contribution to masochism.

D.S.: I was looking at your writing about that recently. Do you want to say something about that?

O.K.: Well, he provided an object relations perspective to masochism in the sense that it didn't derive simply from the very early tendencies to turn aggression against the self. For Fairbairn, and I think rightly so, it was determined much more by the need to maintain the internal relationship with the punishing, frustrating object in order to make that object acceptable to the self and maintain the relationship. The need to rationalize the object's aggression and integrate the bad superego precursor, one might say, with the idealized one by idealizing the reasons for the aggression. This, then, would create a powerful internalized sadistic morality with which the person would agree. This is the part of the self, or the self-representation, that is the Internal Saboteur, in alliance with the internalized bad object. This position, that the self is in alliance with the aggressor, is, of course, clinically very important because masochistic patients don't only attack themselves, but also show a sense of moral superiority and of collusion—the agreement with that which is damaging to them. That deep sense of collusion is very often the most important resistance that one finds: that patients get a sense of profound satisfaction and justice in destroying themselves.

D.S.: And in resisting the psychotherapist.

O.K.: Sure, the process threatens that equilibrium. Fairbairn's observation that, after resolving more advanced superego features, you find these internal persecutors is very central in fact. Independently it had already been observed that sometimes, in advanced stages of psychoanalytic treatment, one finds profound paranoid tendencies. Of course, Melanie Klein also talked about a very early paranoid superego and talked in more abstract terms about the contamination of the idealized superego components by the combination with the aggressive ones. So there was a cruel demand for perfection on the part of the superego. But I think that Fairbairn put this in more directly usable clinical terms.

D.S.: One of the things that I noticed is the way you use that to discuss perversions in your new book, *Love and Love Relations*. You thought he gave us a good way of understanding perversions.

O.K.: Yes. One of the important contributions is his analysis of the escape from deep object relations, and their replacement by partial sexual involvements, pointing to the fact that in perversions often we have to examine not only the implications of the sexual behavior—the unconscious fantasies embedded in the sexual behavior—but also the relationships against which such sexual behavior and its fantasies protect the patient, pointing therefore to the profound preoedipal roots of perversion. This is the general trend of the literature in contrast to earlier analysis of Freud, who saw oedipal frustration and castration anxiety at the center of the dynamics of perversion.

D.S.: It has to do with the earliest object relations.

O.K.: Of course. Now there is a new twist in the development of psychoanalytic thinking, perhaps particularly under the influence of French psychoanalysts, pointing to the archaic oedipal conflict, the early presence in the mother's fantasy— and eventually in the child's fantasy—of father as an agent that separates the mother from the child. So that it may well be that archaic oedipal relationships have to be incorporated into object relations models.

D.S.: "Archaic" meaning that in the mother's internal conception of the oedipal configuration . . .

O.K.: . . . in the mother's internal conception, and therefore in her unconscious relationship to infants of both genders. I have become very interested in recent times in Laplanche's thinking and his theory that, in the interaction between mother and infant, mother emits enigmatic messages. In other words, that the unconscious erotic relationship of the mother with the child, which is codetermined by her own oedipal conflicts, is experienced by the child as erotic messages that the child cannot as yet comprehend. It has essentially an enigmatic quality. Laplanche sees it as the origin of primary unconscious fantasies involving the parents' sexual life, crystalizing in archaic oedipal fantasies and relationships, including both libidinal and aggressive ones. So, he sees both love and aggression as induced by the mother –infant relationship.

D.S.: As induced rather than innate . . .

O.K.: Yes, as induced by the mother–infant relationship not as innate. Leaning on the biological function, but giving it a new symbolic meaning. So, Laplanche sees drives as leaning on the biological function, but not directly being within the biological function. Eroticism is not the same as sexuality, but it leans on sexuality. He uses Freud's concept of *Anlehnung*, of "leaning on" as the psychological relation to the biological predisposition. I think that's an interesting reinforcement of an object relations view including the origin of the drives.

D.S.: The drives, then, are interpersonally determined, which fits with Bion, for instance. There is an interpersonal origin of mind. To return to Fairbairn, his theory can include this concept without being violated, although it's not really quite what he was thinking. He was thinking of mind as originating in the relationship.

O.K.: Yes. His reorganization of the tripartite structure into structure of the central ego, as he called it. He used the term ego but he meant self. In those years that differentiation was not made.

D.S.: That was my impression too. Nobody really talked about self.

O.K.: Which is the consequence of the bad translation from the German into the English because Freud always talked about *Ich* which is the "I." It was Strachey who changed it into the Latin "ego," which made it an impersonal apparatus and took out the subjective quality, which had to be reintroduced by the term self.

D.S.: Freud was much more enigmatic in his meaning.

O.K.: Not enigmatic, but ambiguous. Yes. But it was an ambiguity that corresponds to the fact that what we call ego is really a combination of subjectivity and behavioral aspects, in other words identity and character.

D.S.: Let's talk about Fairbairn's model a bit more.

O.K.: Fairbairn used his model of the six-part structure of the psyche—central ego and ideal object, rejecting ego and object, exciting self and excited object to reformulate Freud's tripartite structure of ego, superego, and id. And independently Edith Jacobson was doing something similar, for example, in her analysis of the superego as being constituted by layers of internalized ideal object, ideal self, bad objects, representations leading from the earliest aggressive or persecutory layer to a second idealizing layer and the third realistic layer, the later superego. She was also describing how real self, ideal self, real object, and ideal object development complicated the internalized object relations within the ego. So both Fairbairn and Jacobson were struggling with a systematic development of the concept that internalized dyadic object relations were the substructures of ego, superego, and id, those three being, in turn, the substructures of the personality, a final superstructure. In other words, this was an open-systems theory of psychic structures to which they both contributed and gave an impetus, which I think we have been trying to develop further. It still is an important task because it links the internalization of early interpersonal experiences of human relations to the development of psychic structure in a way that is clearer and more precise than anybody else's contributions in psychoanalysis. Melanie Klein referred to the nature of early object relations and defensive operations, but she really never developed a systematic view of psychic structure linking her views with those of Freud.

D.S.: She offered much more by way of clinical observation and wonderful clinical experience, but not the systematic development.

O.K.: Fairbairn had a clarity of thinking and of writing. English is my third language, so I'm not an expert to talk about English, but I have been told by people who have an appreciation of the English language that they have the same experience I have. There is a clarity about Fairbairn's thinking and writing—which is not that frequent in psychoanalytic writing.

D.S.: Quite. Well, I think that had to do with his philosophical training and vigorous mind. Just to return: the layering idea is Jacobson's, the layering of experience. That is not in Fairbairn. It is very much in your thinking. And one of the places where you differed with Fairbairn's idea originally was in differentiating between splitting and repression, a differentiation you have made an important building block.

O.K.: Yes. He did not differentiate that.

D.S.: In my reading, he makes splitting and repression functionally almost synonymous functions: two descriptions of something that always happens at the same time.

O.K.: Yes. He worked at something else. At one point—it was like an early outline—when he tried to differentiate the obsessive, the hysteric, the phobic, and the paranoid. He hinted that they are different organizations of internalized object relations. It's a very important point, except that there was a certain simplicity in the way he put the good object inside or outside. The structures are more complex than that. But the idea that they are different "molecular" arrangements of internalized object relations determining the dominant types of pathological character structure—that is very important. I am working on that at this time. I am working on a psychoanalytic classification of personality disorders, in which I am using the concept of a developmental view of psychic structures that can evolve in different directions under the impact of different dimensional features, intensity of aggression, introversion, extroversion.

D.S.: He didn't talk about it in terms of the experience of the external object world's handling of the child. Is that part of your view of it, the building up of the balance of factors?

O.K.: Yes, but he did assume that the actual mother has importance in the development of the child.

D.S.: Yes, and that's why his model is radically different. It gives a place to think about what actually happened.

O.K.: Yes. That is part of the strength of the entire Independent group. I'm thinking that the influence of trauma, which we now know is quite prevalent in certain severe personality disorders, also can be conceptualized in terms of the internalization of traumatic object relations. Fairbairn's outline lends itself to a conceptualization of the internalization of the relationship with the persecutor so that victimized persons internalize both victim and victimizer. You have to deal with both aspects, activated in the mind. Fairbairn points to that.

D.S.: Did you know about his experience with trauma? He was a combat officer in World War I, and then he treated abused children.

O.K.: I didn't know that.

D.S.: He treated sexually and physically abused children in the child guidance clinic at the University. He did write one paper on sexually abused children, and he wrote a paper on abusers, both of them quite good. They have a modern tone.

O.K.: I must confess, I have not ever seen them. I wasn't aware of them.

D.S.: Well, they are in the two volumes of his uncollected papers, *From Instinct to Self,* that his daughter, Ellinor Birtles, and I edited. They certainly weren't well known in the analytic community. And then, of course, the war neuroses were a major part of what he drew on directly. So it has seemed to me not surprising that his theory works well for trauma and traumatized patients.

O.K.: One other aspect of his work that I found stimulating was his analysis of dreams. Like all classical analysts, he used dream analysis quite centrally in his clinical papers, but the way in which he would look for different aspects of the patient's personality to be impersonated by different figures in the content of the dream was, I thought, very interesting and made a lot of sense clinically. Very helpful.

D.S.: And it was radically different.

O.K.: Radically different! And that's an important contribution to dream analysis that is underemphasized in the usual literature. People who are interested in Fairbairn's work don't refer much to that, which I find interesting. I've found it helpful to think that different people in the dream may represent different aspects of the patient's personality split off and distributed in the same way as they also represent split-off aspects of significant objects. So that both self and object are split as role distributions within the dream.

D.S.: Right. It's comparable to using the dream as transference material, but to think of it exclusively as a "short" of the inner world was a radical thought for me when I read it. I'm glad you mentioned the business about the dreams. It has been important to me as well. I have used it with couples and families whose dreams are simultaneously representative of different people in the family or aspects of the couple's life and are also shorts of internal life as it is projected onto them.

Well, is there anything else you can think of that we haven't talked about that's worth mentioning?

O.K.: I think we probably have talked about all the important things. There are always things that we remember afterwards, but I think we have talked about what, at least for me, are essential aspects that accompany me in my daily work and thinking. Particularly this dyadic unit of self-representation and object representation as inseparable building blocks in mental structure.

D.S.: So that even when you talk about affect, actually affect implies that it's connected to the dyadic unit. You can't think of it as a disembodied phenomenon.

O.K.: Absolutely. There is no such thing as pure affect that does not contain an internalized object relation.

D.S.: That means that, if we are talking about treating depressive affective illnesses, we are talking about an illness of relational issues in the individual, not simply translatable to a psychopharmacological intervention.

O.K.: Well, often treatable by psychopharmacological means, because psychopathology of affect predisposes to overloads of depressive or guilt-ridden relationships. So that affects influence the kind of relationship we establish, the same as if having an excessive activation of rage means the internalization of rageful internalized object relations. So the pathology, the exaggeration of certain object relations patterns, may come both from inborn excessive affects and from traumatic situations that activate this affect. But in all cases there is an object relation. Sometimes strategically it may be preferable, if there are strong biological dispositions to affect distortion, as in the case of major affective illness, to treat that biologically. But there are other times, when we are talking about characterological depression, when patients respond best to psychotherapeutic treatment. The same is true, I think, for all affects. One interesting study in this regard is sexual excitement. It is a basic affect that's strangely, or not so strangely, neglected in the literature and even in psychoanalytic writing.

D.S.: It's a funny thing, isn't it, in view of Freud's basing psychoanalysis on sex, how little writing has been specifically about sex as a primary matter?

O.K.: About subjective experience of sexuality, yes. This is an area that needs lots of exploration. The same as we are now exploring the subject of love, which Freud opened up from a new perspective but which was followed up by very few authors, particularly by French authors.

D.S.: Well, thank you very much for talking with me about Fairbairn. It has been a real treat for me.

O.K.: It has been a treat for me to have this opportunity to share this with you. I know that both of us share the view of the importance of object relations theory in psychoanalysis. Fairbairn certainly is one of the basic contributors to it.

3

Developing Connections
Fairbairn's Philosophic Contribution

Ellinor Fairbairn Birtles

When I read Fairbairn's early published and unpublished papers I realized that their intellectual context was of paramount importance to an understanding of his theory of personality development. In the papers published between 1927 and 1939, the starting point is Freudian, but in each paper Fairbairn makes an innovative contribution.

In the unpublished papers, written when he was a lecturer in psychology at Edinburgh University from 1927 to 1935, Fairbairn's orientation becomes much clearer. Thus his philosophical orientation emerges as the crucial factor in any study of his psychoanalytical ideas.

To establish the philosophical origins of Fairbairn's work, I started by researching the syllabus of his first degree, undertaken from 1907 to 1911, in Mental Philosophy at Edinburgh University. My reading of the actual texts he had studied led me to appreciate his reliance on a dialectic account of the human condition as the basis for his theory of object relations. It became apparent that Hegel was the key to this theory. One of the important features of Hegelian philosophy is its connection with an Aristotelian rather than a Platonic account. Initially, Fairbairn was particularly interested in Aristotelian ideas and continued his study of Greek culture, language, and philosophy in postgraduate courses in Strasburg and Kiel Universities. The close relationship between Aristotle and Hegel is therefore important.

During World War I, Fairbairn decided to "become a psychotherapist." This decision followed his visit in 1916 to W. H. R. Rivers's Hospital for "shell-shocked" combatants located in Edinburgh. Accordingly, in 1919 he enrolled as a medical student at Edinburgh University, graduating in 1923. His experience of the "war neuroses," "disturbed" and abused children, and sexual offenders over a period of more than 30 years provided a unique basis for the validation of his theoretical reassessment of personality development. Thus Fairbairn's practical clinical experience enabled him to develop a view of object relations within which infantile deprivation and its corollary of reactive dependence is of specific relevance to an understanding of 20th-century philosophic ideas.

Fairbairn's study of Freudian psychoanalysis began in 1919 with "The Interpretation of Dreams" (Freud, 1900). He later undertook an extensive and thorough reading of Freud's writings, some of which he read in the original German. But, although Fairbairn's ideas were stimulated by Freud, it is important to appreciate that his critical response to them demonstrates a very different philosophic perspective.

Freud's Background

Freud's training in medicine and neurology was based on the dominant scientific theories at the time, which, in turn, were based on physics and mechanics. In these theories, elements constituting a system were seen as separate and indivisible; for example, atoms were immutable. Mechanical systems were seen to consist of discrete parts driven by an external energy source. To take the human person as an example, mind and body were each distinct; hence the body has one energy source and the mind another. Freud's historical position in the European debate about unconscious mental processes was chronologically close to Darwin's (1859). In *The Origin of the Species,* conflict of interest between individuals, species, and the environment became the cause of evolution. At this time, discussions about unconscious mental processes were particularly widespread in Europe. Freud crystalized these ideas about unconscious mental processes into a theory of mental functioning based on the analogy of 19th-century physics.

Fairbairn's training, on the other hand, was in philosophy. Philosophic training is designed to develop the ability to analyze ideas and concepts, identify their basic assumptions, and assess their internal coherence. Fairbairn's post-Freudian position in the debate gave him the advantage of alternative scientific metaphors.

Although only 33 years separated Freud's birth from that of Fairbairn's, scientific ideas had changed dramatically. So, in spite of his insights Freud remains a 19th-century man, while Fairbairn is a 20th-century one. Both men realized that any psychological theory had to be commensurate with scientific laws. Here I am in trouble, for one of the changes from 19th- to 20th-century science was a general agreement that such "laws" are strictly conditional. So I am using "laws" with the conditional rider that such laws are themselves the subject of the current paradigm. The view of science on which Fairbairn based his thinking relied on alternative conceptualisations validated by Einstein's theory of relativity.

Here are Einstein's words from a lecture given by him in Oxford in 1933: "For to the discoverer [in that field,] . . . the constructions of his imagination appear so necessary and so natural that he is apt to treat them not as the creations of his thoughts but as given realities." Here Einstein was drawing attention to the effects on the individual mind of cultural and intellectual influences, or modes of thinking. In the paradigm change from the 19th-century model in which energy and structure were separate, to the 20th-century one, where energy and structure are integral, which Einstein himself initiated with his theory of relativity, the structural model of the steam engine was replaced by that of the composite and constantly interactive atomic system.

Fairbairn's Philosophic Origins

Fairbairn brought to his critique of psychoanalysis a thorough study of Freud's writings combined with an adherence to logical thought that was the result of his philosophic background. There are two distinct traditions within European philosophy. In the Platonic tradition, discrete parts or functions are considered in isolation; the Aristotelian account is integrative, relating the parts to each other within the whole. Freud's view of human nature assumed a Platonic mind–body dualism consistent with the 19th-century scientific view. In this view, the mind and the body are concrete entities. Difference is thus seen as opposition. The connection between mind and body is conflictual, leading to Freud's ideas of necessary conflict between, for example, life and death, id and ego instincts, and the individual and society. Thus, Freud's assumption that the response to conflict must be repression was founded upon what Berlin (1969) calls "negative freedom," that is, *freedom from* interference. A defensive psychology became a fundamental assumption in psychoanalysis.

Fairbairn's critical reorientation of psychoanalysis assumes an Aristotelian view of human nature. As I have noted, this view was expanded in the 19th century by Hegel. His account elaborates a dialectic environment within which "human nature" is defined as integral and participatory. In his model, each individual is motivated by the desire for integration and reciprocity in the human world, which also encompasses a wider integration within the natural world. His model, then, illustrates that oppositional difference can be incorporated by means of changed perspectives.

Fairbairn's psychoanalytic vision originated from his studies in Mental Philosophy undertaken as his first degree at Edinburgh University prior to 1914. The course focused on the psychology of human beings, as exemplified by the structuring of their ideas in such forms as "logic," "ethics," and the philosophies of law, economics, and education. The metaphysical content of the syllabus was influenced by Professor Andrew Seth's (1882) interest in philosophic developments from Kant to Hegel. As we saw Fairbairn extended his studies at postgraduate level. This background, combined with his lecturership in psychology, during which he also taught philosophy, ensured that Fairbairn gained a thorough knowledge of prior and contemporary accounts of subjective experience and unconscious aspects of the human mind.

In Hegel's (1817) account of psychology, the innate capacities for language, symbolization, and rational thought are dependent for their development on an adequate environment. The dialectic exchange between the subject and the other results in a new relationship, or synthesis, which forms the basis for man's capacity for language and thought. Because subject–object relationships encompass a progressive epistemological element, meaning and value, not gratification, provide Fairbairn with primary motivation.

Aristotle was the first Western philosopher to develop a holistic psychology. He based this philosophy on his observations of the effects that one object had on another in terms of the extent to which one was active in respect of the other. Using this methodology, Aristotle was able to develop a psychology in which he moved from the Platonic view in which the *form* of the human being, the body, was devalued and the power of reason exalted, to one in which the *experience* of existing in a world of phenomena is contained *within the form of the individual*. Mind and body thus have equal status. Aristotle (n.d.) wrote, "man is an animal naturally formed for society" (111 127a). The major consequence of a shift from a discrete entity in which human development is preprogrammed to one in which "Man" is identified as a "social" animal is the role of physical and emotional dependence. Having accepted Aristotle's definition that man is a social animal, Fairbairn realized that, because the human infant is totally dependent, this dependency is the dominant psychological factor in early life. It is the child's idiosyncratic experience of total dependence which results in its *perception* of maternal inadequacy. It is for this reason that infantile dependence and its circumstances play such a significant role in Fairbairn's psychoanalytic account.

Schacht (1972) identifies three firm philosophical connections between Aristotle and Hegel (pp. 292–293): (1) where "essence is defined as your very nature." (We would now use the term genetic inheritance, within which rationality is a defining characteristic of humans beings); (2) what Aristotle described as "coming-to-be," the change from potentiality to actuality, where, for instance, the infant has the unactualized potentiality to become a fully rational being; (3) the notion of an "originative source of change . . . in one thing in relation to another." Such changes in living creatures appear to be of their own doing but are actually reactive responses to their experience of the environment. The child's adaptive response to its parents and external reality would come under this category, while the "change" in physical maturity has its source within the child itself. When the environment is satisfactory, "self-realization," the actualization of potential, occurs.

For Hegel (1817) rational decisions have to be self-conscious. Being human is to have the capacity for rational thought and self-reflection. It has been argued that Fairbairn assumes too great a capacity for cognition in the infant. It is one of his arguments against Freud's theory of the Ucs that there is no reason for infantile affective experience to be repressed if it is the result of instinctual stimulation alone. Experience must reach some level of cognition before repression is necessary. Research by Stern (1985) has confirmed the early functioning of cognition in infants. Following Stout (1927), Fairbairn (1943b) argued that "although the mental life of the infant belongs characteristically to the perceptual level, it is not altogether devoid of ideational, and even conceptual, elements" (p. 293).

Now, in Hegel's (1817) own words:

> It is the facts or the contents in our consciousness, of whatever kind they are, that give character or determination to our feelings, perceptions, fancies and figurative conceptions; to our aims and duties; and to our thoughts and notions. From this point of

view, feeling perception, etc. are the forms assumed by these contents. The contents remain one and the same, whether they are merely felt, or felt with an admixture of thoughts, or merely and simply thought. In any one of these forms, or in the admixture of several, the contents confront the consciousness, or are its object. But when they are thus objects of consciousness, the modes of the several forms ally themselves with the contents, and each form of them appears in consequence to give rise to a special object [p. 243].

Here Hegel is describing an unconscious process through which affect is associated with "facts" or "contents" in the mind. It is this association, which may be a complex of affects with the "fact" (the mental image), that is the "special object." Thus, inner objects are composed of "fact" (the image of the object) and the affect, or affects, attached to it. (In the passage, Hegel implies that neutral affect is possible.) For Fairbairn, the mother as the "fact" or "content" is seen in three affective modes: alluring, rejecting, and acceptable or "good." These, then, are the "*forms* assumed by contents." Each form, in conjunction with the "fact" (the mother), then gives rise to the "exciting," "rejecting," and "ideal" objects respectively. Because the mother is defined by three separate affective experiences, she becomes three separate mothers, each embodying a separate relationship with the child.

For Hegel (1821), self-consciousness requires an object from which to differentiate itself; such an object has to be recognized as alien, and, as Singer (1983) writes, a "form of opposition to it":

There is therefore a peculiar kind of love-hate relationship between self-consciousness and the external object. The relationship, in the best tradition of love-hate relationships, comes to the surface in the form of desire. To desire something is to wish to possess it. . . . to transform it into something that is yours and thus to strip it of its foreignness [p. 57].

Singer sees that desire, arising from the need for self-consciousness to find a connection with an external object, "yet finds itself limited by anything that is outside itself.". . . [To] desire something is . . . an unsatisfactory state for self-consciousness" (p. 58). In this "dilemma," Singer notes that Hegel (1807) took the step of making "the object of self-consciousness another self-consciousness." This implies that the object is returned to the external world and has its own autonomy—it is no longer controlled by the subject. This notion of the unsatisfactory nature of encounters motivated by desire became, in Fairbairn's theory, the basic motivation for the splitting of the ego and for the construction of endopsychic structure, personality development, and psychology. By splitting the object into three, Fairbairn (1944) retains limited control of aspects of the object and leaves his "ideal object" free to interact in the external world. This, then, represents the infant's recognition of another "self-consciousness."

The acknowledgment by the infant that the mother is separate also means that the infant itself is perceived by the mother as separate. Self-consciousness is a recognition that the self is an object to itself; that is to say, the condition of self-consciousness is one of ego splitting. Here we can understand Fairbairn's claim that splitting is universal.

Singer (1939) noted that Hegel (1807) made "the object of self consciousness another self consciousness." This is part of the psychological process involved in the capacity for self-reflection. Self-reflection can be understood as knowing that I, myself, am another to myself, as well as being the "other" to another. In Hegelian terms, the living world is an expression of God's self-consciousness (Hegel, 1807), the purpose of which is the total expression of the Absolute Spirit. For Hegel (1821) the apparent form of the Absolute Spirit is the secular State within which individuals form a dialectic whole. As the individual is one self-consciousness living within and reciprocating within another self consciousness, thus, that which is other is also that within which the other is incorporated. Fairbairn (1941) drew attention to this phenomenon:

> The process of differentiation of the object derives particular significance from the fact that infantile dependence is characterized

not only by identification, but also by an oral attitude of incorporation. In virtue of this fact the object with which the individual is identified becomes equivalent to an incorporated object, or, to put the matter in a more arresting fashion, the object in which the individual is incorporated is incorporated in the individual [p. 43].

Human Nature

As noted, Platonic and Aristotelian ideas of "human nature" have opposing assumptions. The Platonic elevation of the mind over the body was consolidated in the Christian church. In the 18th century, in the period of the Enlightenment, Reason became deified (e.g., Reason Personified was crowned in Notre Dame). Hence, education, within a strictly Western mode of the 18th-century *Encyclopédie,* introduced in France by thinkers such as Rousseau and Voltaire, and through which they sought to propagate "all branches of human knowledge" to as wide a public as possible, became the road to emancipation. "Human nature" was defined in terms of progress. Cultural changes were seen as evolutionary in such linear terms as the change from the primitive to the civilized, the irrational to the rational. Human nature was thus seen to be universal; no account was taken of cultural or historical factors. Starting with Rousseau, who himself influenced Hegel, philosophy moved toward reintegration of the mind and body in the individual (e.g., Nietzsche's [1878] accommodation of the Apollonian and Dionysian). But as cultural and historical factors have acquired increasing emphasis in 20th-century philosophy, human nature as a category has become problematic. Ortega (1941) (the Spanish philosopher who studied in Germany for five years after gaining his Ph.D., after which he returned to Madrid) wrote, "Man, in a word, has no nature; what he has is—history" (cited in Kaufmann, 1975, p. 157).

How, then, can the subjective be meaningfully incorporated within the idea of human nature as a construct? What kind of model can we use?

I suggest that Fairbairn's "endopsychic structure" might fill the bill. So let's see how it finally evolved.

Hegel's dialectic psychology provided the base from which Fairbairn's theory evolved. As man was defined first by Aristotle as a social animal, encounters between the self and the other are socially and historically constructed. Society is necessary for the development of human potential, so social relationships are potentially emancipatory. The condition of self-consciousness implies the recognition of an opposition to it, which takes the form of another self-consciousness, so separation is a developmental step in social integration. This condition of mutuality, as Hegel stressed, incorporates the concept of "recognition." That is to say, we exist in the form of a self because we are recognized as another self, in the first instance by the mother. Sartre wrote, "the other is the indispensable mediator between myself and me. . . . [because] I am as certain of his or her existence as I am of my own existence. . . . [through heightened self-awareness] I have an 'objective' self, that is, a 'self for others'" (cited in Holmes, 1996, p. 315). Here we can understand the importance of Fairbairn's (1941) words that "the greatest need of a child is to obtain conclusive assurance (a) that he is genuinely loved as a person by his parents, and (b) that his parents genuinely accept his love" (p. 39) as a condition of healthy mental development.

Scientific Concepts in Psychoanalysis

Now let's look at the scientific frameworks within which Freud and Fairbairn developed their psychoanalytic ideas. In simple terms, the difference can be expressed as that between a steam engine and a benzene ring, or that between Freud's Platonic dualism and Fairbairn's Aristotelian integration. Freud's ideas about energy relied on the 19th-century mechanical view dominated by Helmholtz's (1847) conception of energy as divorced from structure, that is to say that a system or body is essentially inert without the application of an external energy source.

When the energy source is closed off, the system returns to a state of inertia. This is a mechanical view manifested in Freud's theory as (a) repression and (b) the "death instinct." Fairbairn (1930) argued:

> The very conception of a "death-instinct" contains an inner contradiction. All instincts are essentially expressions of life. *The instincts . . . are simply the characteristic ways in which life manifests itself in members of the species.* Unless the term instinct is interpreted in this sense, it is difficult to attach any meaning to it at all. *All* instincts are therefore "life-instincts" [p. 122].

Fairbairn's revised view incorporated 20th-century scientific concepts, such as Einstein's (1905) theory of relativity and the work of Heisenberg, Planck, and many others. In experiments that validated Einstein's ideas, it is the relationship between the observer and the object that defines the event. Truth becomes relative, that is, dependent upon subjective experience. Ideas of atomic structure define potential as an inherent characteristic of structure—it is the carbon double bond that gives the benzene ring its enormous capacity to form new compounds with totally different properties. This is the basis of organic chemistry, in other words, the history of life. Fairbairn ((1951) described "energy as inseparable from structure"; moreover, "the only changes which are intelligible are changes in structural relationships and relationships between structures; and such changes are essentially directional" (p. 176). He openly acknowledged his debt to modern science:

> In the twentieth century atomic physics has revolutionized the scientific conception of the physical universe and has introduced the conception of dynamic structure; and the views which I have outlined represent an attempt to formulate psychoanalytical theory in terms of this conception. The psychology of dynamic structure . . . has the advantage of enabling psychopathological phenomena to be explained directly in terms of structural conformations, and thus doing justice to the unquestionable fact that symptoms are expressions of the personality as a whole [pp. 176–177].

Capra (1982) says, "The systems view looks at the world in terms of relationships and integration" (p. 286). He describes machines as "linear" and systems as "cyclical" (p. 289). Moreover, when machines break down, a "single cause can usually be identified," whereas, in system breakdown, multiple interactive factors may be responsible. Freud's hierarchical structural connections between the superego, the ego, and the id and his view that single traumatic events are pathogenetic are linear; whereas Fairbairn's account implies the gradual accretion of human interactions.

Post-Hegelian Philosophy

Andrew Seth, Fairbairn's professor, was, as mentioned, a post-Hegelian thinker, as was Fairbairn, whose work developed concurrently with that of the Frankfurt School, founded in 1923. These philosophers inherited the Hegelian tradition, used the work of Marx (who was known as a "young Hegelian") and Freud as their starting point. Their brief was to develop a "critical theory . . . uncontaminated by positivism and materialism, and giving due role to the influence of . . . the culture and self image of people in a historical period as a factor in social change" (Blackburn, 1994, p. 146). They "emphasised the interlocking role of psychoanalysis and popular culture in reinforcing the prevailing Western condition of a passive, depersonalized acceptance of the *status quo*." The first generation of thinkers included Marcuse; the second included Habermas. They considered that psychoanalysis could provide a new methodology for an empirical investigation of the subjective. In 1932, Marcuse (1932), discussing his Hegelian roots, wrote "Man cannot simply accept the objective world. . . ; he must appropriate it; he has to transform the objects of this world into organs of his life, which becomes effective in and through them" (p. 16). Turning to individual freedom, Marcuse argued, "The individual cannot be simultaneously free and unfree, . . . unless the person is conceived of as divisible." He defined the "inner" realm as "free" and the external world as "unfree"; this, Marcuse maintained, is the psychological condition of the individual in Western civilization. Fairbairn reversed this position making the infantile "inner" world, which includes defensive repression, as the condition of "unfreedom" and the "outer" world as the arena in which the relative freedom of mature dependence is attainable. Here Marcuse's position demonstrates his acceptance of negative freedom, expressed by Freud as "repression" and by Marx as alienation. Where does Fairbairn stand here? Well, ego splitting is a dissociative process. In his M.D. thesis Fairbairn (1929a) wrote, "Repression is a special form of dissociation of the unpleasant." For Fairbairn, infantile anxiety is the cause of repression; repression is psychical dissociation. As far as Fairbairn (1944) is concerned, while all repression is potentially pathogenic, the degree of repression determines its pathogenicity. Both splitting and dissociative processes are universal, so alienation is a factor in human experience. Dissociation plays a vital role in Fairbairn's account of psychopathology, for example, "moral defence" (1943a, p. 65) or the "return of bad objects." In his early writing he gave accounts of more "normal" expressions of active dissociation operating, for instance, in education. Here Marcuse has affirmed political and philosophic isolationism and Fairbairn continuous adaptation. In 1941 the Spanish philosopher Ortega y Gassett similarly defined freedom as the living capacity for adaptation: "To be free means to be lacking a constitutive identity, . . . to be able to be other than what one was, . . . The only attribute of the fixed, stable being in the free being is this constitutive instability" (quoted in Kaufmann, 1972, p. 156).

Turning to Habermas, Richards (1989) writes, "Habermas proposes that psychoanalysis is the only example of an emancipatory, self-reflective science, or rather that this is so once it is shorn of Freud's theory of biological instincts" (p. 127). In this short statement Richards brings together Habermas's recognition that, if psychoanalysis retains its dependence on a biological instinct theory, its capacity to be either a science or emancipatory will be negated. Very much Fairbairn's own diagnosis.

We have seen how the idea of emancipation has been a thread running through the philosophic and scientific ideas I have outlined here. For Freud, psychoanalysis could provide a tool whereby human motivation could be identified, exposed, and comprehended through analysis undertaken by an "expert." Freud was thus relying on the idea that truth understood rationally can be a way to freedom, a view shared by the Frankfurt School. According to Fairbairn (1929b), the idea of emancipation through psychoanalysis was a dominant feature of the 1929 International Congress held in Oxford, the idea being that complete analysis would result in a Nietzschean "Superman" freed *from his environment*. Fairbairn didn't think much of this idea. But he did, particularly in his early writing, advocate that where societal environments are incompatible with healthy mental development, the external environment should be altered, and not the other way round. Freud's therapeutic aim was to allow his patients to recover their own history by excavating repressed trauma and memories; in these terms, this is a self-reflective model. But Freud insisted that the story must be interpreted before it is "true."

As we have seen, the "truth" is more problematic for us than it was for Freud. Today truth is always constrained within its cultural and historical context. Science, as even Popper (1935) realized, was provisional. All we can hope for is conditional truth. As far as the human mind and its psychology is concerned, psychoanalysis can provide us with subjective histories as the data for scientific investigation. Gadamer (1960) proposed a "reader response" theory of interpretation. This methodology sees dialogue as the only means to achieve meaningful, (truthful) understanding of the "text." A "text," of course, can equally well be a "history." But first the "reader" has to become aware, by means of self-reflection, of his own historicity. That is to say, be aware of his, or her, own culture and its history, as well as its assumptions. Gadamer also maintained that time can fully elucidate the real events. The argument is that the man in the trenches of the Somme can supply only subjective truth; it is only when we can survey the event in the light of documents, hindsight, and the like, that the "truth" emerges. Of course, subjective truth is not untruthful; it is merely partial. Fairbairn (1958) proposes a similarly dialogic methodology for the psychoanalytic encounter: "The subjective aspects of the phenomena studied are as much part of the phenomena as the objective aspects, and are actually more important; and the subjective aspects can only be understood in terms of the subjective experience of the psychologist himself" (p. 78).

We saw that, when "human nature" is defined as ahistorical and universal, that definition cannot serve as the basis for a general model for a universal psychology. It then becomes apparent that changing philosophic ideas played a part in undermining the definition. Fairbairn managed, in his theory of endopsychic structure, to provide us with a universal model, which, because it is formed *within existing relationships* between the developing child and its environment, is culturally, historically and experientially derived. "Man is what has happened to him and what he has done" (Ortega y Gassett, quoted in Kaufmann, 1975, p. 157). Individual infantile experience will vary according to cultural and historical circumstances. Thus, for example, though the *influence* of language will be variable, it will not affect either the capacity for language or symbolization. The infant's experience of unsatisfying relationships will be universal, though its extent will be variable. But Ortega y Gassett used the words "and what he has done" in this way, emphasizing that both aspects of his contention are active. Thus the "happening" and the response become intrinsic. They form a structural relationship within which the child's active response to experience occurs both internally and externally. It is apparent in the external world and becomes incorporated internally as an aspect of his personality. Because it is a "living systems model," Fairbairn's theory of endopsychic development can accommodate any experience of "being in the world," to use Heidegger's phrase. Thus it can be applied as a universal developmental model for human psychology.

So, Fairbairn's contribution has been to form connections between scientific, philosophic, and psychoanalytic ideas, and, above all, to provide a model that fulfills the criteria required by modern versions of these three disciplines.

References

Aristotle (n.d.), *Politics*, ed. S. Everson (trans. B. Jowett). Cambridge: Cambridge University Press, 1988.

Berlin, I. (1969), Two concepts of liberty. In: *Four Essays on Liberty.* Oxford, UK: Oxford University Press.

Blackburn, S. (1994), *Oxford Dictionary of Philosophy.* Oxford: Oxford University Press.

Capra, F. (1983), *The Turning Point.* London: Fontana.

Darwin, C. (1859), *The Origin of Species.* London: Penguin, 1968.

Einstein, A. (1933), On the method of theoretical physics. In: *Darwin to Einstein*, ed. N. Coley & V. Hall. Harlow, UK: The Open University and Longman, 1980, pp. 143–148.

Fairbairn, W. R. D. (1929a), Dissociation and repression. In: *From Instinct to Self, Vol. 1*, ed. D. E. Scharff & E. F. Birtles. Northvale, NJ: Aronson, 1994, pp. 13–79.

——— (1929b), Impressions of the 1929 International Congress of Psychoanalysis. In: *From Instinct to Self, Vol. 2*, ed. D. E. Scharff & E. F. Birtles. Northvale, NJ: Aronson, 1994, pp. 454–461.

——— (1930), Libido theory re-examined. In: *From Instinct to Self, Vol. 1*, ed. D. E. Scharff & E. F. Birtles. Northvale, NJ: Aronson, 1994, pp. 115–156.

——— (1941), A revised psychopathology of the psychoses and psychoneuroses. *Internat. J. Psycho-Anal.*, 22:250–279. Also in: *Psychoanalytic Studies of the Personality.* London: Routledge & Kegan Paul, 1952, pp. 28–58.

——— (1943a), The repression and return of of bad objects (with special reference to the "war neuroses"). *Brit. J. Med. Psychol.*, 29:342–347. Also in: *Psychoanalytic Studies of the Personality.* London: Routledge & Kegan Paul, 1952.

——— (1943b), Phantasy and internal objects. Paper presented February 17 at the British Psycho-Analytical Society. Published in: *The Freud-*

Klein Controversies 1941–45. London: Routledge, Chapman & Hall and the Institute of Psycho-Analysis, 1991. Also in: *From Instinct to Self, Vol. 2*, ed. D. E. Scharff & E. F. Birtles. Northvale, NJ: Aronson, 1994, pp. 293–294.

———— (1944), Endopsychic structure considered in terms of object-relationships. *Internat. J. Psycho-Anal.*, 27:70–93. Also in: *Psychoanalytic Studies of the Personality*. London: Routledge & Kegan Paul, 1952.

———— (1951), A synopsis of the author's views regarding the structure of the personality. In: *Psychoanalytic Studies of the Personality*. London: Routledge & Kegan Paul, 1952.

———— (1958), On the nature and aims of psychoanalytic treatment. *Internat. J. Psycho-Anal.*, 39:374–385. Also in: *From Instinct to Self, Vol. 1*, 1994, pp. 74–92.

Freud, S. (1900), The interpretation of dreams. *Standard Edition*, 4 & 5. London: Hogarth Press, 1958.

Gadamer, H. G. (1960), *Truth and Method*. New York: Crossroad Paperbacks, 1982.

Helmholtz, H. von (1847), Uber der Erhaltung der Kraft. Can be found as "Energy Conservation as an Example of Simultaneous Discovery," by T. S. Kuhn, in *Critical Problems in the History of Science*, ed. M. Clagett. Madison: Wisconsin University Press, 1951, pp. 321–356.

Hegel, G. W. F. (1807), *Phenomenology of Spirit*. Oxford: Oxford University Press, 1979.

———— (1817), *The Logic of Hegel*, from *The Encyclopaedia of the Philosophical Sciences*, trans. W. Wallace. Oxford: Clarendon Press, 1874.

———— (1821), *The Philosophy of Right*. New York: Oxford University Press, 1967.

Holmes, O. (1996), Perceptions of "otherness." In: *People of the Book*, ed. J. Rubin-Dworski & S. Fisher Fishkin (trans. J. de Bres). Madison: University of Wisconsin Press, 1996.

Kaufmann, W. (1975), *Existentialism*. New York: New American Library.

Marcuse, H. (1932), The foundation of historical materialism. In: *From Luther to Popper*, trans. J. de Bres. London: Verso, 1972.

Nietzsche, F. (1878), *The Birth of Tragedy*. London: Penguin, 1992.

Ortega y Gassett, J. (1941), Man has no nature. In: *Towards a Philosophy of History*, trans. H. Weyl, E. Clark & W. Atkinson. Reprinted in 1961 as *History as a System*. In: *Existentialism* by W. Kaufmann. New York: Norton, 1975.

Popper, K. (1935), *Conjectures, Growth and Refutations*. London: Routledge, 1989.

Richards, B. (1989), *Images of Freud*. London: J. M. Dent.

Sartre, J-P. (1956), *Being and Nothingness*, trans. H. E. Barnes. New York: Philosophical Library.

Schacht, R. L. (1972), Hegel on freedom. In: *Hegel*, ed. A. MacIntyre. Notre Dame: University of Notre Dame Press, pp. 289–328.

Seth (Pringle-Pattison), A. (1882), *The Development from Kant to Hegel*. London: Williams & Norgate.

Singer, P. (1983), *Hegel*. Oxford: Oxford University Press.

Stern, D. (1985) *The Interpersonal World of the Infant*. New York: Basic Books.

Stout, G. F. (1927), *The Groundwork of Psychology*. London: W. B. Clive.

◆ Part 2 ◆

Theoretical Connections

To the Past

4

Repression and Dissociation— Freud and Janet

Fairbairn's New Model of Unconscious Process

Jody Messler Davies

In this tribute and investigation into the work of W. R. D. Fairbairn, I think it serves us well to stand back, with some regularity, and observe the extent to which the Fairbairnian concepts we are exploring here herald in a particularly prescient form so many of the dialogues and controversies of contemporary psychoanalytic theory and practice. In this chapter I seek to explore Fairbairn's lifelong struggle with the concepts of dissociation and repression; the Scylla and Charybdis of contemporary trauma theories; the twin concepts inextricably involved in any attempt to reconfigure mental structure and unconscious process in keeping with contemporary relational theory.

That Fairbairn reached any conclusive definition of the differences between dissociation and repression, about their place and function within mental structuralization, is surely debatable. But psychoanalysis has always concerned itself with process above content, at almost every turn, and that Fairbairn was deeply involved in exploring and articulating these two mental phenomena over the entire course of his career is readily apparent. This interest involved Fairbairn, at the very earliest and most formative stages of his thinking, in exploring the

---

Some parts of this paper appeared earlier in Davies (1996).

entire body of late 19th- and early 20th-century literature on dissociation and its place in mental life. This "preanalytic" literature, so called because it pre-dated Freud's renunciation of the seduction hypothesis and his elevation of psychic fantasy above actual object relations, involved also a more decentered, multiply constructed version of self. This pre-Freudian conceptualization was of a self that struggled with experiences of discontinuity and irreconcilable conflict; a self that was involved in an ongoing dialectic between fragmentation and interaction, a self more in keeping with Fairbairnian endopsychic structuralization, and with contemporary relational psychoanalysis, than with the direction ultimately taken by classical psychoanalysis. This early fascination with dissociative processes involved Fairbairn at this formative stage of his thinking, in an in-depth investigation of the work of Pierre Janet and his contemporaries. He chose to write his 1929 doctoral thesis on the differences between dissociation and repression. Early in that 1929 thesis, discussing the long-term influence of Charcot, Fairbairn went so far as to say, "It was, however, in the influence which he exerted upon two of his pupils . . . that his importance for psychopathology chiefly lies. These pupils were Pierre Janet and Sigmund Freud. It is upon the work of these two men that the whole structure of modern psychopathology is founded" (1994, p. 16).

In the course of this chapter I will argue that the body of Fairbairn's work involved him in lifelong dialogues—one manifest, the other latent—with these two men. The more apparent dialogue with Freud speaks to Fairbairn's opposition to much of classical theory; it speaks to his need to "take on," if you will, the more preeminent theory of his day, all the while maintaining, in a manner that often obfuscates his very dramatic departures and original contributions, his allegiance to its professionally powerful infrastructure. While "speaking out loud" to Freud, Fairbairn's work can also be viewed as a more subtly muted, but nonetheless ongoing, discussion, incorporation, and adaptation of the work of Pierre Janet.

In the first part of this chapter I will explore the relationship between Janet's work and Freud's later work on hysteria. I will try to show how Fairbairn's (1944) oft-repeated remark that psychoanalysis needed to "return to hysteria" stemmed from his deep ambivalence about the direction taken by classical psychoanalysis at this early yet crucial juncture of theory building. I will suggest that Fairbairn's ultimate rendering of endopsychic structure is, indeed, more aligned with the dissociation-based mental models of pre-Freudian thinkers, particularly Janet, the most well regarded and prolific of these thinkers, than it is to the ultimate structural model of mind evolved by the Freudian school.

Janet and Freud

By suggesting often that we "return to hysteria" in order to understand psychic functioning, Fairbairn subtly pulls us back to the point at which the works of these two great thinkers, Pierre Janet and Sigmund Freud, diverged. Fairbairn (1929) stated:

> Although Janet and Freud both owe their inspiration to a common master, their researches have led them along different paths. The starting point for the researches of both was the disease to which Charcot's clinical teaching had directed their attention, i.e., hysteria; but Janet in Paris and Freud in Vienna each pursued his own path more or less indifferent to the other. Each reached the conclusion that all the hydra-headed symptomotology of hysteria was the expression of one fundamental psychological process. They differed, however, in their views as to the nature of this process, as well as in the terms which they adopted to describe it. Janet developed the conception of "dissociation," while Freud developed that of "repression" [p. 16].

In conceiving of Fairbairn's work as an outgrowth of his dialogues with Freud and Janet, I have come to view his ultimate rendering of "endopsychic structure" as a significant nodal linch pin uniting contemporary relational and constructivist models of mind with the alternative psychologies that overwhelmingly predominated pre-Freudian theories of mental structure. As such it also forms a necessary and long overdue linkage between contemporary psychoanalysis and other branches of academic exploration, particularly the neurosciences and cognitive psychologies.

Ten years prior to *"Studies on Hysteria"* (Breuer and Freud, 1893–1895), Pierre Janet (1887) began working with hysterical patients in an attempt to make sense of their puzzling symptomatology. His conclusions, which began appearing in print seven years prior to Freud's and Breuer's (1893) "Preliminary Communication," bear a startling similarity to it. Janet came to believe that the memory processes, the typical schemas for integrating new incoming information, provided the essential organizing mental systems. When operating smoothly, most of these processes went on out of awareness. These schemas are flexible, and there is a constant oscillation between the effect of new information in changing the internal structure of organizing schemas and the individual's reliance on these schemas in order to create mental order and internal organization. Thus, schemas affect the way in which each individual views reality, and reality affects the ongoing structural nuances of schemas (Janet, 1889). It is interesting here to consider the Piagetian notions of accommodation and assimilation and to keep in mind that Piaget himself was one of Janet's most influential pupils. The prescience of these ideas is extraordinary, especially when one compares them with contemporary theories on the constructed nature of memory in the empirical work of people like Daniel Schacter (1987), the application to clinical psychoanalysis in work by Irwin Hoffman (1991, 1992), and their application to such contemporary theories of consciousness as those of Donnel Stern (1996).

True psychic trauma, according to Janet (1887, 1889), occurs when the integration of particularly overstimulating, intensely affective uncharacteristic events cannot be incorporated into preexisting schemas and, indeed, overwhelms the mental resiliency to accommodate such schemas to ongoing experience. Where such unintegrated traumatic events occur, Janet (1894) speculated the establishment of what he termed "subconscious fixed ideas," believed by Ellenberger (1970) to be the first mention of a "subconscious" process in the history of clinical literature. Because of this basic incompatability between traumatic events and preexisting cognitive schemas, Janet maintained that hysterical symptoms are related to these splitoff aspects of personality that come to operate and develop as autonomous centers of awareness and activity. He posited that curing hysterical symptomatology necessitates understanding the roots of these subconscious fixed ideas and reintegrating such experiences within the operative organizing schemas of meaning. Janet experimented with both hypnosis and "automatic talking" his own model of free association in attempting such integrations.

Let us compare these theories with Freud's conceptualization of hysterical processes prior to his rejection of the seduction hypothesis.

What is often referred to as Freud's "preanalytic" work mostly concerned his explication of the mechanisms of hysteria. This explanation is considered to be nonanalytic because the origin of the disorder was believed to be rooted in the real adult seduction of young children and therefore its notions of pathology had their basis in the actual, object-related experiences of the child rather than in the elaboration and structuralization of drive-related unconscious fantasy. An unhappy result of this dichotomy between actual, object-related experience and unconscious fantasy is the naive assumption that those who believe in the primacy of formative object relationships ignore the profound impact of unconscious fantasy in the internalization process. Fairbairn's work marks a significant contribution toward addressing this split.

Perhaps most germane to my thesis here, the turning away from the "preanalytic," from the focus on hysterical states and traumatic realities, also implied a turning away from a model of mind that emphasized the dynamic interplay of multiply organized centers of awareness and agency. For Freud, the mechanism of hysteria involved just such a fragmentation of mental processes; the setting up of discontinuous spheres of associational communication; the partitioning of mental contents into noncommunicating centers of awareness and activity; and the now famous "hypnoid state or condition seconde." Breuer and Freud (1893–1895) stated:

> The longer we have been occupied with these phenomena the more we have become convinced that *the splitting of consciousness which is so striking in the well-known classical cases under the form of* "double conscience" *is present to a rudimentary degree in every hysteria, and that a tendency to such a dissociation, and with it the* emergence of abnormal states of consciousness *(which we shall bring together under the term "hypnoid")* is the basic phenomenon of this neurosis. In these views we concur with Binet and the two Janets [p. 12].

And again, in the same paper:

> In hysteria groups of ideas originating in hypnoid states are present and . . . these are cut off from associative connection with the other ideas, but can be associated among themselves, and thus form the more or less highly organized rudiment of a second consciousness, *a condition seconde.* If this is so, a chronic hysterical symptom will correspond to the intrusion of this second state [p. 15].

Although Freud first used the word repression in this paper, to describe this process of psychical incompatability and splitting, it is clear that his description of the process is more in keeping with Janet's descriptions of "traumatic dissociation" than with his later understanding of repression as a defensive manifestation within the topographical model of unconscious, preconscious, and conscious and, the later, structural model of id, ego, and superego. The latter implies a hierarchical structuring of consciousness and unconsciousness, with the goal of keeping certain experiences entirely and permanently out of awareness, whereas the former stresses the failure to integrate certain fundamentally incompatible interpersonal experiences and the vertical splitting of consciousness into independent centers of associational interconnection. In his discussion of the case of Lucy R., Freud himself makes this distinction:

> When this process occurs for the first time, there comes into being a nucleus and centre of crystallization for the formation of a psychical group divorced from the ego—a group around which everything which would imply an acceptance of the incompatible idea subsequently collects. The splitting of consciousness in these cases of acquired hysteria is accordingly a deliberate and intentional one. At least it is often *introduced* by an act of volition; for the actual outcome is something different from what the subject intended. What he wanted was to do away with an idea, as though it had never appeared, but all he succeeds in doing is to isolate it psychically. . . . The therapeutic process in this case consisted in compelling the psychical group that had been split off to unite once more with the ego-consciousness [pp. 123–124].

It thus becomes difficult not to agree with Ellenberger (1970), who concludes:

> Indeed it is difficult to study the initial periods of Janet's psychological analysis and of Freud's psychoanalysis without coming to the conclusion that . . . the methods and concepts of Freud were modeled after those of Janet, of whom he seems to have inspired himself constantly . . . that is until the paths of the two diverged [p. 540].

The Beginnings of Fairbairn's Endopsychic Structure

The divergence I have just referred to—the divergence that led Freud to the discovery of psychoanalysis and left Janet's work all but forgotten—was therefore twofold. It not only involved a turning away from the primacy of formative, traumatizing, interpersonal relationships to the centrality of drive-dominated unconscious fantasy in determining psychopathology, but also implicitly (and to my way of thinking, more centrally) it involved reconceptualizing the model of mind, which had been based on the internalization of childhood traumas into independent and dynamically interactive centers of awareness and agency, to a model of mind that was singular, integrated, and linearly organized around a hierarchy of universal, fantasy-dominated stages of development. While Fairbairn explicitly addressed the first of these Freudian departures, an allegiance to the primacy of object relations, his entire redrafting of psychic structure and organization addresses his equally firm allegiance to the pre-Freudian model of mind, which emphasized the diffficulty in integrating incompatible systems of self–other experience.

Fairbairn's conceptualization of different selves—a libidinal self and an antilibidinal self—and a central ego organized inextricably around distinct but irreconcilable experiences of the object—experiences that are gratifying, overstimulating, rejecting, and depriving—suggests a mental organization in which psychic structures themselves are agentic and dynamically interacting. Distinctly separate centers of awareness and experience construct multiple interactive world visions which subsequently infuse and inform all interpersonal relationships. Unconsciousness is not static and developmentally layered, but shifting in accord with the self perspective mobilized by the dynamics and interpersonal evocativeness of a situation.

Fairbairn addressed some of the weaknesses of the Janetian model by recognizing that the failure of integration in psychic structure was not restricted to trauma, but actually spoke to universal phenomena of irreconcilable identifications and to a fundamentally object relational definition of intrapsychic conflict. Unfortunately, his frequent use of the term splitting when referring to dissociative processes often obfuscated the connection between his thoughts and these pre-Freudian approaches. Fairbairn seemed to reach the compromise of reserving the term dissociation for more trauma-based manifestations of discontinuity in self-organization, while turning to the more widely used term splitting for more normative irreconcilable identifications.

In a very early clinical paper, "Features in the Analysis of a Patient with a Physical Genital Abnormality" (Fairbairn, 1931), written prior to his reconfiguration of endopsychic structure, one can observe Fairbairn's more manifest dialogue with Freud, as well as the more latent dialogue and identification with Janet. Here we see Fairbairn struggling mightily to forge an integration of the Freudian structural model, although his clinical material screams dissociation. Although he keeps asserting that the clinical findings of the case support the tripartite model of id, ego, and superego, it becomes clear in the end that they simply do not. One can almost hear his sadness in this realization . . . the personal giving up of the idealization of Freud. . . . a watershed in the development of his own creative and original thought. Fairbairn ends with a patient who demonstrates what he later calls a "mutiplicity of ego states," a mind divided into personifications (a term later adopted by Sullivan [1953], although with different implications for psychic structure), personifications that adhere to early internalized relationships with others and part-others constructed out of unconscious fantasy; a system of dynamically interacting aspects of self in ongoing relation to the complementary system of internalized others. In this particularly compelling clinical material, one hears Fairbairn listening to his patient and struggling with and ultimately moving beyond his theoretical preconceptions. We hear the nascent underpinnings of what will emerge as his own unique contribution to understanding psychic structure.

I would like to relate some of this clinical material and ask that, for our purposes now, you consider not only the evolution of theory, but three other aspects of this compelling case: (1) the intricately nuanced wealth of clinical information available about the patient's internal world, when one allows such personifications of separate self-states to find their way into the analytic work; (2) the fact that all these separate "selves" described by Fairbairn exist only "in relation to" significant others, for in each case it is the interpersonal dimension of the self-state that breathes life into the personification described (the personification, indeed, becomes a kind of embodiment of an interpersonal fantasy); and, finally, (3) Fairbairn's normalization of such dissociative phenomena, his assertion that what separates such phenomena from even the extremes of actual multiple personalities is not any qualitative difference but, rather, an essentially quantitative distinction:

> Before the present account is concluded, it seems important to draw attention to another remarkable feature of the case—the tendency of the patient to personify various aspects of her psyche. This tendency first manifested itself in dreams; but it came to be quite consciously adopted by the patient during analysis. The most striking and the most persistent of these personifications were two figures whom she described respectively as "the mischievous boy and the critic." The former figure was a preadolescent boy, completely irresponsible and forever playing pranks and poking fun. This boy was frequently represented as annoying the dreamer by his tricks, or as being chased by more sedate figures, whom he mocked as he escaped. . . .
>
> The personification which the patient described as "the critic" was a figure of a very different character. The critic was essentially a female figure. Occasionally, however, a headmaster under whom she had once worked, or some other male figure of a similar character took over the role of critic. When a male figure played this part, he was invariably an authoritative father-figure whose good opinion she was anxious to secure. Nevertheless, the critic was characteristically represented by a serious, formidable puritanical and aggressive woman of middle age. Sometimes this woman was a fanciful individual who uttered public accusations against the dreamer; but more frequently she was represented by some actual female personage to whose authority the patient had been subject in the past. . . .
>
> Usually the dreaming consciousness played the part of an independent onlooker, whose sympathies were sometimes on the one side, sometimes on the other. . . .
>
> The conformity between the three leading actors in this patient's dreams and Freud's tripartite division of mind must be regarded as providing striking evidence of the practical validity of Freud's scheme. It must be recorded, however, that the dream figures so far mentioned by no means exhaust the personifications appearing . . . thus there eventually emerged another figure whom the patient came to describe as "the little girl." Another personification to make entry during the third stage of analysis was the figure of "the martyr". . . .

Here attention must be drawn to the fact that, although "the little girl" and "the martyr" played relatively subordinate roles, their validity as personifications seemed in no sense inferior to that of the critic and the mischievous boy. This fact raises the question whether Freud's tripartite division of the mind has not led us to regard the ego, the id, and the super-ego too much in the light of entities. Such a tendency is an almost inevitable consequence of the topographical method of exposition adopted by Freud in his description of the mental apparatus. His topographical description has, of course, provided us with an invaluable working hypothesis, but it is a question whether any topographical representation whatsoever (here referring to a repression based structure of horizontal repressions) can hope to do justice to all the complexities of mental structure, and whether, so far as psychological theory is concerned, such a mode of representation is not bound eventually to prove misleading [Fairbairn, 1931, pp. 216–217].

Here, I believe, Fairbairn breaks, irrevocably, from the classical, repression-based models of mind suggested by Freud and later by Klein and struggles with the seemingly impossible task of accounting for mental complexity with a linear integrative approach. Later, in the same text, Fairbairn begins his own theoretical journey, a search for an alternative model of mind, that will end with his own conceptualization of endopsychic structure:

As a whole personifications seem best interpreted as functioning structural units, which . . . attained a certain independence within the total personality; and it seems reasonable to suppose that the mental processes which give rise to multiple personality only represent a more extreme form of those which produced the mischievous boy, the critic, the little girl and the martyr. . . . Evidence of the differentiation of these structures is found so consistently in analytical work that their presence must be regarded not only as characteristic, but as compatible with normality [p. 219].

Thus, by 1931 Fairbairn was entertaining a model of mind based on independent, functionally autonomous subsystems: unique representations of self in particular relation to fantasy-imbued representations of others and part-others, determined overwhelmingly by the affective quality and fantasied vicissitudes of the patient's earliest object relationships.

Implications for Contemporary Relational Theory

Perhaps most unique about Fairbairn's endopsychic substructures was their powerful, dynamic, and irrepressibly agentic nature. These were not static mental representations existing placidly in the archives of the patient's unconscious mind. On the contrary, they occupied the stage of the patient's everyday, lived world, "characters in search of an author," as Grotstein (1995) has so persuasively described them. But here the belief that the author will script action for the players is perhaps a misleading assertion. In Fairbairn's schema it is more likely the characters who will propel the play's action by their endless search for peaceful coexistence and self-perpetuation. Indeed, they assure this coexistence and self-perpetuation by sacrificing aspects of their unique character in order to achieve a functional, dearly bought sense of internal order and integrity. The play itself, that action which we can witness at the outermost layers of experience, becomes a compromise that orchestrates and organizes a multiplicity of separate lives, distinct but inextricably intertwined potentials, which may or may not see the light of day, depending on the bargains that have been struck among the players. This play, indeed, will tolerate no single author, for the play itself is nothing more than that on which its characters can agree; it is an action scripted by committee or by those renegades who choose to break form and undermine the agreed upon narrative. For relational analysts, "the play" is most decidedly not "the thing." We are far more concerned with the endless auditions and rehearsals, the needy, yearning, envious, greedy, sometimes diabolical, sometimes poignant maneuvering that goes on behind the scenes; the struggle to explore and resolve oftentimes conflicting systems of internal motivation, that which determines the character and content of center stage, as well as those who become compelling and oftentimes pivotal bit players driving the play's action in very small, almost imperceptible voices. Indeed, the action that holds our attention, is more likely to resemble a three-ring or, better yet, a multiring circus.

That Fairbairn's structures are actors, centers of agency with frequently competing worlds of their own may be seen in another excerpt from the case we have been discussing. Here Fairbairn (1931) recounts the patient's unfolding sexuality:

> At this time also she began to record experiences with men, which she rather aptly designated as "adventures." She (was) required to travel by train when she came for analysis; and these adventures took place characteristically on the journeys to and fro. She began to find that, when her only fellow traveller was a man, she almost invariably attracted his attention; and incidents in which she was hugged and kissed by chance men in railway carriages became not infrequent. This constituted for her a novel experience, which at first afforded her considerable satisfaction. Thus, she frequently recorded that men who passed her compartment when the train was drawn up at a platform would turn back and get into the same compartment. This may have been true in part at least; for at this stage (of the treatment) she certainly exhaled libido [p. 205].

This clinical description portrays a character in search of her own dissociated agency, her own erotic desire; a struggle against what we might aptly call her proclivity for sex in the passive voice. But it also makes clear that it is only when characters become freed from the agreed upon storyline, when they can break loose from that which has been "scripted by committee," that they can become fully known in the psychoanalytic sense. It is only in this more dissociated state that the patient fully realizes one aspect of her unconscious sexual fantasies. Within a relational model, the psychoanalytic space becomes the transitional arena in which each character can be invited in, afforded the opportunity, if you will, to live out his or her unique potential, unfettered by the need for intrapsychic integration and compromise. In an earlier paper, I (Davies, 1996) have termed such use of the transference–countertransference process a "therapeutic dissociation": a process in which the patient becomes capable of bringing such split-off aspects of self into the therapeutic arena; of allowing them to engage with the analyst; and, in so doing, of clarifying the myriad unconscious interpersonal fantasies that drive the patient's story forward. By thus reopening fantasy-driven interpersonal processes foreclosed by overiding integrative forces, we encourage a kind of splitting apart along naturally occurring, developmentally determined fault lines, thereby encouraging a fuller renegotiation of self-organizations and meaning-schemas born of the patient's earliest self–other experience. We are still working in the realm of unconscious fantasy and conflict. But our Fairbairnian roots dictate that such fantasy is always one of self-in-relation-to-other, and our conflicts the illusory embodiments of these fantasies as they breathe fire into the transference–countertransference enactments allowing aspects and part-aspects of self–other schemas that imbue experience with meaning, making it come alive. It is, I believe, to Fairbairn that we owe the centrality of this ongoing dialectic between dissociation and integration, between fragmentation and renegotiation of psychic structure and meaning.

It is intriguing to speculate on what Fairbairn would have made of more contemporary developments in psychoanalytic theory. For although he speculated in his last paper (Fairbairn, 1958) about the role of the analyst in bringing about psychic change, he never seriously struggled with the interactive, kaleidoscopic, dynamically shifting transference–countertransference process between analyst and patient, which has, for contemporary relational analysts, become the all-important interface where intrapsychic and interpersonal relations meet and together construct a world vision. Although Fairbairn was instrumental in posing the question, Who within the patient is speaking? he never quite reached what for many of us has become the complementary question, Who, within the analyst, is listening?

For contemporary relational analysts the transference–countertransference matrix, as coconstructed by patient and analyst, becomes the transitional stage on which the Fairbairnian cast of characters, in ongoing improvisational interaction with the analyst's complementary troupe of players, can, through projective identification and other projective–introjective mechanisms, begin to tell the story of "multiple selves in interaction." Such character-driven dramas as those which unfold from the tapestry of interactive dialogues between patient and therapist become the substance of a new psychoanalytic agenda. The drama progresses, scene by scene, by dint of what we have come to call enactments, that is, the personified embodiments of relationally derived unconscious fantasies as they force themselves outward onto the interpersonally receptive medium of the transference–countertransference experience.

It remains to lay out, in greater detail than is possible here, some of the fundamentals of a dissociation-based model of mind and psychic structure more in keeping with contemporary relational theories and clinical practice. But I would like to end with our debt to Fairbairn. For, when we work in the transference–countertransference arena with multiply derived experiences of self and other, volleying through projective–introjective mechanisms between the personas embodied by the patient and those embodied by the analyst, we are, indeed, traversing an unconscious markedly different from the unconscious of classical theory. This, to my mind, is the unconscious derived from Fairbairn's conversation with Janet; the unconscious Fairbairn sought when he urged us "back to hysteria." This model emphasizes the multiplicity of self–other configurations or self-systems based on an ongoing continuous dialectic between dissociative and integrative processes. It seeks to emphasize the failure of linear, repression-based developmental schemas and hierarchies in capturing the profound complexity of human experience. It is an unconscious that is dynamic and ever-shifting, in accord with the particular evocations of interpersonal context. It is, above all else, an unconscious shaped and enacted by its participants; an unconscious propelled by the conflicts of embodied selves in intimate, gratifying, frustrating, oftentimes maddening union with the limitless world of potential others. Although we have brought Fairbairn's model into a two-person context and enhanced its interpersonal dimensions with an emphasis on projective–introjective processes, our work today would not be possible without Fairbairn's courageous and dramatic departures from the existing doctrine of his day.

References

Breuer, J. & Freud, S. (1893–1895), Studies on hysteria. *Standard Edition*, 2. London: Hogarth Press, 1955.

Davies, J. M. (1996), Linking the pre-analytic and the post-classical: Integration, dissociation, and multiplicity of unconscious process. *Contemp. Psychoanal.*, 32:533–576.

Ellenberger, H. F. (1970), *The Discovery of the Unconscious*. New York: Basic Books.

Fairbairn, W. R. D. (1929), Dissociation and repression. In: *From Instinct to Self*, ed. E. F. Birtles & D. Scharff. Northvale,NJ: Aronson, 1994.

——— (1931), Features in the analysis of a patient with a physical genital abnormality. In: *Psychoanalytic Studies of the Personality*. London: Routledge & Kegan Paul, 1952.

——— (1958), On the nature and aims of psychoanalytic treatment. *Internat. J. Psycho-Anal.*, 39:374–385.

Grotstein, J. (1995), Endopsychic structure and the cartography of the internal world: Six endopsychic characters in search of an author. In: *Fairbairn and the Origins of Object Relations*, ed. J. Grotstein & D. Rinsley. New York: Guilford, pp. 174–194.

Hoffman, I. Z. (1991), Discussion: Toward a social-constructivist view of the psychoanalytic situation. *Psychoanal. Dial.*, 1:74–105.

——— (1992), Some practical implications of a social-constructivist view of the analytic situation. *Psychoanal. Dial.*, 2:287–304.

Janet, P. (1887), L'anesthésie systematisée et la dissociation des phénomènes psychologiques. *Revue Philosophique*, 23:449–472.

——— (1889), *L'Automatisme Psychologique*. Paris: Alcan.

——— (1894), Histoire d'une idée fixe. *Revue Philosophique*, 37:121–163.

Klein, M. (1964), *Contributions to Psychoanalysis: 1921–1945*. New York: McGraw-Hill.

Schacter, D. (1987), Implicit memory: History and current status. *J. Exper. Psychol.*, 13:501–518.

Stern, D. B. (1996), Dissociation and constructivism. *Psychoanal. Dial.*, 6:251–266.

Sullivan, H. S. (1953), *The Interpersonal Theory of Psychiatry*. New York: Norton.

5

A Comparison of Fairbairn's Endopsychic Structure and Klein's Internal World

James S. Grotstein

Object relations, once a daunting new school rivaling first the orthodox and later the classical analytic establishment, has now become so widely accepted that the boundaries between the disparate schools that now espouse it have become less clear. The object relations concepts of Klein differ significantly from those of Fairbairn, and, in turn, each of theirs differs from Winnicott's. All differ significantly from the object relations ideas of ego psychology (Jacobson, Kernberg) and, yet again, from those of the relational (Sullivan, Mitchell) and the intersubjective schools (Stolorow, Atwood, Brandchaft). In the United States those contributors whose works are most in line with both sides of the British Object Relations School (Kleinian and Independent) include Ogden, Seinfeld, and Grotstein.

The idea of object relations began with Freud, first as the background to his theory of infantile sexuality (Freud, 1905), later in his work "On Narcissism: An Introduction" (Freud, 1914), and finally in "Mourning and Melancholia" (Freud, 1917). This last work is of such importance as the source for all object relations theory that I shall spend some time in introducing it so as to set the scene for a comparison between the ideas of perhaps the foremost progenitors of object relations theory, Melanie Klein and W. R. D. Fairbairn.

Freud's Exploration of Internal Objects in "Mourning and Melancholia"

After first exploring the internal object relations of narcissism, beginning with primary narcissism, where the ego chooses the ideal ego as its first love object, and then in secondary narcissism, where "the shadow of the object falls upon the ego," that is, the ego relates to the lost object through internalization and identification (Freud, 1914), Freud (1917) then explored the fate of narcissistic object relations in mourning and in melancholia. He found that a person who has achieved the ability for anaclitic object relations (who had accepted his or her dependency on the object) is able to grieve and mourn the loss of the object without suffering a loss of self-esteem. A narcissist, on the other hand, cannot accept the fact of separation from the object (and thus his or her dependency on the separate object) and is thus unable to tolerate its loss. The narcissist consequently enters into an unconscious fantasy whereby he or she becomes able to deny the object's loss through incorporation of and identification with the object. In other words, the narcissist denies the loss of the object by *becoming the object*—in two distinct ways, as we shall soon see. Clinically, however, these patients seem to develop "side effects" from this internalization. Unlike successful mourners, they develop a melancholia that is characterized by self-criticism and a loss of self-esteem.

Freud intuited from this syndrome that the object that had been internalized within the narcissist's ego had been internalized in two ways, that is, both in the ego and in "a gradient in the ego," the latter of which he termed the *ego-ideal* but that later was to become the *superego* (Freud, 1923). Freud had obviously stumbled on the concept of the splitting of the ego and of the object but failed to explicate this notion of splitting, which was later to become a centerpiece for the concepts of Klein and Fairbairn. Freud clinically intuited that, as a result of this bifurcated internalization of the object, the ego of the suffering narcissist treats himself or herself as if he or she *were* the object. Yet, paradoxically, the very ego that treats that ego as if it were the object is itself a loftier ego (ego ideal), which is also identified with the another aspect of the object. Thus, finally, one aspect of the ego, which is identified with a concordant aspect of the object, exerts a maximum of sadism against another ego, which is identified with a complementary aspect of the object, the latter two constituting the masochistic counterpart to a sadistic couple.

Freud thus formulated an anatomy of melancholy, in which there were four structures in the internal world that combined into two units, one loftier than the other and having the propensity of moral sadism toward the other, whose masochistic surrender to this moral sadism amounts to what we might call a folie à deux (Mason, 1994) or mimesis (Girard, 1972, 1978, 1986, 1987), each being a way of talking about a collusion or a state of mutual projective identification between two individuals or groups to support a common delusion (Grotstein, 1994c, 1995a, b). In other words, this agreement between the sadistic, self-righteous, self-object-relations unit and its masochistic counterpart constitutes a pathological (narcissistic/melancholic) "contract" or covenant.

In his anatomy of melancholy Freud did not include the allegedly normal ego and object relationships that transpire in mourning. Fairbairn (1944) conceived of an original ego (OE) and an original object (OO), each of which underwent splitting upon frustrating experiences and devolved ultimately into a central ego (CE) relating to an ideal object (IO), which together (CE and IO) repressed an antilibidinal ego (AE), which was associated with a rejecting object (RO) and a libidinal ego (LE), which was associated with an exciting object (EO). It is clear that Freud's anatomy of melancholy is the provenance of Fairbairn's endopsychic structures, and it is to the latter's credit that he was able to flesh out this "anatomy" with dynamic structures. Of interest is that Fairbairn used this "anatomy" to emphasize the *schizoid condition*, whereas Freud used it to emphasize the internalized narcissistic object relations of melancholia. As we shall see, Klein, though no stranger to schizoid phenomena, came down on the side of Freud and considered melancholia—and later paranoia—to be variants of pathological narcissism.

Fairbairn's Departure from Freud

The Ariadne's thread that runs through the entirety of Fairbairn's revised psychology of object relations is his criticism of Freud's economic theory, that is, the importance the latter gives to drives and to libido in terms of their propensity to discharge tension rather than being primarily object directed. Because of space limitations I can only allude here to what I believe may have been a misunderstanding, not only on Fairbairn's part, but on virtually all the orthodox and classical analytic world that seemingly followed Freud. It often happens that followers of a great teacher may so reify and concretize the original text that the originality, breadth, and scope of the original message enter into a fateful desuetude and ultimate demise. I am referring to what perhaps may be called "the other Freud," the Freud who was a philosophical humanist, a side of him that contended with his seemingly scientific-positivistic side. In deference to Fairbairn, one can easily read into Freud everything that Fairbairn states. On the other hand, I believe that another credible reading could be stated as follows: Libido and the drives constitute the instruments of the sense of *personal agency* and *subjectivity* for the infant—and his or her "descendant," the adult. When we "cathect" an object with libido, we are not merely "discharging tension"; we are simultaneously certifying the *personal meaningfulness* of the event with the object, thereby rendering it into a *personal experience*. This process is akin to an infant's placing an object in its mouth and licking it with its saliva in order to personalize the object from its erstwhile strangeness. Further, Freud's emphasis on autoerotism was founded on an object relations basis. Freud (1905) stated that weaning from the breast inaugurates the onset of autoerotism.

Thus, the autoerotic zones are conceived by him to be fantasied object substitutes as well as ultimate instruments for relating to the object.

Fairbairn's Endopsychic Structures As Derived from a Patient's Dream

Fairbairn (1944) illustrated his new concept with a dream from a patient who suffered from frigidity:

> The (manifest) dream to which I refer consisted in a brief scene in which the dreamer saw the figure of herself being viciously attacked by a well-known actress in a venerable building which had belonged to her family for generations. Her husband was looking on; but he seemed quite helpless and quite incapable of protecting her. After delivering the attack the actress turned away and resumed playing a stage part, which, as seemed to be implied, she had momentarily set aside in order to deliver the attack by way of interlude. The dreamer then found herself gazing at the figure of herself lying bleeding on the floor; but, as she gazed, she noticed that this figure turned for an instant into that of a man. Thereafter the figure alternated between herself and this man until eventually she awoke in a state of acute anxiety [p. 95].

A summary of the associations is as follows: The man into whom the beaten figure of the patient turned was the patient's husband and also, as it turned out, her father. Thus, the attack was delivered against him as well as her. The actress delivering the attack was also identified with the patient and with her mother. Fairbairn interposes in his own view of the patient's dynamics that the patient behaved as an actress with her husband by disguising her feelings. He also believed that her frigidity represented an attack on both her libidinal ego and, at the same time, on her husband as libidinal object. Thus, the patient, in a libidinal capacity, was identified with her husband as the object of her own aggression. The attacking aspect was identified with the patient and also her mother.

The figures in the dream devolve into ego structures and object structures, according to Fairbairn. The ego structures consist of: (a) an observing ego, (b) an attacked ego, and (c) an attacking ego. The object structures can be divided as follows: (a) an observing object, (b) an attacked object, and (c) an attacking object. When each of the separate egos are matched up with the respective objects with which they are in with libidinal identification, three binary structures emerge: (a) a central self, (b) a rejecting self that is rejected (repressed) by the former, and (c) a self rejected by both of the preceding. What organizes Fairbairn's conception of the patient's plight is his view of the reality of the patient's experiences with her husband and mother, to which she reacts defensively as a "frigid actress."

A Kleinian Formulation of the Dream

Having presented Fairbairn's formulation of his patient's symptom of sexual frigidity and the endopsychic structure he derived from her dream, I should now like to posit a tentative Kleinian formulation, albeit incomplete. The dream and the psychodynamic formulations that emerged from the interpretation of the dream emphasized a contrast between the patient's love relationships with her husband and father, on one hand, and an aggressive or hostile attitude on the other, a hidden ambivalence, as it were. The hatred toward her husband was due in part to his philandering, which we could assign to an intersubjective errancy on his part. Fundamentally, however, it seems that the patient's frigidity represents the final common pathway of a symptom compromise that expresses her envy of the desired object(s). She might have been envious toward her husband because she loved him and needed him and therefore attacked him by demeaning him and the goodness he had to offer her. Parenthetically, we must remember that World War II had not yet ended, and he was away from home presumably for an extended period of time in one of the combatant services—at the risk of his life. This vulnerability of her husband as her current object of love must certainly have reminded her of the fatal vulnerability of her father, who had died in action in World War I. Might not her envy of her husband have been stimulated all the more because of her exquisite vulnerability to the contemplation of his possibly forthcoming death? Here I am suggesting that she may have employed envious attacks against the goodness of her husband as a prophylactic measure against mourning in order to lessen his value since he might have died in combat at any moment. His absence must also be considered in the context of her transference to Fairbairn and his absences, since at that time I believe he was serving as a consultant to the Scottish Command of the British Army; as Bion once mentioned to me, they had served there together approximately at that time. Even if not, the transference implications of the dream are very important and seem to have been neglected by Fairbairn.

What I am suggesting is that the patient may have experienced the revival of her archaic oral dependency in the transference, and, as a consequence, she began to experience envious feelings toward her needed transference object, which became displaced, through projective identification, into her husband, on one level, and into her father, on another—but ultimately those feelings were directed toward her mother. Because of her putative envy, I suggest, not only may she have attacked her beloved husband and father, but also her envious superego may have attacked herself as wife to her husband and child to her father, on both of whom respectively she was and had been dependent. Her envy-inspired attacks against the part-object penis (as husband and father) also extends to her mother's breasts. In his interpretation of the patient's dream, Fairbairn fails to allot significance to the patient's thwarted oral dependency on her mother. I should like to amend what I believe was his oversight and suggest that all three objects—mother, father, and husband—are condensed montages and are interchangeable for each of the three object positions in his endopsychic structure and that the patient (as infant, child, and adult) qualifies for each of the three ego positions—all in the transference to Fairbairn.

Now, to elaborate the subject of envy and its transformations from the Kleinian perspective. The first transformation that resulted from the patient's unconscious envious attack against the breast—or penis-part-object—was the fantasied mutilation of the breast or penis, which she thereupon incorporated and with which she introjectively identified. Being thence identified internally with a damaged, and thus impotent, breast-penis, the patient correspondingly experienced frigidity symptomatically. According to the Kleinian way of thinking, we become what we believe we have done to our objects. This particular transformation or transmutation constitutes a *complementary* one.

The second transformation resulting from the envious attack against the breast-penis was one in which the enviously attacking infant aspect of the patient changed the image of her object(s) into a *concordantly* attacking object, which is thereupon internalized and introjectively identified with as a superego, which in turn attacks the ego(s) and the objects with which the latter identifies. From these two transformations we can envision a hapless infant (patient) who not only is weakened into frigid "impotence" because of an identification with the attack*ed* object but who also becomes further weakened by an enviously attack*ing* superego.

This is not the end of the difficulties for this frigid victim. There are yet a third and fourth transformation in store for her—the consequences of her envious attack against the parental intercourse, which are also internalized similarly to the aforementioned. Thus, the third transformation is the patient's libidinal ego's being victimized by a coalition of exciting object and rejecting object, the parental couple. The fourth transformation is her using that posture as a passive–aggressive maneuver to keep the parents apart (by way of projective identification). This maneuver would be called the *depressive defense* and corresponds to an internalization of the objects triumphed over by the use of the manic defense. In other words, the patient, in her

·oedipal rage, may have become activated by an unconscious fantasy in which she, by actively being frigid, employed projective identification in order to make the parental couple frigid. It works this way: The infant uses his or her own body as an unconscious effigy image in such a way as to pretend that there is no separation between her and her objects. Thus, she lies between them and magically controls their intercourse by her frigidity, similarly to catatonics who believe their actions control the world and in turn are controlled by the world. Elsewhere (Grotstein, 1994c, 1995) I have termed this mechanism the *depressive defense*, which represents the internalization of the manic defense; that is, by exercising control over oneself, one magically controls the objects with whom one is projectively identified.[1] The possibly oedipal nature of the patient's frigidity is significant, I believe, especially in the light of the fact that her father died in combat in the Great War while she was still a child.

Earlier I mentioned that all four objects (analyst, husband, wife, and father) qualify for all three object positions in the endopsychic structures. Similarly, the patient qualifies for all three ego positions. One wonders, however, where to assign the normal libidinal ego (self) or its normal dialectical counterpart, the assertive self. I should like to posit that, analogously to Winnicott's (1960, 1963) positing the existence of a "being (object-relating) self" and an "active (object-using) self" as the normal antecedents of the "true" and "false" selves respectively, I believe that Fairbairn may well have come around eventually to postulating a normal endopsychic structure but one situated topographically in the preconscious rather than in the unconscious—because of his injunction, with which I am in agreement, that good objects do not need to be internalized (except for defensive purposes), only unsatisfying ones. The system preconscious would be the reservoir for the legacy or memory of satisfying experiences with reliable objects as opposed to the

---

[1] This concept of self as effigy image and its relationship to the manic and depressive defenses constitutes a significant contradiction to the now popular, and I believe erroneous, concept of interactional projective identification.

unconscious, which is the reservoir for the concrete internalization of unreliable but needed objects that putatively need to be controlled and processed dissociatively.

It is of no small interest that Fairbairn's concept of endopsychic structures accommodates both the preoedipal (two-person) and oedipal (three-person) situation. We have seen already how the splitting of the objects in this case and of the corresponding egos that relate to them can be dialectically accounted for in the binary oppositions of:

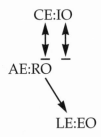

where CE, AE, and LE all stand for separate aspects of the patient and where IO, RO, and EO stand for first the maternal object in three aspects and then the paternal object in three aspects (which also include the analyst and husband). Finally, in the oedipal situation, the maternal object, as in this case, occupied the role of the primitive oedipal superego (RO) whereas the father was the exciting object (EO). Perhaps both mother and father occupied the IO position.

The symptom of frigidity is accounted for consequently on the basis of splitting or dissociation, which was described in Klein's (1946) concept of the paranoid-schizoid position and the schizoid mechanisms that underlay it, that is, splitting, projective identification, magically omnipotent denial, and idealization, each of which is implicitly active in the dynamic relationships between endopsychic structures. Fairbairn's critique of Klein was, unfortunately, never updated to include her then newer views of the schizoid state and her views of the premoral stage of infant development, which the paranoid-schizoid position had come to represent (Grotstein, 1993, 1994a, b, 1996b). Thus, I believe that Fairbairn's model of endopsychic structures is incomplete insofar as it fails to represent the normal situation; but, having said that, I also believe that his model is able to accommodate Klein's internalized objects as well as his own endopsychic structures.

A Comparison Between Klein's and Fairbairn's Conceptions of Internal Objects

Fairbairn and Freud picture the composition of the internal object somewhat differently from Klein's version. We have seen that, although Freud did explicate the process of introjective identification with the ego that occurs when the object is internalized, he discussed the two aspects of the ego as if they were also separate from the internalized object(s) with which the former are identified. Fairbairn, while clearly specifying the process of identification between the subsidiary egos and their (part-)objects, also mentioned that there simultaneously exists a *libidinal relationship between them*. There is yet another aspect of Fairbairn's conceptions of objects that informs his object relations theories which is radically at odds with those of Klein— and Freud. Fairbairn followed in the tradition of Ian Suttie (1935) and, before him, the object relations ideas that originated in Budapest with the works of Ferenczi (1916) and Herrman (1936) in particular and later of Balint (1968)—that emphasized the prime and organizing importance of the external object as a decisive player in an infant's and child's psychological development. This emphasis on the primary importance of the object was in contrast to the object relations concepts that Freud had left incomplete but in which he seldom if ever discussed the importance of the external object in its own right. Abraham's (1924) object relations concepts likewise emphasized the instinctual vicissitudes of relations to the objects, both internal and external, and consequently avoided the issue of external deprivation and trauma.[2]

Except for Suttie and Sullivan, Fairbairn was the first psychoanalyst not only to espouse the importance of the malfunctioning of external objects (trauma, deprivation) but also to anatomize them as endopsychic structures in direct proportion to the infant's and child's experiences of their damaging effects. This formulation presented a metapsychological problem that contemporaneous orthodox and classical analysts, as well as Klein, were unable to contemplate. The problem was as follows: orthodox and classical psychoanalytic theory was dominated by the conception of primary narcissism, which imposed the idea of a prementational state in which the infant could not clearly register external trauma, and of the oedipus complex, a late phallic happening that only retrospectively elaborated preoedipal (pregenital) experiences. Even Klein, who disavowed the theory of primary narcissism, followed closely upon Freud in valorizing primary process as the infant's only instrument in processing the data of its emotional experiences. We now know from infant development research that an infant is capable of accurate and realistic perception from the very beginning, and Fairbairn is now accorded the credit for presciently formulating this idea (Stern, 1985, 1989).[3] Let me summarize the problem: Freud believed in the existence of primary narcissism, which, when taken to its limits, implies no mental or perceptual capacity for an infant. Thus, it cannot perceive or experience the trauma that it endures. Fairbairn and Klein disavowed primary narcissism in favor of primary object relatedness, but Klein followed Freud in valorizing the hegemony of primary process (unconscious fantasy), and Fairbairn, by contrast, valorized the primacy of reality perception (secondary process), *to which*

---

[2] Recall that Klein had been in analysis with Ferenczi as well as Abraham, but her later ideas seem to owe more to the latter than to the former, except that Ferenczi was the first to encourage her to become a child analyst.

[3] Later I shall propose the concepts of the *dual track* and *autochthony* (*creationism*) as reconciliatory bridges between the two points of view.

unconscious fantasy is always obligatorily subservient. As I hope to show, I think that all the points of view are accurate and constitute differing ways of looking at infantile experience.

It is important to recognize that Fairbairn's endopsychic structures are formed in accordance with Freud's (1914) idea that "the shadow of the object falls on the ego." This postulate predicates that the ego on which the (internalized) object's shadow falls is altered according to the Procrustean limitations imposed by the contours of the object. Yet, by internalizing the unsatisfying (but needed) object, Fairbairn seems to be suggesting that the infant passive–aggressively retains its sense of *agency* as a self by internalizing the troublesome object and then identifying with it internally—even to the point, possibly, of projectively reassigning the fantasy of agency to the object internally so as to direct a maximum of sadism toward it (in both its forms, EO and RO)—"the devil made me do it!" (where the devil is EO and RO).

According to Ogden (1983), internal objects do not "think." The subject who creates the internal object through projective—and then introjective—identification creates an amalgam in which he or she can identify with the "self" aspect of the object or with the object itself or with both. This distinction evaporates, however, in the Kleinian version, where projective and introjective identifications alchemize the two into an alienated, indivisible, and therefore unique "third form."

Klein's internalized objects, on the other hand, constitute *third forms,* that is, chimerical or monstrous demonic forms that represent a condensation of the infant's projective identification of self in addition to the modification of the image of that hybrid form by introjective identification (Grotstein, 1996c). The long and short of it is that, whereas the Freudian internal object and Fairbairn's endopsychic objects are objects per se and are conceived of as seemingly separate from their corresponding egos, identification notwithstanding, the Kleinian internal object is no longer the original "object" per se. It becomes a transmuted or transmogrified third form. It becomes a seamless amalgam of an exaggerated self indivisibly intermixed with an altered image of the erstwhile external object. Neither would find itself recognizable in the final product once it has entered into the alchemy of transmutation.

The Ontology of Endopsychic Structures

Elsewhere (Grotstein, 1994b), I have postulated that, having been given conceptual life, as it were, a sense of subjective "I"-ness, subjectivity, and mental life becomes projectively attributed to each of these structures, egos and objects alike. Every creature or form in the unconscious, no matter how alienated from the sense of self, is fantasmally and imaginatively imbued with life, subjectivity, affect, and consciousness, as well as with conation (sense of agency, determination, will to survive and thrive). Under the concept of *divide et impera*, Fairbairn, after Freud (1914), attributed a maximum of aggression to the repressing egos (CE) but particularly to the AE (internal saboteur) in its relationship with RO and a maximum of libido to LE in its relationship to EO.[4] Thus, the main ingredients of mental life with which Fairbairn imbues his internalized objects and subsidiary egos are *libido* and *aggression* in that descending order of importance. Klein, on the other hand, imbues her internalized objects (which, unlike Fairbairn's, include the subsidiary egos) with destructiveness and libido in an order of importance that is the reverse of Fairbairn's. She does something else, however, that Fairbairn seldom gives mention to: she imbues her internalized objects with omnipotence, thus their authority to be superegos. From this point of view, EO (which to her would indivisibly include LE) would become a corrupt superego, and RO (which would include AE) would correspond to a sadistic superego.

---

[4] Freud (1917) assigned a maximum of *sadism* to the ego ideal and to one aspect of the internalized object that had been internalized "in a gradient in the ego." This maximized sadism was directed toward the ego itself and the other aspect of the object that had been internalized.

What she misses, however, is the nature of the ongoing relationships between the differentiated structures.

A word is in order about the nature of the relationships that transpire amongst the internalized objects and subsidiary egos. A state of libidinal trance or idealization takes place between LE and EO and also between AE and RO, since each respective relationship is characterized by a sense of total hypnotic surrender to the authority that LE invests in EO and AE in RO. To that we add the ingredient of omnipotence supplied by Klein, and we can then understand why it is so difficult for each of the subsidiary egos to be rescued, repatriated to CE, and rehabilitated— because of a tenacious love–hate attachment to omnipotent internal objects. The nature of LE's masochistic bondage to AE (and RO) is complicated and perhaps labyrinthine. LE adores EO, "knows" that it should not, and cannot help itself. It therefore enters into a secret collusion with AE to submit to the latter's "corrective" hostility toward it, but, in the process, following Freud's (1917) melancholic paradigm, EO is indirectly punished because of LE's identification with it. A primitive Byzantine morality or criminal ethic, is in operation, behind which is a hidden order or covenant of choreographed rules of behavior between the various denizens of this macabre world. It is the quintessence of folie à deux (Mason, 1994) or *mimesis* (Girard, 1972, 1978, 1986, 1987), a phenomenon in which two or more individuals so seamlessly symmetrize their relationship through mutual projective identification that they are in total accord, but may need to express their individual differences by mutually appointing a scapegoat to embody those differences, even if the scapegoat is the self, as it most commonly is. Thus, CE and IO collude to scapegoat the four denizens of endopsychic structure; AE and RO likewise collude against LE and EO; and finally LE and AE collude against EO, the latter of which, after all, is not only the other side of RO but, more importantly, is the other side of IO. Further, CE/IO may collude with AE/RO against LE/EO in melancholia, whereas LE/EO may collude with CE/IO against AE/RO in mania.

Subsidiary Egos as "Second Selves" (Alter Egos)

Another interesting comparison between Klein and Fairbairn in terms of endopsychic structures harkens back to a major difference in the clinical as well as theoretical emphasis that each respectively gives to the egos, central as well as subsidiary, on one hand, as opposed to the objects, IO, as well as RO and EO, on the other. In his scholarly and definitive study on the meaning of the term object in the works of Freud, Klein, and Fairbairn, Mitchell (1981) calls attention to its transience with Freud, its fundamental importance in the external as well as in the internal world with Fairbairn, and its internality with Klein. Put another way, to Fairbairn the internalized object owes its existence to its having failed as an external object, the latter being always of primary importance to the infant. Thus, the object is internalized *because it cannot be mourned—owing to its disappointing nature!*[5] To Klein, the external world ultimately becomes the mediator of the demons and terrors that owe their provenance to the death instinct. The external object either confirms it, reinforces it, or mitigates its intensity. The Kleinian emphasis falls consequently on the ego—and on the objects created or transformed by the ego through projective and introjective identification.

In analysis we invariably see many different aspects, parts, or seemingly separate personalities emerging from the patient from time to time and often from moment to moment. I recall a combative borderline male patient who, after having threatened me almost physically the session before, handed me a note upon leaving the next session which stated, "Don't pay any attention to him! He's only trying to make trouble between us!" Another psychotic patient dreamed that she was trying to escape a frightening man who had been pursuing her. She ran for cover

---

[5] The need for the infant to internalize the needed object that disappoints because it cannot be mourned speaks to Freud's (1917) melancholic paradigm, a factor that seems to have eluded Fairbairn when he insisted on the schizoid rather than on the melancholic nature of internalized objects. Seen from this dual-track advantage, both paradigms apply.

into a radio station and then, at the last moment, cried out, "Help, he's stealing the microphone from me!" The point is that we all exist as loose confederations of subselves whose seeming differences from our core selves become all too manifest in analysis. Thus, we may find ourselves identified with and dominated at any given moment by any of the six (or more) components of the endopsyche.

Now to return to Klein and Fairbairn. The ultimate meaning that subtends, orders, and choreographs Kleinian thinking is the unconscious determinism—or, as I would now modify, revise, and extend it—the sense, myth, or belief in one's putative determinism as psychic creationism or imagination—any or all of which depend on the ego alone and in its own subjectivity and right of agency. Thus, from this standpoint, again to return to the all but lost canon of orthodox Freudian and Kleinian analysis, all the personages that appear in the manifest content of an analytic session or in a dream in that session are, in effect, *shadows of the ego* (in the Platonic sense). They are *alter egos* of the analytic subject who are externalized into the forms and images of others in order to highlight and explore important aspects of oneself at one remove.

Autochthony (Creationism) and the Dual-Track

I now wish to take a brief detour through orthodox and classical analytic technique in order to shepherd these aforementioned ideas to their final destination. The task of orthodox analysis in particular, and of classical analysis to a somewhat lesser extent, was to introduce the patient to his or her unconscious mind and to the psychic determinism that ultimately ordered all his or her volition, thoughts, dreams, and behavior. A rough "translation" of this point of view would be as follows: The events of one's life that affect one constitute autobiography. How one was unconsciously predisposed to experience the event subjectively is the sole subject of analysis. I have modified the orthodox/classical canon of psychic determinism by suggesting the concept of *autochthony*, or *creationism*; that is, the idea that one unconsciously believes that one created the good or bad external or internal situation from aspects within oneself because of projective identification (Grotstein, 1996a). Further, autochthonous creationism obligatorily parallels and precedes rational thinking, and its purpose is to allow the infant the ability to establish a sense of agency and subjectivity for himself or herself. Autochthony follows from Klein's (1929) concepts of personification and projective identification (Klein, 1946, 1955) and from Winnicott's (1969, 1971a) concepts of the subjective object and playing (Winnicott, 1968, 1971b). Autochthony (syncretism, self-creationism) is the principle that accounts for an infant's belief that she or he has created himself or herself and the objects in his or her cosmos—much like the Infant God of *Genesis*. According to this principle, the infant must first create the object before it is able to discover or explore it—so as to establish a sense of self-as-agent. The arrival of object events that preempt the infant's "creation" of them is what we term trauma.

Whereas absolute psychic determinism played a major role in orthodox, classical, and Kleinian formulations, Fairbairn and other relational analysts went to the other extreme and emphasized the importance of the perceived reality of the external objects—at the expense, I believe, of the infant's sense (fantasy) of agency. Yet, after he formulated the first (except for Sullivan's) theory of *realistic causality*, Fairbairn ultimately fell back on autochthony as the infant's belief that either its love was bad (schizoid position) or its hate was bad (depressive position) for the objects to have been bad in the first place.

Thus, there has been a dual track in psychoanalytic metatheory in regard to the genetic metapsychological point of view. According to the dual track, an infant can be imagined to be a "Siamese-twin" in many perspectives. Thus, one can portray the infant as being paradoxically the author (agent, cause) of its experiences with objects and the hapless victim of them at the same time. Another aspect of this dual track is the conception that the infant is both separate from mother and simultaneously indivisibly connected to her. Klein's point of view discards the concept of primary narcissism. Winnicott's (1960a), while seemingly endorsing the orthodox/classical point of view of an objectless primary narcissism, alters it in his suggestion that "there is no such thing as an infant. There is only an infant and its mother" (p. 39) to put forth his own concept of object relations (as opposed to object usage): that the initial stage of development before object usage consists of the object relations between the infant and its holding environment mother, an entity that I have called the *background object* (now *presence*) *of primary identification*. Thus, the infant can be conceived of as being both separate and not separate from mother from the very beginning.

Another aspect of a dual track is the object-related agendas for the infant. Whereas Freud's protocol seems to privilege auto-erotism at the expense of object relatedness, one can readily read into his work a significantly different view, as I have already stated, one that represents the obligatory forerunner of what we have traditionally called object relations—that of choosing the self as one's first object. We may recall that Freud (1914) stated that the id chooses the ego as its first love object just as the ego chooses its ideal ego (p. 94). He also said that in the beginning the ego is first and foremost a body ego (Freud, 1923). Tausk (1919) and Federn (1952), on the other hand, proposed that the infant is born as an inchoate psyche, which then must discover its body self (and ego, too, presumably) by "identification through projection."

What I am suggesting here is that Freud's libido principle may have lent itself to too narrow a reading, one that may have ultimately become a *mis*reading because of the emphasis Freud placed on "instinctual discharge" and the "pleasure"—and later the "pleasure–unpleasure principle." My own reading today would be as follows: The drives are *semiotic signifiers* of need, which ultimately personalize *desire* as the infant's uniqueness, its fingerprint for life. Libido, in the guise of need, constitutes a complicated *signified* in its own right insofar as it condenses the unknowable terror of annihilation; that is, the newborn infant may at first experience hunger as a nameless centrifugal terror. The drives that proclaim this terror are frightened/frightening messengers of anticipated danger or disaster which constitute a call for help to the maternal object. Libido, as the pursuer of pleasure, imparts personal meaning to the objects of the infant's experience and therefore personally valorizes the object, while at the same time it defines the self in terms of how and with whom it has pleasurable desire. The choice of the object that *releases* one *defines* one. Thus, libido constitutes the defining instrument of personalness and of subjective uniqueness.

Yet another aspect of the dual track is the dialectic between power and powerlessness. The concept of the drives emerged in part in the *Zeitgeist* of German Romanticism culturally and Brentano's notion of *intentionality* and Nietzsche's idea of the Dionysian *will to power* philosophically. While it is true that power does constitute a significant motif in human development, as the maturational protocols of virtually all schools attest, there is another aspect of drive that is so obvious, that, like the unconscious itself, it lies in broad daylight, unnoticed. I refer to the realization that the drives proclaim weakness, emptiness, powerlessness, hunger, need, desire, *absence*. What we have unwittingly done is to enter into a manic defense of theory in which we have reversed the valence of powerlessness into the power of the drives and have represented them as coming from a bin of iniquity, the "seething cauldron," rather than understanding that the unconscious itself is an "alter ego" that plaintively, if not articulately, informs us of our needs, desires, and absences in sophisticated, cryptic code. Our manic defenses deny the need, contemn the message, and scapegoat and caricature the messenger, the drives. Ultimately, as the drives become organized and integrated into one's sense of identity, agency, and subjectivity, they always retain their dialectically ambiguous nature. Put another way, we hear our weakness through the power of our terror. We have only to watch infants to realize the truth of this hypothesis.

The Relationship of Endopsychic Structures to Klein's and Fairbairn's Positions

Earlier I mentioned that Fairbairn's endopsychic structures display a coherence of interrelationships whose versatility allows for two-person as well as three-person relationships. This versatility extends to its ability to accommodate Fairbairn's schizoid and depressive positions and Klein's paranoid-schizoid and *depressive positions*. I have compared Klein's and Fairbairn's conceptions of the positions in earlier contributions (Grotstein, 1994a, b). A synopsis of their respective points of view follows. Klein (1935) first developed the conception of the depressive position to account for clinical phenomena that emerged in child analytic situations which were characterized by the young patient's anxiety about the putative damage his or her destructiveness had inflicted on his or her objects, both internal and external. Later, she formulated the concept of the paranoid-schizoid position to designate a cluster of infantile anxieties that occurred around three weeks postnatally (Klein, 1946). The characteristic of these anxieties was their paranoid or persecutory nature because of their origins in splitting and projective identifications from the infant into the object. The depressive position came to connote an awareness of the real object, of its separateness, and a fantasied awareness of the putative damage that the infant may have caused the object to suffer, following which it seeks to conduct a restoration and reparations of the object. It is important to remember that Klein's metapsychology is based on Freud's psychic determinism; thus, unconscious fantasies, which are the direct mental manifestations of the drives, are primary. External reality either mitigates or confirms their nature.

Fairbairn, on the other hand, conceived his schizoid position as one in which the infant realistically appraises an unsuitable object environment to which it must accommodate at its own expense by internalizing the bad aspects of the object(s), splitting it first from the original object (OO), then resplitting it internally into an exciting (EO) and a rejecting object (RO), and then splitting off aspects of its own ego to follow these objects into repression (LE and AE). Since the trauma involved here occurs in the preambivalent stage, Fairbairn believed that the infant is not in touch with its hate; thus, it is its neediness and love that is bad.

Fairbairn's conception of the depressive position is not congruent with that of Klein. He based its provenance, like that of the schizoid position, on Abraham's (1924) concept of infant development, which postulated a preambivalent stage to which Fairbairn assigned significance for the establishment of the schizoid position, and an ambivalent phase in which teething, and thus aggression, becomes prominent. With the onset of aggression toward the object, the infant tends to become remorseful about the putative damage its hate caused to happen to the object(s). Parenthetically, it is of some interest that, even though Klein and Fairbairn begin at opposite poles as to the issue of infantile psychopathogenesis (Klein valorizing the primacy of unconscious phantasy and Fairbairn the veridicality of the infant's perception of external reality, Fairbairn ultimately reconciles with the orthodox/Kleinian view—that of autochthonous creationism or psychic determinism—that the infant believes that the badness of its objects is due to the fact that its *love* is bad (schizoid position) or that its *hate* is bad (depressive position). Put another way, even though Fairbairn postulated an endopsychic structure based on the infant's need to comply with the realistic badness of its needed objects and thereby enter into a schizoid compromise, his endopsychic structure is anything but schizoid beneath the line of primary repression. The endopsyche is inherently schizoid in its basic structure but is melancholic in its psychodynamics—whether the origin of the internalized objects are based on reality or fantasy.

Even though Klein and Fairbairn seem to be coming from opposite points of view, we can see not only that they ultimately reconcile in part, but also that every one of the six (or more) endopsychic structures can represent the point of view of actual traumatic reality or that of the primacy of unconscious fantasy.

In other words, one can reconcile both perspectives by using the dual-track theorem in which two differing theories of causality can simultaneously be valid. In the clinical reality of the analysand, each of the repressed internal objects can be thought of as being realistically perceived and also as being fantasmally (imaginatively) created. For instance, it is easily conceivable that LE, to which Fairbairn assigns consummate integrity and primal innocence, could believe that it has tried to subvert, manipulate, and excite its needed object out of separation anxiety and thus comes to believe that it has seduced and corrupted this object, thereby transforming it into a depraved, compromised, and exciting object (EO) that retaliates by attempting, in turn, to seduce and compromise LE and also, by way of its "Siamese-twin," RO, seek to punish LE. RO could also owe its source to LE's envious attack on the needed object, thereby transforming it into RO, and so on.

If we conceive of the infantile neurosis as a dialectic between a realistic traumatic neurosis (Fairbairn) and an autochthonously (imaginatively) created one (the psychic reality of Klein), then we may come closer to the appreciation of the actual clinical situation (Grotstein, 1994d).

There is a final point on the depressive position to which I should like to make reference. I have already cited the differences between Fairbairn's schizoid position and Klein's paranoid-schizoid position. Fairbairn's conceptualization of the depressive position overlaps Klein's in terms of the infant's sense of badness due to hostility. Fairbairn narrowly limits this phase to the origin of teething—and thus to biting and its consequences—whereas Klein assigns the origin of the infant's destructiveness largely to the death instinct and sees this destructiveness as existing from the beginning. Recently, Likierman (1995) divided the depressive position into an initial *tragic* phase (in which there is felt to be no hope because of the extent of the felt damage to mother), which is followed by a *moral* phase, in which the infant develops remorse, begins to mourn, and institutes reparative/restorative measures. If we were to assign these phases to Fairbairn's endopsychic structure, we could picture phase one (the tragic one) as the basic "anatomy of melancholy," which he terms his schizoid structure, that is, where LE is the ultimate underdog under a double repressive attack—by CE/IO and by AE/RO. The second phase, the moral one, could be visualized as the beginning of a benign coalition between LE and CE/IO in which the latter would come to the former's aid in conducting reparations and restorations of the damaged object, which amounts to allowing an integration between RO, EO, and IO—and thus with LE, AE, and CE (Rinsley, 1987).

Finally, perhaps one of the subtlest differences between the ideas of Fairbairn and Klein in terms of the positions is the postmodern issue of the *Subject*. In disclaiming the idea that an infant incorporates good (satisfying) objects, Fairbairn leaves no room for the concept of the incorporation of the *legacy* of the experience, a necessary process for growth that is fundamentally dependent on *mourning*. Additionally, his concept of the depressive position and its successors, the transitional stage, and adult interdependence do not specifically anticipate, as do Klein's concepts of the depressive position, that the development of whole object relations is the dawn of the awareness of mother's *Otherness* as ineffable *Subject*.

References

Abraham, K. (1924), A short study of the development of the libido. In: *Selected Papers on Psycho-Analysis*. London: Hogarth Press, 1948, pp. 418–501.

Balint, M. (1968), *The Basic Fault*. London: Tavistock.

Fairbairn, W. R. D. (1944), Endopsychic structure considered in terms of object-relationships. In: *Psychoanalytic Studies of the Personality*. London: Tavistock, 1952, pp. 82–136.

——— (1952), *Psychoanalytic Studies of the Personality*. London: Tavistock.

Federn, P. (1952), *Ego Psychology and the Psychoses*. New York: Basic Books.

Ferenczi, S. (1916), *Contributions to Psycho-Analysis*, trans. J. I. Suttie. Boston: Badger Press.

Freud, S. (1905), Three essays on the theory of sexuality. *Standard Edition*, 7:125–245. London: Hogarth Press, 1953.

——— (1914), On narcissism: An introduction. *Standard Edition*, 14:67–104. London: Hogarth Press, 1957.

——— (1917), Mourning and melancholia. *Standard Edition*, 14:237–260. London: Hogarth, 1957.

——— (1923), The ego and the id. *Standard Edition*, 19:3–66. London: Hogarth Press, 1961.

Girard, R. (1972), *Violence and the Sacred*, trans. P. Gregory. Baltimore, MD: Johns Hopkins University Press.

——— (1978), *Things Hidden Since the Foundation of the World*, trans. S. Bann & M. Metteer. Stanford, CA: Stanford University Press, 1987.

——— (1986), *The Scapegoat*, trans. Y. Freccero. Baltimore, MD: Johns Hopkins University Press.

——— (1987), *Job*. Stanford, CA: Stanford University Press.

Grotstein, J. (1981), *Splitting and Projective Identification*. New York: Aronson.

——— (1993), A reappraisal of W. R. D. Fairbairn. *J. Bull. Menninger Clin.*, 57:421–449.

——— (1994a), I. Notes on Fairbairn's metapsychology. In: *Fairbairn and the Origins of Object Relations*, ed. J. Grotstein & D. Rinsley. New York: Guilford, pp. 112–148.

——— (1994b), II. Endopsychic structures and the cartography of the internal world: Six endopsychic characters in search of an author. In: *Fairbairn and the Origins of Object Relations*, ed. J. Grotstein & D. Rinsley. New York: Guilford, pp. 174–194.

——— (1994c), Projective identification reappraised: Projective identification, introjective identification, the transference/countertransference neurosis/psychosis, and their consummate expression in the crucifixion, the Pietà, and "therapeutic exorcism": Part I. Projective identification. *Contemp. Psychoanal.*, 30:708–746.

——— (1994d), The infantile neurosis reassessed: The impact upon it of infant development research. Accepted for publication in a series for the Reiss-Davis Child Study Center, Los Angeles, CA, pp. 43–80.

——— (1995a), Projective identification reappraised: Projective identification, introjective identification, the transference/countertransference neurosis/psychosis, and their consummate expression in the crucifixion, the Pietà, and "therapeutic exorcism": Part II. The countertransference complex. *Contemp. Psychoanal.*, 31:479–511.

——— (1995b), The infantile neurosis reassessed. In: *The Handbook of Infant, Child, and Adolescent Psychotherapy*, ed. S. Mark & J. A. Incorvaia. Northvale, NJ: Aronson, pp. 43–80.

——— (1996), Autochthony and alterity: Psychic reality in counterpoint. *Psychoanal. Quart.*, 66:403–427.

——— (1997a), "Internal objects" or "chimerical monsters?": The demonic "third forms" of the internal world. *J. Anal. Psychol.*, 42:47–80.

——— (1997b), Fairbairn and his growing significance for current psycho-analysis and psychotherapy. In: *Psychoanalytic Versions of the Human Condition in Clinical Practice*, ed. P. Marcus & A. Rosenberg.

——— (1997c), The dual-track theorem and the "Siamese-twinship" paradigm for psychoanalytic concepts. Unpublished manuscript.

Hermann, I. (1936), Clinging-going-in-search. *Psychoanal. Quart.*, 45:5–36.

Klein, M. (1929), Personification in the play of children. In: *Contributions to Psycho-Analysis, 1921–1945*. London: Hogarth Press, 1950, pp. 215–226.

——— (1935), A contribution to the psychogenesis of manic-depressive states. In: *Contributions to Psycho-Analysis, 1921–1945*. London: Hogarth Press, 1950, pp. 282–310.

——— (1946), Notes on some schizoid mechanisms. In: *Developments of Psycho-Analysis*, ed. M. Klein, P. Heimann, S. Isaacs & J. Riviere. London: Hogarth Press, 1952, pp. 292–320.

——— (1955), On identification. In: *New Directions in Psycho-Analysis*, ed. M. Klein, P. Heimann, S. Isaacs & J. Riviere. London: Hogarth Press, 1952, pp. 309–345.

Likierman, M. (1995), Loss of the object: Tragic motifs in Melanie Klein's concept of the depressive position. *Brit. J. Psychother.*, 12:147–159.

Mason, A. (1994), A psychoanalyst's look at a hypnotist: A study of folie à deux. *Psychoanal. Quart.*, 63:641–679.

Mitchell, S. A. (1981), The origin and nature of the "object" in the theories of Klein and Fairbairn. *Contemp. Psychoanal.*, 17:374–398.

Ogden, T. (1983), The concept of internal object relations. *Internat. J. Psycho-Anal.*, 64:227–241.

Rinsley, D. B. (1987), A reconsideration of Fairbairn's "original object" and "original ego" in relation to borderline and other self disorders. In: *The Borderline Patient, Vol. 1*, ed. J. S. Grotstein, M. Solomon & J. A. Lang. Hillsdale, NJ: The Analytic Press, pp. 219–232.

Stern, D. (1985), *The Interpersonal World of the Infant*. New York: Basic Books.

——— (1989), The representation of relational patterns: Developmental considerations. In: *Relation Disturbances and Early Childhood*, ed. A. J. Sameroff & R. N. Emde. New York: Basic Books, pp. 52–69.

Suttie, I. (1935), *The Origins of Love and Hate*. New York: Matrix House, 1952.

Tausk, V. (1919), On the origin of the "influencing machine" in schizophrenia. *Psychoanal. Quart.*, 2:519–556.

Winnicott, D. W. (1960a), The theory of the parent–infant relationship. In: *The Maturational Processes and the Facilitating Environment*. New York: International Universities Press, 1965, pp. 37–55.

——— (1960b), Ego distortion in terms of true and false self. In: *The Maturational Processes and the Facilitating Environment*. New York: International Universities Press, pp. 140–152.

—— (1963), Communicating and not communicating leading to a study of certain opposites. In: *The Maturational Processes and the Facilitating Environment*. New York: International Universities Press, pp. 179–192.

—— (1968), Playing: Its theoretical status in the clinical situation. *Internat. J. Psycho-Anal.*, 49:591–599.

—— (1969), The use of an object. *Internat. J. Psycho-Anal.*, 50:711–716.

—— (1971a), The use of an object and relating through identifications. In: *Playing and Reality*. New York: Basic Books, 1971, pp. 86–94. [Also in: *Psycho-Analysis: Theory and Practice*. Cambridge, MA: Harvard University Press, 1989, pp. 218–227.]

—— (1971b), Playing: A theoretical statement. In: *Playing and Reality*. New York: Basic Books, 1971, pp. 38–52.

—— (1971c), Playing: Creative activity and the search for the self. In: *Playing and Reality*. New York: Basic Books, 1971, pp. 53–64.

—— (1971d), Creativity and its origins. In: *Playing and Reality*. New York: Basic Books, 1971, pp. 65–85.

6

The Dialectic Between
W. R. D. Fairbairn and Wilfred Bion

Jeffrey Seinfeld

This chapter demonstrates the complementarity and effectiveness of bringing together the work of W. R. D. Fairbairn and
Wilfred Bion as an explanatory model for a clinical case discussion. Bion and Fairbairn were unusual psychoanalysts in that
they both had a strong interest and background in philosophy.
In fact, their interests were nearly identical—they studied the
classical Greeks and the German idealist tradition of Kant and
Hegel, Bion being somewhat more influenced by Kant and
Fairbairn by Hegel. Bion was among the first of psychoanalysts
to recognize the interpersonal as well as intrapsychic dimensions of projective identification, emphasizing the importance of
the caregiver in containing the infant's anxieties. Bion was also
well aware of the social aspect of human being in his pioneering
early work with groups. He shared this point of view with
Fairbairn who described the individual as a social animal.
According to John Sutherland (1994), Fairbairn and Bion knew
and liked one another and appreciated each other's work.

   W. R. D. Fairbairn (1941) presented the fundamental thesis of
object relations theory in his statement that individuals are
inherently and fundamentally object seeking. This view implies
that an ego exists from birth and has at least a vague, pristine
sense of the object it seeks. Wilfred Bion (1962) described such
innate inclinations as preconceptions and suggested that they
are realized through experience with reality and thereby become

conceptions. To provide a philosophical basis for Melanie Klein's theory that infants possess an apriori knowledge of objects as a part of their instinctual endowment, Bion was drawing on the Platonic and Kantian belief that mind provides the form of experience. This idea of a preconception of the object is compatible with Fairbairn's theory as long as it is emphasized that the characteristics and attributes of the object world become known to the infant through actual experience.

These views may be further clarified by drawing on the work of John Bowlby, the renowned infant researcher and ethologist who referred to himself as a Fairbairnian. Bowlby (1968) suggested that social animals are genetically preprogrammed to have an innate apprehension toward predators. Social animals have survived by the evolution of innate mechanisms that keep them grouped together thereby providing protection from predators; the newborn and young animals have a much better chance of survival by remaining close to others. Thus, there may be a preconception of the predator (bad object) and a preconception of an object required for survival (good object). Libido serves the ego seeking the object needed for survival, and aggression serves the model of fight/flight behavior on behalf of the ego apprehensive of the predator.

Fairbairn's and Bion's views of the internal world have much in common. Fairbairn (1941) described the personality as fundamentally schizoid, whereas Bion believed a part of the personality is inevitably psychotic. Fairbairn (1941) said that the infant needs to be loved as a person in its own right if it is to develop an autonomous self. Deprivation of love is felt as emptiness. As the experience of hunger is felt as physiological emptiness, deprivation of love is felt as psychic emptiness. Deprivation and emptiness arouse the desire to control, possess, and transform the object. Internalization is understood as an effort to possess the other omnipotently. The person endeavoring to possess the object ends up being possessed by it. For Fairbairn (1941), self and object become known in a Hegelian developmental struggle of possession, identification, and differentiation. Human development and differentiation often resemble the difficult journey of Odysseus and his crew as they struggle to outwit the demons, sirens, cyclops, and witches threatening to thwart their long journey and deprive them of freedom. In fact, these mythological demons personify the internal bad objects described by Fairbairn as exciting, rejecting, enticing, bewitching, engulfing, and persecuting. As James Grotstein (1994) points out, the internal world of objects is felt by the patient to be a world of demons, witches, monsters, angels, ghosts, and spirits. The patient feels trapped inside an internal hell comprised of split-egos relating in trancelike surrender and idealizing loyalty to intimidating, frightening, persecuting, exciting, and rejecting objects.

Fairbairn (1958) viewed splitting as a reaction to environmental trauma. For Fairbairn, however, this situation could not be adequately described in terms of a purely passive shattered self. Rather, Fairbairn described the splitting of egos and objects by the central ego as an active process. This view is supported by Sutherland's (1994) view of the self as an active, autonomous agent. The complementarity of the work of Bion and Fairbairn is most evident in this view of splitting as an active process.

Bion (1967) described a psychotic part of the personality as always coexisting alongside a nonpsychotic part of the personality. One part of the personality will usually dominate over the other, and they will have different levels of ego organization, functioning, and stability. A person diagnosed as psychotic will therefore still have a hidden nonpsychotic part of the personality, and a person diagnosed as neurotic will have a hidden psychotic core. Bion stated that the borderline and psychotic patients that he treated often had a violent hatred of the frustrating aspects of reality. In one of his most original contributions, Bion (1967) said that these patients hate not only reality but also the parts of the personality—the perceptual apparatus, consciousness, and ego functioning—that establish contact with reality. Bion described attacks on the capacity to think, to perceive, and to know. There are attacks on linkages and the perceptual apparatus that links the individuals to others. The psychotic attack on linkages is a form of radical splitting, serving to destroy the awareness between self and object. Bion describes the means by which splitting occurs. One has only to think of a typical situation in which an intelligent patient continually and blindly repeats the same self-destructive patterns of behaviors or engages in the same self-defeating pattern of relationships and the exasperated therapist thinks "Can't this patient see where this is going?" or "Can't this person see what is going on?" Bion's theory suggests that it is the attack on the capacity to think that prevents the patient from seeing what is happening and allows for the activation of split egos and objects.

Bion (1967) believed that frustration is the major determinant of psychotic states. The incapacity to tolerate frustration of instinctual drives is, he thought, the chief factor in the infant's rejection of reality. Bion (1962) did, however, take into account the environment in the importance he attributed to the caregiver, containing frustrating experience. Fairbairn (1958) believed that frustration is always experienced as rejection and that separation from the object is the original, or primary, source of anxiety. From a Fairbairnian view point, the activities of splitting and attacks on the perceptual apparatus are not to deny the frustration of instinctual drives but rather to destroy the awareness of traumatic separation from the needed object. Grotstein (1990) and Frances Tustin (1990) point out that some patients suffering from constitutional or environmental deficiency experience separation as if they were falling into a black hole or bottomless void. Fairbairn has, on occasion, been criticized for placing too much weight on the environment and not enough on constitutional biochemical factors in the etiology of schizoid pathology (Greenberg and Mitchell, 1983). In fact, his theory can easily take into account biochemical constitutional factors. A child with such deficits will have an even greater need for the object and be more likely to suffer frustration interpreted as rejection and even greater anxiety when separated from the object.

Fairbairn (1941) wrote his seminal papers on object relations theory before Melanie Klein (1946) and Bion (1962) developed the concept of projective identification. Fairbairn focused on the schizoid individual and how a conscious central adaptive ego relates to an idealized environment in a superficial, constricted fashion by splitting off and repressing negative experience. This enables the individual to remain in contact with an idealized outer world as seen through "rose colored glasses." The work of Klein and Bion shows how borderline and paranoid patients often are unable to repress their internal bad objects, and feeling persecuted within, project them back onto the external world. There is a dialectic in the views of Bion and Fairbairn regarding the creation of the object world. Bion (1962) illustrates how the infant creates its world through projective identification, whereas Fairbairn (1958) illustrates how the world becomes part of the infant through introjective identification. I suggest that treatment from a Fairbairn-Bion perspective involves interpreting splitting and the associated attacks of the perceptual apparatus and containing the patient's terror, despair, and rage as he or she separates from internal bad objects. The following clinical case will illustrate some of these views.

Case Example

Alice, a middle-aged woman, recalling the loss of her mother several years before, suffered every December. She had a difficult childhood and experienced severe deprivation in the first year of life. Her mother was an adolescent when she gave birth to Alice; her father was an alcoholic and a gambler. Alice's mother was unable to focus on her own parenting because she felt hopeless and depressed over her husband's problems. In the first few years of her treatment, Alice became aware that she had been her mother's helper to make herself so needed that she would not be abandoned. She described her mother as a narcissistic woman who devoted all her attention to her glamorous appearance and an affair with a neighbor. Alice worked hard to do well in school and later worked as a teacher.

She married a man who was an alcoholic, like her father. She had a child and attempted to provide her daughter with everything she had missed. Her husband left when the daughter was four years old. The daughter was compliant and cooperative, but when she reached adolescence she became rebellious, trying to separate from her mother. The daughter later moved out of state and lived with roommates. Alice was disappointed that her daughter never finished college, but the daughter did find a job to support herself. She did not earn much money and sometimes sought help from Alice. She was conflicted about her dependency needs and often became hostile when seeking help. Alice then felt rejected and rejected the child in turn. When Alice did provide her daughter with material help, she expected her daughter to follow her advice as to how she should live her life and became resentful when she didn't.

Holiday Crisis

Alice was in a crisis between Thanksgiving and New Year's Day. The daughter had called Alice complaining of being tired of her working conditions and asking if it was all right to quit. Alice agreed but then later wondered if she wanted the daughter to be dependent. The daughter quit her job and found herself more dependent on her mother. She approached Alice for help in a demanding and angry way, and Alice felt that her daughter's vocational problems pointed to Alice as being a failure as a mother. The daughter visited on Thanksgiving and fought with her mother. Alice told her to leave and never to return and the daughter stormed out. Alice said that as soon as the daughter arrived she had announced that she was only staying overnight and leaving the next day. The daughter said she had hardly slept the night before, and Alice accused her of poor planning.

In her treatment sessions Alice complained that she no longer had a daughter. She said that she no longer cared and she wasn't going to go crawling to her or give in.

I asked how it affected her to think that she no longer had a daughter. She said she felt like dying—that since her husband left she lived only for her daughter and that after her mother died it was even worse. So, if she did not have a daughter, what did she have? There was no point to living.

I interpreted that it wasn't that she no longer had a daughter. The trouble was that now she felt she had a demon daughter and that she had lost her good daughter. I emphasized that she was not thinking of herself as without a daughter but rather as herself persecuted by her daughter.

She wondered what if her daughter never called, what if they never spoke to each other? That is what she meant by no longer having a daughter.

I reminded her that this was the anniversary of her mother's death. I said that the feelings about the conflict with her daughter were colored by her feeling abandoned by her mother. I reminded her that it was her mother she would never see or hear from again and that she was feeling possessed by this sense of an abandoning mother and of herself as an abandoned child.

Alice said that she had been withdrawing from several of her friends. She wished to go out but then recalled occasions when her friends had disappointed her and she therefore no longer wished to go.

I told her that she was seeing everyone in the image of her abandoning mother, that the anniversary of her mother stirred up the memories of disappointment, rejection, and rage associated with her relationship with her mother. I recalled what she had told me about the severe deprivation in her first year of life. "It is this early feeling of being abandoned, stirred up by the anniversary of your mother's death, that you are reliving," I told her. "This abandoned part of you comes out saying it's not going to crawl to your mother, daughter, friends or anyone anymore. It feels it cannot trust anyone, so it is better not to depend on anyone, and to be alone. You then lose whatever good aspects there are in your relationship with your daughter and with other people."

Alice says that when she feels this way it seems that there are no good aspects to her entire life; it is at this point she feels like disappearing or dying. During the next few sessions, Alice would alternate between reflecting on the way that she sometimes saw her life as all bad and hopeless, and feeling as if her life was, in fact, all bad and hopeless. These oscillations occurred quite rapidly, sometimes repeatedly during the same session. Describing all the negative aspects in her relationships with her daughter and friends, she insisted that she could see nothing positive in any of her relationships and therefore might as well give up. I then commented that she was silently attacking her capacity to perceive any of the evidence of a connection between herself and her daughter or to think about relationships in anything but a negative way. I made this interpretation repeatedly and also reminded her of occasions she had described that suggested some evidence of caring between herself and her daughter. I said, "The problem is that in infancy you did not have a good-enough connection to your mother, so you have no experience of a foundation that is sustained even when there is an absence or a fight. If you had a sense of the connection I'm describing, you would feel the possibility of you and another person caring for one another even when you are separated or having a fight."

Alice replied that she felt what I said was important even though it was only intellectual. She still felt terrible. It was a physical feeling in her chest. It nevertheless gave her some "food for thought" over the next few days. I said the fact that she was beginning to think was very important.

When we met again, Alice said that the last few days had been interesting. After the last session she went to sleep, still feeling bad. She woke up still feeling depressed, but there was something different. There was a school project she had been putting off for weeks because she never felt she had enough energy. On this day she felt energetic and motivated to do it. This was significant because she did not force herself. She was supposed to do this project with another teacher. When Alice approached, the other teacher looked frightened. Alice realized she had not spoken to this teacher for weeks, and she must have looked so irritable that when she approached her colleague, she must have expected Alice to be angry. When she realized what Alice wanted, her face changed its expression and she was quite friendly. On the next day Alice met a friend who lived in her building. The friend had been expressing concern and calling and looking in on Alice. Alice had been putting her off but now she spoke to the friend and did not feel she had to force herself. Alice stated that one of the most important differences now was that she could think about what was happening between herself and other people and not immediately interpret everything from the standpoint of feeling abandoned. She was able to fig-ure out how to approach her daughter in a constructive fashion.

Agoraphobia and the Patient's Fear of Autonomy

Alice continued to have a difficult winter, though her relation-ship with her daughter improved. Alice had always been agora-phobic, and at one time she feared leaving her house. She was able to manage her anxiety well enough to learn how to drive but continued to fear driving at night, in the rain, or in less than perfect conditions. Alice had to drive a long distance to work each day, and it was an especially snowy season. If there was any snow or ice, she typically did not go to work. She knew her behavior was phobic because other teachers who lived as far away or even further away managed to get to work. This winter the weather was so bad so often that she was forced to face her fear of driving in inclement conditions.

Fairbairn (1941) described agoraphobia as a form of separa-tion anxiety. The security of home is felt to represent merger and identification with the object. Thus, leaving home arouses sepa-ration anxiety because it represents separation from the internal object. Alice's increased mobility and the lessening of her agora-phobia meant that she was becoming more autonomous. She started to become seriously depressed again, however, as she felt stressed out by the bad weather conditions and increasing demands on her. Alice said she knew everyone felt stressed out by having to travel in this difficult weather, but she felt that for her something more happened. She began to feel that the snow was intended to persecute her personally. She said. "It sounds crazy, but it isn't just that the snow is difficult and dangerous to get around in; rather it's that it's snowing to make it difficult for me." She felt that the snow meant to stop her from going about her business, to obstruct her, to make her feel suicidal. She said that she felt these thoughts made her feel as discouraged and defeated as when she felt that everyone in her life was bad. She lost all perspective, could no longer think straight. It was as if a demon were let loose in her mind.

Alice acknowledged that over the years she had become better able to express her natural inclination toward autonomy, although she felt she was still not autonomous enough to handle her current situation. She described how slowly she drove in the snow and how all the other cars passed her and she sometimes arrived late to work. She wished to go faster but feared doing so and hated herself for it. I remarked that the bad weather thwarted her wish for autonomy. Being thwarted so aroused her rage , but she had nowhere else to express it so she turned it against herself.

Alice concurred that she wished she could be left alone to go about her business and that she felt frustrated and angry that things wouldn't let her be. I interpreted this feeling of being thwarted and not allowed to do her own thing must be a reliving of how she had felt in childhood. Alice replied that she had never been left alone. She never remembered any peace. Whenever she wished to do something by herself, there was always a crisis. Either her mother needed her help or her father and brothers fought. It was a crazy house. There was always a crisis, and they never left her alone. Now the weather repeatedly stopped her from going about her business and made her life hectic, she felt much the same way.

I interpreted that the weather she felt to be persecuting her and thwarting her autonomy felt like a reliving of her family not letting her be and thwarting her autonomy.

The Moral Defense and the
Projection of the Bad Object

The winter remained stressful for Alice. She had a difficult class of children, and the administrators and teachers were all under much pressure. Alice felt distressed that her children were so difficult and complained to the administration, who, in turn, criticized her. She was in a rage that her children were disorderly. She described bitter fights with teachers and administration. At times, she'd think of quitting or hurting herself. She felt that the children, administration, other teachers and the weather were all part of her fate to suffer. I commented that such thoughts were evidence of the internal attacks on her capacity to think and perceive accurately. I also remarked that she might take these difficult feelings personally because of an underlying feeling that she deserved to be punished and to suffer. At first she vehemently denied this possibility, insisting that she believed that the administrators, teachers and children were bad and she didn't believe that she was bad or deserving of her miserable fate.

Although she denied believing that she was bad, she readily acknowledged feeling that she always needed to be perfect. She recalled many occasions that demonstrated how perfectionist she was. Her apartment must always be perfect; when she invited friends, she must prepare everything perfectly. She felt that she must always be beyond reproach. She recalled that another teacher said that he was concerned about her, concerned that she was going to get sick. He said she took the children's misbehavior too much to heart, and that she tried to do the impossible. She now realized that she blamed herself for the children's being difficult and expected that the administration was going to blame her and fire her or transfer her. She therefore went on the attack and blamed them before they could blame her. In the following sessions, Alice could see that this fear was not based on reality but was a reliving of childhood anxieties. She recalled that her mother always had said that she was a difficult child. She felt that unless she helped out and was not difficult or demanding, she would be sent away. She tried to be perfect and beyond reproach.

In describing the moral defense, Fairbairn (1958) stated that the child internalizes the badness of the object to preserve the needed external object as good. The child then feels that the parent treats it badly only because the child is bad and deserves such treatment. The child may enact the moral defense by becoming perfect and beyond reproach so that the parent will no longer punish or reject the child. Alice took this step and tried to be as good as possible and sacrificed herself to the object. Here it can be seen that a further step may occur. The object may continue to treat the child badly even though the child has sacrificed itself to the object and endeavors to be perfect. It is here that the projection comes in. The person may now project all the internalized badness back into the external object. The person may then say they deserve to be loved. They are now not seeking to be loved as a person in their own right— simply for who they are—but rather because they have used the moral defense and therefore deserve to be loved because they have sacrificed themselves to the object. They demand to be loved not for themselves but for not having a self, for surrendering it. This was the dynamic revealed in the case of Alice.

References

Bion, W. (1962), *Learning from Experience*. New York: Aronson, 1983.
———— (1967), *Second Thoughts*. New York: Basic Books.
Bowlby, J. (1968), *Attachment and Loss, Vol. 1*. London: Hogarth Press.
Fairbairn, W. R. D. (1941), A revised psychopathology of the psychoses and psychoneuroses. In: *Psychoanalytic Studies of the Personality*. London: Routledge & Kegan Paul, 1952, pp. 28–58.

———— (1958), On the nature and aims of psychoanalytic treatment. In: *From Instinct to Self, Vol. 1*, ed. D. Scharff & E. F. Birtles. Northvale, NJ: Aronson, 1994, pp. 74–94.

Greenberg, J. & Mitchell, S. (1983), *Object Relations in Psychoanalytic Theory.* Cambridge, MA: Harvard University Press.

Grotstein, J. (1990), Nothingness, meaninglessness, chaos and the black hole: II. The black hole. *Contemp. Psychoanal.*, 26:377–407.

———— (1994), Notes on Fairbairn's metapsychology. In: *Fairbairn and the Origins of Object Relations*, ed. J. Grotstein & D. Rinsley. New York: Guilford, pp. 112–150.

Sutherland, J. (1994), *The Autonomous Self*, ed. J. S. Scharff. Northvale, NJ: Aronson, pp. 303–330.

Tustin, F. (1990), *The Protective Shell in Children and Adults*. London: Karnac.

◆ Part 3 ◆

Theoretical Connections

To the Future

7

Fairbairn's Object Seeking
Between Paradigms

Stephen A. Mitchell

One of the clearest lessons to be gleaned from the enormous body of Freud scholarship that has become a field of intellectual history in its own right is that major theoreticians can be read in many, many different ways. A second lesson is that it is probably a mistake to expect any great innovator to really grasp the revolution he or she is participating in. Since the theoreticians are standing in one world view and struggling to give birth to another, they cannot possibly envision what the full fruition of their efforts will be. Thus, Loewald (1971), Habermas, and Lear, each in his own way, argue that Freud only incompletely understood the revolution he himself was effecting. And Ogden has argued not only that it is impossible to understand Melanie Klein's work without having read Freud, but that it is impossible to understand Freud without having first read Melanie Klein, since the work of Klein and others brought to life potentials that were germinal in Freud's writings.

Object Seeking: Drive or Ground?

Jay Greenberg (1991) regards Fairbairn as, in one fundamental respect, less revolutionary as a theorist than Fairbairn took himself to be. He argues that all psychoanalytic theories must contain a theory of drive, either explicitly or implicitly. He goes on to claim that, although Fairbairn presented his object relations theory as an alternative to traditional drive theory, a close reading reveals a hidden drive concept in Fairbairn's vision, a kind of crypto-drive theory. Greenberg believes that unless a theory espouses a complete and thoroughly naive environmentalism (Edgar Levenson is the only proponent he can find for such a viewpoint), a concept of drive is essential. Presuppositions about drive define what the individual brings to interaction with others. Without drives, the individual would be merely passive putty, shaped by external, social influences. In this view, theorists who eschew *Freud's* drive theory necessarily substitute an alternative theory of drive to account for that which draws the individual into interactions with others and for the way in which an individual records and is shaped by those interactions.

One might ague in response that Fairbairn's object seeking *is* a kind of drive, in much the same way that Bowlby saw attachment as a drive. Emmanuel Ghent (personal communication) has suggested naming these kinds of motivations *d*rives (with a small d) to distinguish them from *D*rives (with a big D) reserved for Freud's sort of sexual and aggressive drives. But, interestingly, Greenberg argues that Fairbairn's notion of "object seeking" cannot itself be considered a drive (and I imagine he would feel the same way about "attachment"), because it is too vague and indeterminate. All psychoanalytic theories depict individuals as seeking objects. The question is, What are they seeking objects for? For Freud, objects are sought for sexual and aggressive discharge. For Sullivan, objects are sought for the satisfaction of various integrating tendencies. In itself, as Greenberg reads it, object seeking means nothing; it is an empty slogan, restating the obvious and making none of the selective motivational claims that make a theory interesting and useful, with all the attendant risks.

So, why *do* babies and other people seek objects? What exactly makes an object an object? An object can become meaningful, psychologically speaking, Greenberg asserts, only because it serves some purpose, provides some sort of gratification, meets some need. Thus, any object relations theory presupposes some basic need or other that objects are sought to meet. In Greenberg's reading, Fairbairn believes that objects are sought for the gratification of oral dependency. In this view, Fairbairn has substituted for the complexity of Freud's dual drive system a simplistic one-drive system. Although Greenberg's analysis is persuasive and he finds passages in Fairbairn's papers to support it, I believe Fairbairn was also after something more fundamental, which he never developed fully or clearly, and I want to try to get at that more relational project.

To argue that we need a concept of drive to describe what the individual seeks in interactions with other people presumes that the individual qua individual is the most appropriate unit of study. It assumes that the individual, in his or her natural state, is essentially alone and then drawn into interaction for some purpose or need. I believe that Fairbairn (like Sullivan) was struggling toward a different way of understanding the nature of human beings as fundamentally social, not as *drawn* into interaction, but as *embedded* in an interactive matrix with others as their natural state.

In what sense does a bee seek other bees? In what sense does the wolf or zebra seek other members of its pack or herd? It seems cumbersome and improbable to regard this gregariousness, or object seeking, as expressive of a discretely experienced need, like hunger or sex, which emerges from time to time, when the individual bee or wolf or zebra feels lonely, requiring other members of its kind for satisfaction. Many animals are, by their very nature, social beings and can exist as normal creatures of their specific type only as part of the group. Fairbairn, Sullivan, and other architects of the relational model were redefining the nature of the human psyche as fundamentally social and interactive. Fairbairn was suggesting that object seeking, in its most radical form, is not the vehicle for the satisfaction of a specific need, but the expression of our very nature, the form through which we become specifically *human* beings.

To define humans as relational is quite different from specifying object seeking as a particular drive. Human beings are oxygen-breathing organisms; we are not driven to seek oxygen (except if it is suddenly withdrawn). It is simply what we are built to do, and we do it without intentionality. Human beings are also language-generating creatures. In the heyday of behaviorism, language was assumed to be an instrumental act that emerged in an individual for some purpose because it was reinforced. Now language is generally regarded as an emergent property of the human brain. Thus, Steven Pinker (1994) describes language as an instinct precisely because "people know how to talk in more or less the sense that spiders know how to spin webs . . . spiders spin spider webs because they have spider brains, which give them the urge to spin and the competence to succeed" (p. 18). Now, there are many controversial theories about the evolutionary adaptive purpose or purposes that originally, eons ago, selected for language development. But, Pinker is suggesting, the young spider begins to spin his web not because he is hungry or because he intuits his need for webs as the basis of his livelihood, but because spinning webs is what he is designed to do. Similarly, babies generate sounds, and eventually language, not for some instrumental purpose, but because they have human brains, and that is what we are wired to do.

Human beings, starting as small babies, seek other human minds to interact with not for the satisfaction of some discrete need, but because we are wired to respond visually to the human face, olfactorily to human smells, auditorily to the human voice, and semiotically to human signs (Muller). We are designed, in many, many ways we are just beginning to appreciate, to be drawn into interaction with other human beings, and this design is necessary for babies to be able to use their brains to become specifically human, language-generating creatures, with specifically human minds. It was Fairbairn's most far-reaching contribution to be among the first to intuit that the establishment and maintenance of relationships with others is as fundamental to the nature of the human organism as oxygen-breathing. Greenberg is right to point to the importance Fairbairn attributes to oral dependency, but, in my view, this reflects not the true, underlying significance of "object seeking," but rather Fairbairn's incomplete emergence from Freud's unquestioned starting point of an individual organism driven by needs.

Greenberg reads Fairbairn as offering a motivational system, necessarily based on drives, rather like Freud's, but lacking Freud's richness and complexity. A common, closely related but somewhat more appreciative reading (Pine, Eagle) portrays Fairbairn as offering something new and useful, but something wholly compatible and integratable with classical drive theory and the structural model. Why not combine a one-person *and* a two-person model, the intrapsychic *with* the interpersonal? Winnicott and Khan (1953) wrote an early review of Fairbairn's work in which they criticized him for asking the reader to make a choice between Freud and Fairbairn. But why is a choice necessary? Doesn't it make sense that human beings are both pleasure seeking and object seeking?

This strategy, while admirable in its inclusiveness, reflects a fundamental misunderstanding of what Fairbairn was up to. A "two-person" perspective, the frame of reference Fairbairn and Sullivan shared, might be defined as follows: the best way to understand persons is not in isolation but in the context of their relations with others, past and present, internal and external, actual and fantasized. It should be immediately apparent, although this is routinely missed, that such a perspective includes individual persons, but sets them in a particular context that, it is argued, is the best context for understanding what is most interesting about them, psychoanalytically speaking.

The argument for a hybrid model that combines one- and two-person perspectives represents a confusion of conceptual levels. It empties out the individual persons from the two-person model and then claims that we need a one-person/two-person hybrid to bring them back. But the individuals were accounted for in the two-person model all along—how could they not be? What would it mean to have a two-person model without individual persons? A model describing the events between people but not the people themselves? Consider as an analogy the movement in astronomy from an earth-centered model to our current model of the solar system, a shift from a view of the earth in its unique splendor at the center of things to a repositioning of earth in a larger context or field, along with other planets, in orbit around the sun. A hybrid modelist might argue that the earth is not sufficiently represented in the solar model. Why not have both an earth- and a sun-centered model? What we need is a mixed model so we can have it all, or both models in a paradoxical, dialectical tension with each other. But to make that argument, you first have to take the earth out of the solar model to justify the need for a hybrid. The solar model provides a full account of the earth, its specific geology, weather systems, flora and fauna, *but in a broader context*, and that is the crucial difference. To explain some things on earth, like the local physics of billiard tables, one need not refer to the sun and other planets. For others, like annual weather cycles, it is crucial to do so. It is never necessary to step out of the solar model; not all parts of it are used in thinking about every problem. A hybrid, earth-centered/sun-centered model purchases a shallow inclusiveness at the price of incoherence.

Similarly, Fairbairn understood very well that human beings seek pleasure. He was not disputing that. He was suggesting that Freud stopped his account, his understanding of pleasure seeking, too soon. By making pleasure seeking a fundamental motivational principle, *the* fundamental motivational principle of drive theory, Freud did not understand it in its proper context, the object-relational field. Why do people seek pleasure? For Fairbairn, the best explanation is not that pleasure seeking, as drive discharge, is a fundamental property of mind, but because pleasure seeking, like all other dynamic processes, occurs in the context of object seeking, because pleasure is a powerful medium for the establishment and maintenance of connections with others. This reordering of priorities is precisely what makes Fairbairn's model such a powerful explanatory framework for just the sort of phenomena Freud's hedonic model foundered on: masochism, negative therapeutic reactions, the repetition compulsion. If pleasure seeking is not available, people seek pain, because pain provides the best channel to others.

A hybrid model based on the dual principle that people are fundamentally both pleasure seeking and object seeking is certainly a possible framework, but it is no longer Fairbairn's theory and does not include Fairbairn's, except in a diminished, cardboard-cutout sense. Fairbairn provided an account of pleasure seeking, recontextualized within object seeking. The hybrid model takes pleasure seeking out of Fairbairn's model as a rationale for resuscitating the traditional drive model, just as the astronomical hybrid would have to take earth out of the solar model as a justification for reviving Ptolemy. The psychoanalytic hybrid is not a broader perspective, which includes both Freud and Fairbairn, because the Fairbairn it includes is a collapsed version, deprived of its broad, explanatory power. It is a version based on a reading of Fairbairn in which "object seeking" is understood as a discrete motive propelling an individually constituted organism, like Freud's Drives, rather than as the very nature of that organism, wired to be actualized only through exchanges with other minds.

Bounded Individuals and the Problem of Internalization

Fairbairn's position between paradigms becomes manifest in his struggle with what he clearly found to be the bedeviling problem of the motivation for early internalization, a position he kept changing and revising from one paper to the next. Because Fairbairn regarded people as most fundamentally reality oriented, directed toward actual people in the interpersonal world, he wrestled again and again with how and why those actual experiences with real people are first established internally. And the most common criticism of Fairbairn's work has been directed precisely at his commitment to the notion that internalization takes place, in the beginning, because early objects are "bad" or "unsatisfying," leaving out the ways in which "good" experiences are taken in.

From my point of view, Fairbairn started off on the wrong foot with regard to this question, because he did not fully appreciate the implications of viewing the individual mind in a relational context with other minds. To pose the question, What is the motive for the first internalization? is to begin with the premise that there is a fundamental differentiation and boundary between inside and outside. This is a premise that Fairbairn inherited from Klein. If something from outside is found inside (which is what we mean by internalization), then we have to explain how it got there. Whereas Klein believed that boundary was regularly traversed through phantasy-driven expulsive/ projective and incorporative/introjective processes, Fairbairn (1954) thought that internalization was explainable only in terms of specific acts of defense. "I do not regard introjection of the object as the inevitable expression of the infant's instinctive incorporative needs—as something that just happens, so to speak" (p. 16fn).

Psychoanalytic authors have been struggling with the central tension between sameness and differentiation at least as far back as Freud's (1921) statement that, in the beginning, object cathexis and identification are indistinguishable. If Freud had given these primary identifications more weight, he might have moved in the direction that Fairbairn did, depicting libido as object seeking rather than pleasure seeking. Fairbairn (1941) picked up the notion of primary identification from Freud to "signify the cathexis of an object which has not yet been differentiated from the cathecting subject" (p. 34). But, although Fairbairn mentioned primary identifications from time to time, he did not give them explanatory weight when it came to accounting for the earliest derivation of our inner worlds. If Fairbairn had given these identifications structure-building significance, he might have regarded primary internalizations as residues of developmentally early object relations, perhaps distinct perceptually but undifferentiated affectively and psychologically.

What if one assumes that there is no discrete psychological boundary for the baby at the start? That the baby begins life fully embedded in a presymbolic (Lachmann and Beebe) relational matrix composed of interactions with caregivers? What if one assumes that a sense of oneself as a separate individual and of objects as differentiated others is only gradually constructed, over the course of early development, out of this undifferentiated matrix? Then the sense of oneself as populated with presences of early significant objects would not have to be accounted for by some discrete, intentional, defensive process. Intensely emotional experiences with others early in life and, on an unconscious level throughout later life as well, might involve a diffusion of boundaries between self and other so that it is not possible to know precisely who is who. Pleasurable and unpleasurable, good and bad senses of oneself as like one's parents, in fact, *as* one's parents, would continually be rediscovered throughout life, because they would constitute the starting point, the ground out of which a differentiated framework of self and others develops. On this point, Loewald (1971) grasped the way in which the very concept of the "object," which Fairbairn took for granted, is itself is developmental construction:

Objects are not givens. On the contrary, a highly complex course of psychic development is required for environmental and body-surface stimuli to become organized and experienced as external, in contrast to internal, and for such sources of stimulation, gratification, and frustration eventually to become objects, in any acceptable sense of that word, for a subject or self. Hand in hand with this came a growing recognition of the fact that, what from an external (i.e., nonpsychoanalytic) observer's point of view are called objects, are indispensable and crucial factors in the organization of psychic functioning and psychic structure. In other words, what is naively called objects plays an essential part in the constitution of the subject, including the organization of instincts as psychic phenomena and of the subject's developing "object relations"; and what is naively called subject plays an essential part in the organization of objects [p. 127].

The emphasis Klein and Fairbairn placed on the boundedness of the individual was an important antidote to the earlier Freudian concept of objectless, primary narcissism. Unfortunately, this movement toward a view of the baby as object related from the start was linked to a view of the baby as separate from the objects he was seeking. This trend was further developed in the work of some infant researchers (like Daniel Stern), who portray a quite differentiated baby who clearly knows who is who. But perceptual discrimination is very different from affective embeddedness, as current writings on transference–countertransference phenomena make increasingly clear. As Adam Philips (1995) has put it, "When two people speak to each other, they soon become inextricable: words are contagious" (p. 22).

We need to move toward a more sophisticated way of thinking about the dialectic between union and differentiation, in which they are regarded not as opposites but as blended together in different forms on different levels. Thus, it is possible to combine Loewald's (1971) notion of primary affective unity with objects with Stern's (1985) notion of perceptual differentiation from objects. We might imagine this tension in terms of the kind of pattern achieved by potters who use crackled glazes, where the surface of the pot is, in one sense, an unbroken unity and, in another sense, broken into bounded fragments with clear boundaries.

Impulses and Guilt

George, a man in his mid-20s whose wife had abandoned him as unexciting and distant, discovered in analysis the implications of his early relationship (ages 4–6) with his beloved uncle, which had been fully sexual, possibly including oral and anal penetration, being dressed in women's clothes, and being tied up. Over several years of productive analytic work, these memories and associated dynamics had been extensively explored and in many respects relived in the transference with a skilled female analyst. George had allowed himself, with great trepidation, to remember and fantasize about these experiences, which he found conflictual but very stimulating. He experimented with cross-dressing and masturbated to S&M scenarios provided by similarly oriented individuals on the Internet. He had recently begun a relationship with a woman, which he had been finding quite satisfying, emotionally and sexually, but the lure of the memories with the uncle and the various masturbatory forms through which he reenacted them was still powerful.

How are we to understand the nature of these impulses? What are they? Consider a session following a weekend that George had spent with his girlfriend, having lots of very satisfying sex. As he was saying good-bye to her, George found himself thinking about the always available electronic trysts involving cross-dressing and S&M play-acting. He pushed the thoughts away, wanting instead to savor the weekend, with its sexual and emotional intimacies. But he could not get the thoughts of the electronic possibilities out of his mind. They became more and more exciting and irresistible. He wrestled with them, but unsuccessfully, and, on returning home, found himself succumbing to what he experienced as ego-alien impulses to seek out these kinky, masturbatory experiences.

Now, there are many possible ways to understand this sequence. From a hybrid framework, one might regard George as caught in the grip of an intense conflict between the object seeking of his interpersonal intimacies with the girlfriend and an addictive pleasure seeking that remained from his early sexual traumas. But that interpretation would not be Fairbairn's, and it would not be making the fullest use of Fairbairn's contributions. Fairbairn wrote about impulses as "disintegration products" of failed personal relations, but the most interesting use to be made of Fairbairn's perspective here is in the unpacking of George's experience of the impulse itself.

As the analyst explored the texture of George's wrestling with his impulses, it began to seem as if that struggle itself repeated his experience with his uncle. The impulse, like the uncle, was experienced as a powerful force outside himself, a force that tempted him into something pleasurable but forbidden and frightening, a force that was stronger than he, a force that eventually overcame him and to which he eventually surrendered. Thus, although he experienced the impulse as a depersonalized tension, a drive perhaps, it seemed clinically most useful to understand it as a pared down, symbolic representation of his uncle. In George's surrender to an irresistible, pleasure-providing impulse, he was reenacting, through an internal object relationship, his very much object-related connection to his uncle, which had, in an important sense, become threatened by his more mutual, higher level intimacy with his girlfriend. In Fairbairn's terms, it was the threat to and allegiance with his internal relationship with his uncle that was the motive for his actions, not pleasure seeking in itself.

Many people feel overcome by their rage rather than their sexuality. I worked with someone a while ago whose father used to blow up in volcanic explosions and beat him. And he himself, as a grown man, felt periodically overcome by similar violent bursts of temper. We came to understand that he experienced his father as thoroughly controlled by his mother in virtually every way imaginable and that he felt a secret thrill in his father's explosions even though he was also the terrified victim of them. By regarding rage, both in his father and in himself, as a depersonalized force of nature, he was celebrating what Fairbairn would understand as a libidinal tie to his father, free of the mother's perview.

Fairbairn (1954) speaks of patients who identify their genitals with the exciting object, as something external to their central self, which entices them and lures them and to which they surrender. These kinds of patients, like George, illustrate the utility of not regarding object relations as distinct and on an equal footing with pleasure seeking or sexuality and aggression, in a spirit of ecclecticism. Among the most radical implications of the perspective that Fairbairn was developing is the notion that the experience of sexuality and aggression does not represent the eruption of sheer biology into subjective experience, but that these experiences are shaped, their meaning determined, their location within the matrix of multiple self-organizations fixed, by early object relations.

And from my point of view, George's sense of his uncle and his perverse connections to him as a powerful and reliable internal presence does not have to be accounted for as the result of a discrete psychic event of internalization. I find it more compelling to regard them as the residue of an early experience in which the uncle and those intense moments with him were experienced as part of George himself, in the context of general parental neglect and an absence of intense emotional experiences that were more constructive and affirming.

Consider a second patient, Will, a 45-year-old corporate executive, who came for psychoanalysis because "bad" dreams made it very difficult for him to sleep at night. The dreams portrayed diffuse anxiety situations in which he had a great deal to do and was intensely nervous about having forgotten something that would mushroom into a disaster. In reality, he had a great deal of responsibility on his job, and sometimes the content of the dreams referred to actual concerns and obligations. He was very dubious about psychoanalysis but felt desperate about his sleep problems. His wife, Anne, a believer in psychoanalysis, thought he had deep emotional conflicts and convinced him to come.

Not too many sessions into our work, Will revealed that he thought of himself as having suffered a kind of disaster 15 years earlier from which he never really recovered. He had been married previously, from his early to his late 20s, to Gail, a woman he had thought he loved. He had begun a flirtation with Anne that turned into an affair, which he found himself, despite desperate efforts to disentangle himself, simply unable to give up. The affair began during Gail's pregnancy, and, when his daughter was two years old, he left to live alone for four years. During this time, he did not allow himself really to be with Anne, tried several times to return to Gail, felt extremely tortured for having left his wife and daughter and for not having told Gail the truth about the existence of another woman, which seemed so awful that he simply could not bring himself to tell her. Finally, he told Gail about Anne, but that only made things worse. Eventually, Anne gave him an ultimatum—marry her or the relationship was over. He married her, and they have been more or less happily married, with two children, for the past 10 years.

The problem is that he cannot forgive himself for what he did to Gail and his daughter. Nor will Gail forgive him. In their financial and pragmatic dealings over time with the daughter, he is overly accommodating, to the great distress of Anne. Gail was the only child of close-binding parents who had lovingly, in some sense suffocatingly, taken Will into their family and adopted his large family as their own. They were devastated by the breakup of their daughter's marriage. Will feels that he has damaged their lives as well. It did not take long for us to recognize that the dreams might refer not just to his work situations but also to his sense of failed obligations with respect to his first marriage. He recalled that a horrible aspect of his trysts with Anne was the nagging sense that something terrible might happen to Gail and his daughter while he was off enjoying himself.

Despite his wife's prodding, Will avoided psychotherapy for many years because he was dubious about the whole idea of unconscious motivation. More importantly, he views psychoanalysis as part of a modern (perhaps postmodern) culture that allows people to avoid taking responsibility for their actions. He loathes public officials who do terrible things, betraying the public trust and their private relationships and who then appear on television saying something facile like, "Mistakes were made. I was wrong. But how big of me to admit my crimes; everybody makes mistakes. Please vote for me in the next election." Will is afraid that I will try to explain away his past actions and talk him out of his guilt, which he thinks he *should* maintain if he is to retain any sense of integrity. Yet it is incomprehensible to him that he did what he did, and he often found himself in gatherings of friends making long, intense speeches criticizing people for doing precisely what he himself had done.

Briefly, Will is one of five children of first-generation immigrant parents. His father's father was a very hard-working man whose working-class job disappeared during the Depression. Will's father had to give up plans to go to law school in order to support his younger siblings. Will's parents worked extremely hard and saved their money to put their own children through college and graduate school, and they succeeded admirably. Will's father died quite a few years ago, but he remains an extremely powerful presence in his life, as an ideal figure whose devotion to family was a superordinate value. Part of the pain of Will's own life is the sense that his father, who never met Anne, would never understand how he could have betrayed his first wife and child.

My first take on Will's story (countertransferentially speaking) was one of admiration. I felt he was right to feel guilty for what he had done, and I admired his social critique of facile, psychopathic posturing by public figures. After a while, I felt he had suffered enough. (Of course, all these reactions were mediated through my own marital history, values, conflicts over guilt, etc.) We explored in detail his childhood conflicts and guilt in relation to both parents, his experiences of his two wives and the way they represented different aspects of himself and his family history, and so on. Although he viewed his adultery as a sexual fall of almost Biblical proportions, it became clear that his second wife made possible the expression of a whole different dimension of him, one concerned with fun and pleasure, whereas his first wife fit into the extremely dutiful, often anhedonic themes of his family of origin. (Of course, it was much more complicated; I am being very reductive here for purposes of brevity.) He began to feel that now, knowing more about himself as he did (partly through our work), he should have consulted a couples therapist at the time. I agreed. Perhaps the first marriage could have been saved. He really did not think so, but at least he would have felt later that he had tried. But none of this seemed to ease his self-punitive guilt.

How should we understand Will's guilt? The traditional psychoanalytic assumption would be that this guilt about an act in his adulthood masked an earlier, oedipal guilt for forbidden sexual desires. This model suggests that interpreting the underlying childhood fantasied crime would relieve the suffering. Fairbairn believed that guilt was often the vehicle for a powerful, underlying object tie and that trying to relieve the guilt would merely drive the attachment to the internal object deeper into repression. Indeed, Will's fierce determination not to let himself off the hook seemed to suggest precisely what Fairbairn predicted.

Several different interactions between us contributed to deepening the work and transforming Will's experience in ways that I find illuminated by the most radical implications of Fairbairn's perspective.

One turning point followed what might be considered a countertransference enactment, in which I inadvertently took on the role of the "bad," guilt-inducing object. I had begun to find Will's guilt a bit sanctimonious. He was going on about his concessions to Gail over holiday plans, in which his daughter, as usual, would spend most of the holiday with her mother; he would bend himself out of shape to make this possible, and Anne, as usual, was angry and resentful. What struck me, for the first time, was how little time his daughter had spent with Will's extended family, which consisted of all kinds of interesting aunts, uncles, and cousins. In his deferring to Gail, his daughter's life had been truncated around the small family consisting of her mother and grandparents, when, in reality she had another, bigger family that she was deprived of. As I encouraged Will to explore his feelings around these choices, he conjured up an image of Gail and her parents with his daughter at the holiday table, with an empty chair, the one he had vacated, like that of Tiny Tim at the end of *A Christmas Carol*. He had ripped this family apart by leaving, and he was bound to do whatever he could to ease their continuing pain.

Out of an initial irritation of which I became aware only retrospectively, I asked him what he thought his daughter would feel when she had grown up and tried to understand why she had been deprived of time with his extended family. Was she being deprived to ease his guilt? It struck me for the first time that, rather than actually bearing the guilt for what he had done, Will was denying it by appeasing Gail, as if he could, in fact, buy her off for his crime. By fixing this image of the family that was rendered asunder and still missing him (Gail, by the way, had actually remarried), he was fixing it in time so that his crime could still be atoned for rather than become an actuality of the past. My guilt-provocation and subsequent interpretation had a big impact on him; eventually, his concern about my values and appeasing them became a focus for exploration. My original intervention, however, in which I was, in a sense, speaking with the voice of his parents but with a different set of priorities, seemed important in opening up the closed circle of his self-punitive guilt.

A second line of inquiry began with an exploration of Will's flirtations with other women during the course of his first marriage, events that he treated as unexplainable aberrations. I suggested that he had difficulty in acknowledging to himself various aspects of his own sexuality and sense of adventure that were impossible for him to integrate into his first marriage, that were very important in drawing him toward his second wife, and that found a satisfying place in his second marriage. In these qualities he was different from his father in ways he had trouble coming to terms with, and the narrative of his seduction by Anne and his fall from grace served to externalize this facet of himself, thereby making him incomprehensible to himself.

A third important series of sessions involved Will's struggle with religion.

He had been raised Catholic and served as an altar boy, but his church attendance had lapsed when he was in college. Now, although not particularly religious, he was interested in attending church and possibly in providing a religious education for his children. His marital status as a divorced and remarried man, however, created obvious problems. He said a return to the church was impossible. I did not know too much about this, but asked a lot of questions; and it turned out that there were congregations it was likely he could join. The problem was that he did not approve of those congregations. Eventually, I noted that he seemed to be protecting a particular ideal of the church from corruption by people like himself.

Later we explored his stance on divorce, which I suggested seemed to involve his upholding the Vatican's position on the irreversibility of marriage. He felt misunderstood. As a progressive intellectual, he did not abide by the Church's teachings on these things; he accepted birth control and abortion. As we discussed these different issues, it became apparent that, although he valued the Church's teachings on issues like the sacredness of prenatal life, he felt there was a broader context, third-world poverty for example, that required a reconsideration of those ideals in the light of other concerns. I suggested that he had not been similarly able to recontextualize and update his ideal of marriage, taken from his parents. That his second marriage was so much more satisfying than the first seemed to have no bearing on his holding on to the ideal of the indissolubility of his first marriage. We agreed that there was something at stake in preserving a sense of continuity with his father and his ideals, despite the price it exacted from him in terms of guilt.

Over the course of several months during the second year of treatment, things began to change. Will drew clearer lines in his negotiations with Gail and began to appreciate ways in which his guilt was punishing toward Anne. He gradually found himself committing himself to his second marriage, owning it in ways he had previously been unable. He recently had the following dream:

> Anne and I were walking to the train station, as if going to work. There was a crowd of people. We missed the train, and then tried to take an elaborate walk around the perimeter of the station to get to another entrance to catch the next train. We were going down a covered walkway into a tunnel. To get to the train platform, you had to go up a ladder. Anne went ahead of me.

Ahead of her, another guy climbed up into a square opening of light and stepped out of sight. As soon as Anne disappeared in that opening, a train suddenly rushed by. I realized with horror that the opening was onto the tracks themselves. The train must have hit her. Car after car goes by; it seems as if it is taking forever. After the last car, I spring up to look around. On a patch of grass, Anne and several other people are sitting. They are all alive, shaken, with bumps and bruises, but no serious injuries. Anne is crying and I go to comfort her. I look up, and standing there is my mother and my (deceased) father. They look like they did in the 1970s, before they got very gray. It is a miracle. Anne can see them too. Then they comfort Anne also, and we all embrace.

Despite his doubts about psychoanalysis and dream interpretation, Will saw this dream as highly significant, representing his own acceptance of Anne in a way he hadn't before and a reconciliation of the part of him that was involved with her with the part of him that was devoted to his parents' ideals. I added only that I thought it might be interesting to think of the train, with the slow violence of car after passing car, as him as well, in his relentless violence toward Annie and the part of himself that was connected with her and had come alive in their relationship. He resonated strongly with this notion.

For me, this example illustrates the power of using Fairbairn's model in its most radical form, rather than collapsing it to create hybrids. Will was involved with pleasure seeking and guilty impulses, to be sure. But the most useful framework for understanding his struggles seemed to be one that views conflictual pleasure seeking and guilt in the context of conflictual allegiances to significant others, present and past, internal and external, actual and fantastic. Interestingly, such a framework makes it possible to regard guilt with greater existential vividness and centrality, without the customary psychoanalytic reduction to infantile themes. Guilt can be understood as reflective of the very real and inevitable betrayals generated by conflictual loyalties to multiple significant others and multiple versions of oneself.

Will's dream also raises for me the question of the fate of good objects, of good experiences with objects, and, ultimately, of the analytic object. Because Fairbairn regarded internal objects as compensatory substitutes for crucial missing connections with actual others, relative progress and health is depicted as a kind of exorcism. This idea seems right to me, but not sufficient. I believe that good and loving experiences also leave internal residues, sometimes not wholly integratable with each other because they are lived in different, multiple versions of self with others. I think we will make fullest use of Fairbairn's contribution when we find a way to describe the ways in which residues from the past can coexist, interpenetrate, and enrich experience in the present, much as Fairbairn's thinking from a long time ago has enriched our own experience.

References

Beebe, B., Lachmann, F. & Jaffe, J. (1997), Mother–infant interaction structures and presymbolic self and object representations. *Psychoanal. Dial.,* 7:133–182.

Bowlby, J. (1969), *Attachment and Loss, Vol. 1.* New York: Basic Books.

Fairbairn, W. R. D. (1941), A revised psychopathology of the psychoses and psychoneuroses. In: *Psychoanalytic Studies of the Personality.* London: Routledge & Kegan Paul, 1952.

—— (1954), Observations on the nature of hysterical states. In: *From Instinct to Self, Vol. 1,* ed. D. E. Scharff & E. F. Birtles. Northvale, NJ: Aronson, 1994, pp. 13–40.

Freud, (1921), Group psychology and the analysis of the ego. *Standard Edition,* 18:65–43. London: Hogarth Press, 1955.

Greenberg, J. (1991), *Oedipus and Beyond.* Cambridge, MA: Harvard University Press.

Habermas, J. (1968), *Knowledge and Human Interests.* New York: Beacon.

Lear, J. (1990), *Love and Its Place in Nature.* New York: Farrar, Straus & Giroux.

Loewald, H. (1971), On motivation and instinct theory. In: *Papers on Psychoanalysis.* New Haven, CT: Yale University Press, 1980, pp. 102–137.

———— (1976), Primary process, secondary process and language. In: *Papers on Psychoanalysis*. New Haven, CT: Yale University Press, 1980.

Muller, J. (1996), *Beyond the Psychoanalytic Dyad*. New York: Routledge.

Ogden, T. (1989), *The Primitive Edge of Experience*. Northvale, NJ: Aronson.

Phillips, A. (1995), *Terrors and Experts*. London: Faber & Faber.

Pine, F. (1990), *Drive, Ego, Object, Self*. New York: Basic Books.

Pinker, S. (1994), *The Language Instinct*. New York: Morrow.

Stern, D. (1985), *The Interpersonal World of the Infant*. New York: Basic Books.

Winnicott, D. & Khan, M. (1953), A review of Fairbairn's *Psychoanalytic Studies of the Personality*. *Internat. J. Psycho-Anal.*, 34:329–333.

8

The Good, the Bad, and the Ambivalent
Fairbairn's Difficulty Locating the Good Object in the Endopsychic Structure

Neil J. Skolnick

Taken by Melanie Klein's (1935, 1946) elaborate descriptions of the dramas that unfold in, and determine the internal psychic reality of, the infant, Fairbairn also focused his attention on explicating the processes by which a child incorporates and then situates self and object relationships in the internal world. He (Fairbairn, 1940, 1944) frequently addressed his theoretical revisions to both Freud and Klein, and gradually his respectful disagreements with their ideas could be found to do nothing less than offer drastic alterations of both of their theories. His radical departures are still being discovered and rediscovered today. Those who study Fairbairn's remarkably elegant theoretical opus are often amazed by the extent to which he presaged many of the paradigmatic shifts that characterize much of relational theorizing today. Where Freud (1923) spoke of an ego that was empowered by the forces of the id, Fairbairn (1946) posited dynamic structures that are in nature similar to the contemporary concept of self as put forth by self psychology theorists (Kohut, 1971; Robbins, 1992) as well as current trends in intersubjective theory (Stolorow and Atwood, 1992) that caution

    I would like to thank Stephen Mitchell for his helpful comments in preparing this chapter.

against static reifications of psychic structures. In fact, Fairbairn did away with the id as Freud had conceived it and replaced it with an irreducible need for people to create and maintain relationships with others. Whereas Klein (1935, 1946) focused her attention on the darker forces of the death instinct and accorded their aggressive essence primary importance in determining psychic structure, motivations, and developmental course, Fairbairn, by contrast, focused his theoretical attention on the primary importance of the child's early environmental objects. Whereas Klein spoke of the influence of our instinctual phantasmagorical inheritance on shaping the fate of the external world as it lodged within the psyche, Fairbairn, by contrast, turned his attention to the real aspects of the real environment and their fate in the internal endopsychic structure, particularly as it ran up against the need of the child for human loving connections. Whereas Klein described the earliest knowledge of the world as rooted in projection, Fairbairn started the developmental ball rolling with introjection. These are just a few of the fundamental shifts he proposed and wrote about. And like his psychoanalytic predecessors, he rooted his ideas in the time-honored method of clinical observation.

I have for years, in my own clinical work, been struck by the somewhat embarrassing quandary that I find both Klein's and Fairbairn's ideas equally useful in informing my thoughts about, and actions toward, patients. I ignore, as I suppose we all do and must do (or at least I imagine we all do and must do) the gross and at times grotesque inconsistencies and incompatibilities between these two theoretical systems. I can, without the appropriate chagrin, lapse into holding mutually exclusive theoretical explanations about my patients and ignore obvious contradictions as if they were inconvenient nuisances. I resolve such inconsistencies in a number of ways. My presumption is that the readers of this volume are familiar with some of them. I can unabashedly ignore them. That's the easiest route. I can also, although with some unease, claim "different theoretical strokes for different folks," squashing some patients into some models and other patients into others. Or—and this is person-ally the least satisfying alternative—I just shrug my shoulders and relegate theoretical inconsistencies to the inherent ambigu-ity and uncertainty embedded in the nature of our work. So where my analytical mind, as informed by Klein, might hear the rumblings of predetermined, phylogenetically programmed narratives as primary determinants of current psychic function-ing, my Fairbairnian ear wonders about the early experiences of the person and the abilities of the early others to love and con-vince of their love. In the same breath that I talk about the effects of sadistic parental attacks, I might refer to the same patient's masochistic fantasies as determining the internalized representation of a sadistic parent (or sadistic analyst). This approach to resolving theoretical inconsistencies, by the way, has received a new sanctioning by appeal from postmodern deconstructionistic thinkers who often make a call for embrac-ing and celebrating the paradoxical. Thus we can synthesize dialectical poles or deconstruct them, both at times useful and both at times clouding inconsistencies in our thinking. Unfortunately, and as we all know too well, sadly, we cannot always have it both ways.

With this in mind, I present here for your consideration a way in which we might begin to think about a possible integra-tion of one aspect of Fairbairn's and Klein's differing concep-tions of the internal world. Specifically, I address the somewhat glaring discrepancy between the two in their place for good objects in this world. Very briefly stated, Klein puts them there and Fairbairn does not.

The divergent conceptualizations of the Fairbairnian and Kleinian object have been explicated by a number of theorists, notably Grotstein and Rinsley (1994) and Mitchell (1981) among others. To highlight these differences, Mitchell has described a number of incompatibilities between Klein's and Fairbairn's concepts of the origin, nature, and functions of internal objects. The difference that I focus a spotlight on in this paper is Fairbairn's idea that the internal unconscious world of objects is

devoid of good objects. I propose that a clarification and alteration in Fairbairn's theory of development can allow for the
place of good objects in the unconscious, while maintaining the
basic integrity of his fundamental concepts.

For Fairbairn (1944), the endopsychic unconscious is structured by the child's internalization of interactions with aspects
of his or her parents that fail to meet his or her psychological
needs, that is, with bad or unsatisfying objects. The child, when
faced with the intolerable feelings that arise in the face of not
being loved or not having his or her love recognized, resorts to a
disintegration of ego or self. Consequently, he or she establishes
a closed internal world that contains organizations of split-off
pieces of self, dynamically structured by and in interaction with
split-off pieces of the other. Whether the split-off pieces of the
other are exciting or taunting, rejecting or failing, they all have
their roots in parental provisions that were lacking; that is, they
all have their roots in bad objects.

Others, most notably Sutherland (1963), Kernberg (1980), and
Grotstein and Rinsley (1994), have modified Fairbairn's conceptualization of the internal self and object tie to make way for a
larger role for the affects as providing self- and object links.
They nonetheless adhere to his basic plan of the endopsychic
structure as separate self- and object systems fashioned out of
bad interactions with early others. Sutherland maintained
Fairbairn's focus on the failing parent as influencing these structures, Kernberg focuses on constitutional factors, while Grotstein
insists that constitutional and environmental factors can be
"simultaneously encompassed" (p. 133) despite their seeming
incompatibility" (as an aside, Grotstein has mounted the most
ambitious attempt to integrate Fairbairns and Klein's perspectives and his "dual-track" approach presents us with a good
example of our being asked to embrace the paradoxical).

Noting that for Fairbairn the internal world of objects is a
gratuitous concept in the economy of healthy as opposed to
pathological functioning, Mitchell (1981) has criticized Fairbairn's
inability to account for the internalization of good objects. He

states, "Perhaps the greatest weakness of Fairbairn's system is his failure to account for the residues of good object relations and the structuralization of the self on the basis of healthy identifications" (p. 392).

This paper, in large part, picks up where this criticism leaves off, and I will argue for a correction in Fairbairn's theory. Fairbairn's notion of a primarily evil endopsychic underworld lacking much influence by good objects is unsatisfactory. From several levels of discourse, both theoretical and clinical, I believe there is an argument to be made for including a process by which good objects are internalized, identified with, and structured into the endopsychic self, where they remain out of conscious awareness but where they exert an active influence on interactions with the external world much the same way bad internalized objects do.

In order to provide a context for the critiquing of Fairbairn's ideas about the internalization of good objects, let me begin with a very brief review of his description of the development of the endopsychic structure.

For Fairbairn (1944), the establishment of the endopsychic structure, while universal and inevitable, represents a fall from grace. Buffeted by the inability, both expectable and those ranging to the traumatic, of the early others in one's life to respond to what is needed, especially in the realms of dependency and love, the child's ego shatters from its pristine integral unity and, by way of the processes of splitting, introjection, and repression, ensconces the failing characteristics of one's early objects in the repressed internal object relationships of the endopsychic structure. Indeed, for Fairbairn our unconscious exists as a kind of intrapsychic hell, populated only by split-off pieces of bad objects (either exciting or rejecting) along with the fragments of ego structure they abscond with and relegate to the unconscious, in particular, the libidinal and antilibidinal egos.

Identifications with good objects are, conversely, accorded express tickets to heaven, the celestial realm Fairbairn (1944) dubbed the Central Ego. As structured into the central ego, good objects remain conscious and readily available for open, flexible interaction with worldly matters and people. Thus, according to Fairbairn (1944), good objects are nowhere to be found in the internal, unconscious world. Good objects, that is, those pieces of our parents that meet Winnicott's (1965) criteria for "good enough" mothering (p. 145) remain integrally connected to our central ego. These central ego/good-object self-units influence and potentiate, if not determine, our healthy functioning. The integrity, strength, and robustness of our ego in its numerous pursuits is, for Fairbairn (1944), derived from its early experience and identification with adequate parents.

How does this happen? Fairbairn (1946) maintained that the child is born with a whole integral ego oriented toward whole others and ready to connect, wired to relate, if we may. (Indeed, current mother–infant research [Stern, 1985; Beebe and Lachmann, 1992] provides support for this idea of an infant with an ego that has great ability to affect as well as be affected by its environment from birth.)

Should the parents fail to love the child for whom he or she is and fail to accept the child's spontaneous offers of love, the experience for the child is unbearable at the least and traumatic at the extreme. In reaction to the failures of psychological provisions, the infant defensively splits the object into good and bad parts and internalizes the bad, which it further splits into its taunting and rejecting aspects. These split-off 'bad' aspects of the parents are banished to the unconscious, along with pieces of the child's ego, those pieces of the self that develop in the context of and interactions with the unsatisfying aspects of the parents. These split-off bundles of part-self and part-other in dynamic relation to each other exist in the unconscious, as Rubens (1984) argues, as "split off subsystems of the self" (p. 434), which continue to exhibit powerful effects on conscious thought, affect, and behavior. The person caught up in repetitious, self-defeating, and painful patterns is somehow enacting powerful unconscious self-and-other relationships that were structured through repeated interactions with a failing parent.

Ogden (1983) expands this idea and notes that a person is identified with both the subject and the object in these internal dramas, and can therefore enact either role. He states:

> Fairbairn's insight that it is object relationships and not objects that are internalized opened the way to thinking of both self- and object components of the internal relationship as active agencies, "dynamic structures" [p. 89].
>
> In this light, I would suggest that the internalization of an object relationship . . . would result in the formation of two new sub organizations of the ego, one identified with the self in the external object relationship and the other thoroughly identified with the object [p. 99].

And what is the intrapsychic fate of the parent who is responsive to the child? What becomes of the parental attributes that rise to the occasion and provide for love and recognition? How does the "good-enough" (Winnicott, 1965) parent become internalized and ensconced in the child's self- and object subsystems? Fairbairn had a lot of difficulty consistently accounting for the internalization of the good object, and his theory is riddled with inconsistencies and confusion regarding this subject. He at different times accounted for the internalization of the good object in the following different ways:

.1. Fairbairn (1944) maintained that there is no primary internalization of a good or satisfying object. For him, internalization was a matter of defensive coercion. The bad part-object, the part of the parent that does not satisfy the infant's needs, is internalized in order to shift the locus of control to the infant. There is no need then to defend against the satisfying experiences of relating to a good object who meets the infant's needs.

2. Fairbairn (1943) stated that the good object is internalized by way of the moral defense. This was in essence a temporal model of internalization. That is, in response to internalizing the bad object, the child subsequently internalizes the good object to compensate for the possible threat to self-organization that comes with being identified only with unsatisfactory object

experiences. As he is oft quoted, "It is better to be a sinner in a world ruled by God than to live in a world ruled by the devil" (p. 67).

3. Fairbairn (1944), in a 1951 addendum, posited that the earliest internalization is that of a preambivalent object, one that "presented itself as unsatisfying in some measure as well as in some measure satisfying" (p. 135). It is only later, when the parent fails and the infant confronts an ambivalent internal object, that the infant splits off the overexciting and overfrustrating aspects of this object and represses them (as the exciting and rejecting objects) along with the pieces of the central ego they are in interaction with, namely, the libidinal ego and the antilibidinal ego, respectively.

While Fairbairn left it for future theorists to resolve the inconsistencies in the timing and nature of the internalization of good objects—and, indeed, the issues appear to get muddier the closer one looks—my reading of where he landed was that, while good objects may be internalized (although the timing of this is never quite clear), they are never repressed. They are never forced by the central ego to dwell in the unconscious endopsychic structures, maintaining self- and object ties that defy conscious awareness. Instead, what remains of the good object, after being shorn of its unsatisfying badness, remains attached to and in interaction with the central ego. It takes the form of an ego ideal informing the core of the superego.

Rubens (1984) has advanced Fairbairn's thought by making a qualitative, rather than a topographical, distinction between the internalization of good and bad objects. In essence, he maintains that objects are internalized in two ways, structuring and nonstructuring. Bad objects are subject to structuring internalization. As they are repressed, they form fairly rigid self- and object subsystems that are structured into the unconscious endopsychic structure. Here they reside, in fairly closed-off systems that remain vital as they manifest in maladaptive patterns and psychopathology. By contrast, good objects are never subjected to structure-generating repression. There is no self-splitting and no formation of endopsychic structure with a good object. Instead, nonstructuring internalizations of good experiences with an object result in either memory or the conscious organization of experience. As Rubens states, "It is clear from this position that nonstructuring internalization does not result in the establishment of any 'entity' within the self, but rather results in an alteration of the integration of the self, or in the production of a thought, memory or fantasy within the self" (p. 437).

While his conceptualization of nonstructuring internalization of good objects represents a thought-provoking enhancement of Fairbairn's concept of central ego, it still fails to account for repressed good objects.

Clinical Evidence for Unconscious Good Objects

To turn to the clinical arena, a fairly common outcome of psychoanalytic treatment is that as a person demonstrates improvement, one overt reflection of the improvement is the return to consciousness of a heretofore unconscious, yet decidedly good, object relationship. Take, for example, a father who is inexorably recounted during the course of treatment as brutal but now is reorganized in the patient's experience as a caring, though somewhat inept man struggling under the constraints of his own conflicts, and a memory appears of his caring concern for a child's unhappy disappointment on a first date. The bitter, depressed, and removed mother is recalled as relaxed, singing, and happy on a picnic outing. Consider the following dream fragment:

> A patient of mine, Derek, reported this dream within a week of his father's death. He was standing in an exquisitely appointed lobby. As he was admiring the rich architectural compositions his father entered and embraced him lovingly. Derek experienced an unexpected welling of powerful and reciprocal loving feelings toward his father.

This brief dream fragment came as a total and utter surprise to Derek, who was not aware of ever having experienced loving emotions toward his oft-described tyrannical father. In his 37 years, he was not aware of a single time when he regarded his father with anything but intense fear and contempt. Indeed, he seemed particularly unmoved by his father's recent death and was conscious only of a pervasive relief to be "rid of the bastard" at last. Prior to this dream his father existed for him almost exclusively as a demeaning and destructive tyrant, with no shades of ambivalence around the edges, a unidimensional tormentor. Of particular note was Derek's attitude toward the dream: he expressed true puzzlement and dismissed it as an aberration unworthy of any attempts at associations.

Derek came into analysis with the dual complaint that he lacked an ability to experience love toward others and that he was not productive at his chosen profession, songwriting. That he possessed significant talent and creativity was substantiated some eight years prior to our meeting, when he wrote a song that achieved critical acclaim. Subsequently, he was unable to write and, feeling exceedingly blocked and frustrated in his work, he resorted to drugs and brief sexual encounters with women to fill a life largely occupied by nothing. He had a relationship with a woman that spanned the time of his professional success, but he became disenchanted and emotionally dead as his professional success deteriorated. He regarded this woman initially as an angel who evoked his creativity in muselike fashion. He was, however, now unable to muster positive feelings toward any woman and entered treatment despairing of the possibility of loving again.

Following the dream, Derek began to have an increasing number of fond recollections of his father. Earlier scenes of his father in a dictatorial rage competed with momentary memories of a kind, caring man who had great difficulty expressing his warmer feelings. Alongside a father who only criticized and discouraged was one who was encouraging and proud. His father's business exploits now gave him the admirable shadings of a self-made man. At first Derek was puzzled. Preferring to hold on to an image of his father as a petty tyrant, he resisted these memories. He could not entertain an image of his father that included both fond and hated memories, although he openly recognized that they both existed and that his struggle to accept the kinder father was perplexing to him.

In the transference, almost the reverse situation was occurring. His previous and tenaciously held positive attitude toward me began to show cracks as I became increasingly worthy of his contempt. Actually, to say that this represented the reverse situation is not entirely correct. The emergence of positive feelings toward his father and less than positive feelings toward me could be considered two manifestations of the same process, that of a foray into what Kleinians might consider the depressive position with its hallmark event, the advent of ambivalence. He was indeed gradually able to embrace a more ambivalent picture of his father, and he was likewise able to recognize his own identifications with both the loving and the tyrannical aspects of him. These changes paralleled a similar shift in his ability to embrace loving as well as not so loving feelings toward me and others. He began dating a woman for whom he reported having loving feelings, and, while bemoaning her shortcomings as a muse, he decided to marry her. (I feel compelled to add the caveat that this brief clinical vignette, like most, is a highly oversimplified and linear description of a lengthy, forward-and-back process that bumped along this way and that way for a long time.)

Derek's evolution in treatment was not unlike that of many of our patients, who, as they progress in psychoanalysis and become more able to tolerate ambivalence, begin to access not only bad memories of early others but also surprisingly loving ones as well. Attempts to understand these memories within the framework of Fairbairn's split self and object systems lead to unsatisfactory dead ends.

For example, the psychic situation for Derek might, from a Fairbairnian perspective, consist of a structured unconscious in which he would have split off and repressed the tyrannical aspects of his father (the rejecting object) in interaction with a split-off part of his ego, identified with the rejecting object (the antilibidinal ego). This system would continue to manifest in his creative and loving blocks, his attacks on his creativity and his inability to love. Similarly, the enticing, taunting aspects of his father (the piece of him that promised recognition but failed to provide it) would remain ensconced in the endopsychic structure in interaction with an unrealistically hopeful organization of self. This organization might be reflected by the part of Derek that searched endlessly for a muse, one who would enable him to fulfill his grandiose strivings for stardom. The kinder, more accepting, and encouraging aspects of his father that appeared in the dream and during the course of treatment might be viewed as a good object ensconced in and suffusing Derek's central ego, where it might exist in memory, but not subject to repression. If we consider the force with which Derek resisted these memories of a kind father, however, we might then posit they had indeed been repressed and were no longer easily understood as unstructured connections to a central ego.

Alternatively, through another Fairbairnian prism we might be tempted to view these favorable memories as manifestations of only bad self and object organizations in the endopsychic unconscious. These kinder memories would represent, then, exciting objects in interaction with the split-off libidinal ego, that is, his hopes for his father's recognition that were repeatedly dashed. This explanation, however, is equally unsatisfying because, for Fairbairn, exciting objects typically exist in taunting, aggrandized, or exaggerated forms; and Derek's descriptions of his father as a kinder soul were modulated and realistic.

Therefore, neither of these attempts to understand the retrieval of Derek's good memories in accordance with Fairbairn's pronouncement that there are no good objects in the endopsychic structure appears satisfactory to me. There is too much resistance to their becoming conscious for us to locate them unequivocally in the memories of the central ego. And they lack the aggrandized or idealized nature of an exciting object in the unconscious. Derek's surprise at the fond memories and his struggle to keep them conscious bespeak some psychic force, or resistance, that actively maintains them out of awareness. For Fairbairn (1943) such a force would not be an acceptable explanation because for him the psychic force maintaining repression was the unbearable nature of the bad object which interfered with the child's desire for connection. Instead, Derek's dream and his uncovered memories appear to embody the sustained and satisfactory aspects of a good object relationship that were lost to the forces of repression.

To turn now to another clinical observation, Fairbairn's object relational approach, not unlike other relational approaches that relegate the drives to secondary importance, runs into difficulty when trying to account for the intensity of our motives, their qualitative forays into the extreme. Once we denude our behavior of the primary and powerful underpinnings of sexual or aggressive tension-seeking quiescence, where are the constructs by which we can understand the motivational thrust and intensity of our everyday passions? By everyday, I mean the more or less healthy intensity that can imbue any pursuit, romantic or otherwise. Such scenarios include the at times inexplicable yet powerful investment of our selves in a person or endeavor—be it the passionate pursuit of a desired romance, the passions that fuel our professional goals, the passionate enjoyment of a cherished hobby, or the fleeting passions of a night on the town. The seething underworld of steamy, tumultuous, instinctual forces has great appeal, often greater appeal than some of our relational constructs have.

It is important to note that, when considering passionate experience and phenomena, I am not referring to the self-defeating, masochistic, and ultimately painful connections to the world that are overt manifestations of a more or less closed internal world of bad object relationships. The split-off and at times inexorable pursuit of bad objects motivated by the structures of the endopsychic unconscious might appear passionate (like Derek's passionate pursuit of a muse or his quest for fame), but it is probably more correctly called compulsive. Indeed, Fairbairn (1943) did make the point that the greater the amount of ego relegated to the closed world of the unconscious, the more compulsive a person's behavior will appear to be in the pursuit of bad objects.

Although Fairbairn (1944) never addressed the issue of passion directly, he most likely would have located the sources of healthy passion in the success of the central ego in achieving sought-after object ties. As the mother greets the child's needs with pleasure and a measure of her own passion, so would the child identify with and incorporate into its self a potential for passionate investments. This process would fall under what Rubens (1984) described as the "unstructured internalizations" of the healthy central ego as it internalizes the satisfying provisions of the good object. It seems to me, however, that Fairbairn's concept of the strivings of a central ego, shorn of its badness, as providing the wellspring of our passions seems to fall flat. It lacks the seemingly stormy and inexorable strength of our passions, the at times inexplicable, but realistic enough pursuit of dreams and follies embedded in our lives, literature, art, and culture.

One additional clinical experience suggests the presence of good, though repressed, self- and object organizations. The workings of the central ego shorn of its badness seem insufficient to account for the tenacity of our patients, particularly our most disturbed, who come to analysis regularly, repeatedly, and harboring hope, despite the affect storms, disintegration, and chaos that can pervade the therapeutic relationship. Why do they keep coming, even when their experience of us is primarily as taunting devils or outright persecutors? Of course, this issue overlaps that of hope, but I think it also contains a degree of what we might consider to be realistically optimistic, hopeful self-organizations fashioned in large measure by contact with satisfying aspects of a parent but remaining out of conscious awareness. As in the learning of a new skill, say, playing an instrument, the difficulties, disappointments, and narcissistic injuries inherent in the learning process, and the perseverance we can display in spite of them, have parallels in the persistence with which our patients consistently return to our offices, over and over despite vitriolic attacks, empathic disappointments, and experiences of disintegration. Are these just the workings of the central ego's connection to fulfilling objects? I don't think so. Persistence is informed by a certain inexplicable quality in which an understanding of the driving force and intensity is not readily apparent. It seems to me that this experience cannot be rooted in a more or less conscious or preconscious functioning of a central ego. I maintain that it, too, is a manifestation of a part of oneself that developed in interaction with hopeful and encouraging pieces of one's parents but operates from a place out of awareness.

These three clinical phenomena—the appearance of heretofore good object relationships during the course of treatment, the often inexplicable imbuing of our behaviors with passionate fuel, and the persistence with which our patients continue in treatment—suggest the existence, in the unconscious, of a world of repressed good objects that remain out of awareness, but very much vital, as they effect our conscious motivation, affects and behavior much as do the torturous, unconscious bad objects.

The Unconscious Good Object

Fairbairn's difficulty in locating these good object relationships in the unconscious can be traced to two separate but overlapping confusions in his theory. The first involves the timing of the structuring of the endopsychic unconscious and; the second, his failure to distinguish adequately between split object experience and ambivalent object experience. To elaborate these points, let us briefly digress to review a few more of his key concepts in order to provide a context for these criticisms.

Fairbairn (1941) elevated the importance of the quality of the object relationship to center stage. In one fell swoop he redefined the oral, anal, and phallic stages of development by focusing on the changing nature of a child's dependent relationship on the object and not the libidinal excitation of changing bodily zones. Thus, a child navigates a developmental course from absolute dependence on another to a mature dependence on others, not by way of the successful resolutions of oral, anal, and phallic crises. Fairbairn's earliest stage in development, corresponding to Freud's (1918) and Abraham's (1924) oral stage and centering on the child's unconditional dependence on the object, he relabeled the period of infantile dependence. He divided this stage into early and late periods, each with its accompanying conflict, which is exacerbated by a depriving environment. The early period encompasses relations with an essentially preambivalent whole object. The child relates to the object primarily through primary identification and internalization, processes that, for Fairbairn, are essentially indistinguishable at this stage. There is no ambivalence toward the object; the choice for the child is to accept or reject the object. The accommodations, ranging from the pathological to the more or less normal, that are necessitated when the object fails to meet the child's needs are coterminous with the establishment of the endopsychic structure.

The late oral period, by contrast, involves an ambivalent relationship with the object. The conflict for the child at this latter point is how to love an object without destroying it with hate. These early and late periods correspond roughly to Klein's (1975) paranoid/schizoid and depressive positions respectively.

One of the hallmarks of Fairbairn's (1944) theory is his emphasis on the earliest period of development, the period of infantile dependence, as the time when endopsychic structure is laid into the cornerstone of character. Further development of ego and object relationships is basically overlaid onto, or fused with, these earliest structurings (1944). A careful reading, however, reveals that he was unclear and inconsistent about the actual timing of events. At times he (Fairbairn, 1944, 1946) treated the early and later stages as one stage contributing to the establishment of the endopsychic structure; at other times he (Fairbairn, 1941) made a clear distinction between the early and later stage. He considered the earlier, schizoid period to be the crucial time for establishing the endopsychic world and relegated the later period, with its depressive issues to one of lesser importance.

He was similarly inconsistent about the appearance of ambivalence during this early development. According to Fairbairn (1941), there is no ambivalence in the early schizoid period. Later, however, Fairbairn (1944) claims that the structuring of the endopsychic structure is, indeed, the structuring of the child's original ambivalent attitude toward the mother: "For what the obstinate attachment of the libidinal ego to the exciting object and the equally obstinate aggression of the internal saboteur towards the same object really represent is the obstinacy of the original *ambivalent* attitude" (p. 117, italics added).

One wonders how ambivalence can be structured if it has not yet appeared on the scene.

Seemingly a minor, hairsplitting point, this inconsistency becomes of utmost importance when one considers the phenomenology of ambivalence. As I have already noted, Fairbairn failed to make an important distinction between the experience of ambivalence and the experience of splitting. Ogden (1986) makes the well-taken point that ambivalence is not

> a matter of consciously and unconsciously loving and hating the same object at a given moment. . . . The critical achievement in the attainment of ambivalence is the fact that the person one hates is the *same person* whom one has loved and unconsciously still loves and hopes to openly love again [pp. 88–89].

Thus, ambivalence requires the temporal maintenance of affects or attitudes toward the same person, despite moment-to-moment fluctuations and swings. And, more important, ambivalence fuels a hope that one will return to a loving state again.

Splitting, on the other hand, lacks a historical continuity; it involves affects and attitudes that are constantly and magically being created, reversed, and recreated. The person one loves one moment is not the same person one hates the next, and the "I" who does the hating is not the same "I" who does the loving. In one state, there is no knowledge of the other state; hope has no meaning in splitting. I maintain that the original attitude toward the primary object structured into Fairbairn's unconscious endopsychic structure is not one of ambivalence, but one rooted in splitting. When the original object fails to meet the psychological needs of the child, the intolerable feelings that arise lead to a splitting of the object and self and these split self- and object subsystems remain very separate. Like hope, ambivalence has no experiential meaning in splitting.

Fairbairn's early and later stages of primary dependence need to be more clearly distinguished, as they are in Klein's (1935, 1946) paranoid/schizoid and depressive positions. A clear delineation between the early and late oral periods sets the stage for an understanding of how the repression of the good object might occur in Fairbairn's model without excessive strain on its internal consistency.

The stages can be more clearly delineated by considering their core conflicts and defensive operations. The task for the child during the early oral period is to accept or reject the object, and the primary mechanism used by the ego to negotiate failures of the object is splitting. By contrast, the primary task of the later oral period is to maintain a whole object when it fails and is attacked by the child's aggression, which is also the problem of establishing ambivalence. And it is in dealing with the problem of ambivalence, with its at times unbearable conflicts, that the action of repressing good objects, along with their interactions with loving pieces of self, is ascendant.

The development of the endopsychic structure as Fairbairn described it, particularly with its establishment of the three ego/object systems (Central Ego/Ideal Object, Libidinal Ego/ Exciting Object, and Antilibidinal Ego/Rejecting Object) continues to have great merit in this new system. The establishment of the endopsychic subsystems, then, predates the establishment of ambivalence, and likewise it results in structures devoid of the experience of ambivalence. Again, the unbearable situation for the dependent infant is contact with an object that fails to meet its psychological needs. This situation leads to a splitting of the object, and these splitting operations lead to a relatively complete dissociation of separate self- and object subsystems in which loving and hating self and object interactions are kept experientially very separate. (For an excellent description of the differences between splitting and repression, see Davies and Frawley, 1994.) My patient, Derek's, unyielding idealization of women as potential creative muses can be considered a behavioral illustration of the splitting process as Fairbairn described it.

In the later oral stage, largely ignored by Fairbairn, the problem of a failing object changes for the child. With the establishment of the endopsychic structure, and its compensatory internal split-off self- and object subsystems, the child now has a relatively whole, good object, shorn of its badness, firmly connected to and interacting with its conscious central ego. But good objects are not always good. Being "good-enough," they inevitably and necessarily must fail, as has been amply noted by object relations and self psychology theorists (Winnicott, 1965; Kohut, 1971). It is when faced with the failures of these primarily whole and primarily good objects—the good objects that have already become structured into the central ego—that the child must struggle with the problem of ambivalence, that is, maintaining this object as good, despite powerful angry feelings being directed toward it. What becomes unbearable for the child at this point is not that the child's very psychological existence is threatened, as it is with earlier experience with a failing object, but, rather, that the experience of *conflict* toward its cherished object is now unbearable. The reconciliation of powerful anger and the need to maintain a much needed connection presents the child with an enormous problem.

The problem I am describing is not unlike the one described

by Klein (1935) regarding the establishment of ambivalence during the depressive crisis. There are several important differences, though. In keeping with his (1943) disavowal of the death instinct, the problem of ambivalence for Fairbairn resides in the child's angry responses to a failing object, not to the taming of and tolerance for his or her own endogenous aggression, as put forth by Klein. Aggression for Fairbairn (1944) is always reactive. The imperative for the child is to maintain a relationship with a real object that does not meet its needs, that frustrates and evokes anger. The failing object for the Kleinian child is largely determined through the projection of aggression, which arises a priori from the death instinct.

Another important difference is that, for Fairbairn, the task is for the child to *maintain* whole-object functioning despite its being buffeted by ambivalence; whereas, for Klein, the task is to integrate and *achieve* whole-object functioning. Fairbairn throughout maintained that the human infant is born with a self that is oriented toward whole-object functioning from birth. It is inevitable environmental failures that create the splitting and structuring of the endogenous world. For Klein, the child moves from part-object functioning to whole-object functioning as it interacts with loving others.

As I noted, the feelings of both love and hate toward the same person present the child with an enormous problem. It is just this struggle to maintain a good connection with a whole but failing object that ushers in the experience of ambivalence, with its concomitant feelings of unbearable conflict. It is this conflict, then, that propels the child at Fairbairn's later oral stage to split off and repress good part objects. This conflict-driven maneuver serves a function not unlike Klein's manic defenses; the splitting and repression of good object ties eases the child's conflict through a denial of the value possessed by the good object. The maintenance of a connection with a whole object who fails, a whole object who evokes ambivalence, is a Herculean and probably lifelong task. Not unlike Klein's manic defenses, the repression of goodness can aid in its achievement.

One ramification of this alteration to Fairbairn's theory is that it places conflict back on center stage as a primary mover and shaker. Often, in discussions of early splitting, the motivating force of conflict is ignored or relegated to later developmental significance. As Mitchell (1988) has noted, relational theories that employ the metaphor of the infant tend to ignore the significance of conflict in psychic functioning. Fairbairn's internal world, devoid of good objects as he had it, can take on the proportions of a cataclysmic battle between ultimate good and evil, a psychic Armageddon. Allowing for conflict tempers this tendency and substitutes for Armageddon the complex negotiations of a Mideast peace negotiation—neither side is on the side of the angels, or devils, and God is on neither, or perhaps both, sides. This internal scenario more accurately represents the state of affairs when we are attempting to understand our patients' experience of ambivalence.

The inclusion of good objects in the unconscious internal world might also enhance the ability of those working from a Fairbairnian perspective to remain closer to a patient's experience of ambivalence. All too often, the emergence of good interactions (either in the transference or in an external arena) are conceptualized by the analyst working from a Fairbairnian perspective as the manifestation of an exciting object tie that needs to be made conscious *as a bad object relationship*, one that ultimately needs to be disavowed. In this fashion, the appearance of my patient, Derek's, loving father in his dream (or perhaps the transference implications of the image) might have been dismissed as but another example of a split-off expression of his idealized relationship with a bad, taunting father. Viewing the image as a loving aspect of his father that has been repressed, the patient (and analyst) can begin to embrace this aspect of the father and ultimately integrate it into an expanded perception of his father as a whole though ambivalently felt figure. The patient will possess an increased ability to view and accept himself and others in more integrated, expanded, albeit ambivalent, ways.

My guess is that many of us who work from an object relational perspective are already helping patients to embrace passionate and life-affirming aspects of themselves and others that
have been lost to repression. The problem for me has been that,
unless one subscribed to a Kleinian conception of the depressive
position, with its emphasis on the taming of aggressive drives in
order to achieve object integration, there was no place within
Fairbairnian theory that allowed us to talk about uncovering
unconscious good-object relationships, relationships with roots
in actual interactions with real others. Good objects for Fairbairn
were always connected only with the conscious and whole central ego.

Which brings me back to my stated quandary at the outset of
this chapter, that I may find myself working from diametrically
opposed theoretical positions, with, at times, what feels like
reckless abandon. The ideas I present here are but preliminary
to a potentially heuristic and fruitful theoretical direction. The
inclusion of repressed good objects in a Fairbairnian schema
may help bridge the gaps between Klein's and Fairbairn's blue-
prints for the inner world.

References

Abraham, K. (1924), The influence of oral eroticism on character formation. In: *Selected Papers of Karl Abraham*. London: Hogarth Press.

Beebe, B. & Lachmann, F. (1992), The contribution of mother–infant influ-
ence to the origins of self- and object representations. In: *Relational
Perspectives in Psychoanalysis*, ed. N. Skolnick & S. Warshaw.
Hillsdale, NJ: The Analytic Press, pp. 83–119.

Davies, J. M. & Frawley, M. G. (1994), *Treating the Adult Survivor of
Childhood Sexual Abuse*. New York: Basic Books.

Fairbairn, W. R. D. (1940), Schizoid factors in the personality. In:
Psychoanalytic Studies of the Personality. London: Routledge & Kegan
Paul, 1952.

——— (1941), A revised psychopathology of the psychoses and psychoneuroses. In: *Psychoanalytic Studies of the Personality*. London:
Routledge & Kegan Paul, 1952, pp. 28–58.

———— (1943), The repression and return of bad objects (with special reference to the "war neuroses"). In: *Psychoanalytic Studies of the Personality.* London: Routledge & Kegan Paul, 1952, pp. 59–81.

———— (1944), Endopsychic structure considered in terms of object relationships. In: *Psychoanalytic Studies of the Personality.* London: Routledge & Kegan Paul, 1952, pp. 82–136.

———— (1946), Object relations and dynamic structure. In: *Psychoanalytic Studies of the Personality.* London: Routledge & Kegan Paul, 1952, pp. 137–151.

Freud, S. (1918), From the history of an infantile neurosis. *Standard Edition,* 17:17–122. London: Hogarth Press, 1955.

———— (1923), The ego and the id. *Standard Edition,* 19:12–66. London: Hogarth Press, 1961.

Grotstein, J. S. & Rinsley, D. B., eds. (1994), *Fairbairn and the Origins of Object Relations.* New York: Guilford.

Kernberg, O. (1980), *Internal World and External Reality.* Northvale, NJ: Aronson.

Klein, M. (1935), A contribution to the psychogenesis of manic-depressive states. In: *Contributions to Psychoanalysis, 1921–1945.* New York: McGraw-Hill, 1964.

———— (1946), Notes on some schizoid mechanisms. In: *Envy and Gratitude and Other Works, 1946–1963.* New York: Delacorte Press, 1975.

Kohut, H. (1971), *The Analysis of the Self.* New York: International Universities Press.

Mitchell, S. A. (1981), The origin and the nature of the "object" in the theories of Klein and Fairbairn. *Contemp. Psychoanal.,* 17:374–398.

———— (1988), *Relational Concepts in Psychoanalysis.* Cambridge, MA: Harvard University Press.

Ogden, T. H. (1983), The concept of internal object relations. *Internat. J. Psycho-Anal.,* 64:227–241.

———— (1986), *The Matrix of the Mind.* Northvale, NJ: Aronson.

Robbins, M. (1992), A Fairbairnian object relations perspective on self psychology. *Amer. J. Psychoanal.,* 53:247–261.

Rubens, R. L. (1984), The meaning of structure in Fairbairn. *Internat. Rev. Psychoanal.,* 11:429–440.

Stern, D. (1985), *The Interpersonal World of the Infant.* New York: MA: Basic Books.

Stolorow, R. & Atwood, R. (1992), *Contexts of Being.* Hillsdale, NJ: The Analytic Press.

Sutherland, J. D. (1963), Object relations theory and the conceptual model of psychoanalysis. *Brit. J. Med. Psychol.,* 36:109–124.

Winnicott, D. W. (1965), *The Maturational Processes and the Facilitating Environment.* New York: International Universities Press.

———— (1975), *Through Paediatrics to Psychoanalysis.* New York: Basic Books.

9

Fairbairn and the Self
An Extension of Fairbairn's Theory by Sutherland

Jill Savege Scharff

Who is Sutherland and how does he relate to Fairbairn's theory of endopsychic structure? John D. Sutherland was Fairbairn's major expositor and biographer. He was analyzed by Fairbairn in Edinburgh prior to going to London for formal psychoanalytic training. For most of his distinguished professional career, he remained in London, where he earned the nickname Jock and held the position of Medical Director of the Tavistock Clinic from 1947 to 1968. As a long-time consultant to the Menninger Clinic and a visitor to Austen Riggs, he brought his knowledge of institutional process and structure to the United States, where he also had a considerable influence on the training of psychiatric residents in those training programs. As editor of the *International Psycho-Analytic Library*, the *International Journal of Psycho-Analysis*, and the *British Journal of Medical Psychology*, and cofounder of the Scottish Institute of Human Relations in 1970, Sutherland (and, through him, Fairbairn) had considerable impact worldwide on psychoanalytic literature, psychiatric institution building, mental health care delivery, training, and research. At the age of 83, he published his excellent biography *Fairbairn's Journey into the Interior* (Sutherland, 1989). Earlier papers and reminiscences collected posthumously in *The Autonomous Self: The Work of John D. Sutherland* (Scharff, 1994) elaborate Fairbairn's influence on Sutherland, the development of Sutherland's psychoanalytic voice, its facilitation by his biographical research on Fairbairn and by his self analysis, and its emergence as his theory of the autonomous self (Sutherland, 1993).

The Influence of Fairbairn's Theory on Sutherland

Sutherland introduced me to Fairbairn's ideas. His one-hour lecture was enough to convince me that Fairbairn's theory of internal object relationships in dynamic relation fit the facts of my human experience. There I was, a young woman enjoying a secure professional self as a junior psychiatrist, while in my personal life resolving family issues of dependency, anger, control, and rejection prior to choosing a husband who would be good for raising a family with, and, in the meantime, observing friends with their babies. The theory helped me to make sense of my personal life relationships and the mother–baby pairs that I knew, and it held up in the clinical situation of individual therapy and in the therapeutic community where I worked at the time. Later, when I went to work for him in Edinburgh as a community psychiatrist, Sutherland showed me how Fairbairn's theory extended itself to understanding the functioning of groups in the community (Savege, 1973). He had an unusual capacity for moving between areas of complexity from the individual to the insitutional, for building bridges within psychonalytic schools, and for integrating psychoanalytic theory with evolutionary theory and social process (Kohon, 1996).

Like Fairbairn, his first analyst and mentor, Sutherland conceived of the self as a dynamic structure from the moment of birth, a holistic ego that would structure itself in response to experience. He taught Fairbairn's view that the pristine ego that emerges from the ideal environment of the womb is unscathed at birth. As the infant finds that he is no longer able to get his physiological needs met automatically or remain one with his mother, he is exposed to delay, hunger, discomfort, and dependency on his mother to notice and take care of him. The ego defends itself from anxious affect generated by the inevitable frustrations of dependent wishes by the nurturing mother by splitting off bad experience and introjecting and repressing it. It then further splits the bad experience into its rejecting and exciting aspects according to whether the tone of the ego's affect states during the unsatisfactory or downright overwhelming experience was either craving, in response to overstimulation and rejection, or rageful in the face of neglect and rejection. Then the ego splits off libidinal and antilibidinal parts of itself to partner the exciting and rejecting objects along with the corresponding affects of longing and rage respectively.

Fairbairn emphasized the defensive introjection of bad experience in psychic structure formation and did not see a role for the introjection of good experience which had not been a problem and did not call for defense (Sutherland, 1990b, cited in Scharff, 1994). Fairbairn's theory challenges many of us to account for the good object with which many people are identified (Scharff and Scharff, 1987; see also Skolnick, this volume). According to Sutherland, Fairbairn intended us to take for granted the nondefensive internalization of good experience with the mother as the ideal object retained in consciousness, where it suffuses the personality.

Sutherland emphasized Fairbairn's concept of the *dynamic* relation between the central ego and the ideal object in the central relationship system in consciousness and the repressed rejecting and exciting object relationship systems. Following Dicks (1967), Sutherland extended Fairbairn's theory to explain the way in which the interaction among the various internal object relationships determines future experience and leads the person to find new relationships that might confirm or modify early object experience (Sutherland, 1963).

Like Fairbairn, Sutherland could not accept the idea that the infant is an inchoate mess of impersonal impulses lost in its mother until the ego develops. Like Fairbairn, he was convinced that the ego is present at birth and that the fundamental human drive is the drive to be in an ongoing, meaningful relationship, not simply to have pleasure or discharge of tension. He distinguished this drive for relatedness from the drive for attachment. He found Bowlby's (1969, 1973) work on attachment critically important and agreed that the frustration of attachment needs leads to aggression and fear in humans as in animals. But in humans Sutherland saw attachment as contextual, not primary in aim, simply a necessary condition for the gestation of the self. For attachment, the infant needs the mother's self to relate to at least as much as it needs her physical proximity and care. The self in gestation follows its own built-in plan that controls the differentiation of its structures and maintains their independence, continuity over time, and eventual modification at higher levels of development.

Following Fairbairn (1944, 1963), Sutherland developed a biosocial concept of the self in which the drives were subservient (see Scharff and Birtles, 1994). He extended Fairbairn's description of psychic structure built from infantile experience in the mother–infant dyad to include continuing structure building and modification throughout the life cycle in groups and institutions, a development that he thought was needed to provide psychoanalysis with an evolutionary arm to ensure its viability in the 20th century (Harrow et al., 1994). He did this by integrating Fairbairn's theory with his own knowledge of open systems, holograms, and evolution theories, in accordance with his preference for process rather than structure (Bertalanffy, 1950; Miller, 1965). To be fully flexible and relevant to the changing environments of contemporary culture, Sutherland thought that psychoanalytic theory must be applicable to individual, marital, family, and group life, at all phases of the life cycle. Only such a fully social, fully intrapsychic approach could encompass the full range of human experience and development.

Sutherland's primary concern was with the self, how it develops and is sustained in interaction with others, and with society and its institutions. This view led him to study the conditions under which the mental health professional self could prosper, namely, to be a part of a caring professional system larger than oneself. These ideas were brought to life at the Tavistock Clinic, through its democratic management system and its human relations training courses, and in Scotland, through community mental health initiatives that he designed while at the Royal Edinburgh Hospital and later at the multidisciplinary Scottish Institute of Human Relations.

Remaining in contact with Fairbairn, Sutherland discussed with him his work at the institutional level, and the two mulled over clinical case material and manuscripts. Fairbairn liked the idea that he had a friend at the illustrious Tavistock Clinic in London, a city that to Fairbairn seemed quite remote, the more so because of his avoidance of train travel. Sutherland stayed in touch with Fairbairn's widow and was given full access to notes that he had left behind after his death. Sutherland was drawn to write a biography of Fairbairn and wrestled with the problem of how much of Fairbairn's self-revelatory material to share with the public. He concluded that Fairbairn had left the notes on purpose and, in the spirit of scientific research, wanted his object relations and symptomatology to be made known posthumously so that they could be linked to his need for a radical revision of Freudian theory.

Sutherland found Fairbairn to be a reserved, formal person lacking in ordinary masculine aggressiveness (not at all how Ellinor Fairbairn Birtles remembers her energetic dad). Sutherland (1989) wrote in his biography that Fairbairn grew up in a restrictive environment with a Calvinist father and a mother who was forbidding of sexual curiosity. Fairbairn resented his modest, stay-at-home father for not being more of an authority in their household, which was dominated by his ambitious mother's expansive ideas of society, further education, and proper behavior. Fairbairn's mother was an antilibidinal figure as far as boyish masculinity was concerned, and yet she was a libidinal force for encouraging him to fulfill his potential in the academic world. On the basis of Fairbairn's posthumous notes, Sutherland argued that resentment about his father's parochial, unambitious attitude, his passivity, and his diminished status in his mother's eyes led Fairbairn to feel that his own young adult success in his mother's eyes had killed his father off. When his father actually died, Fairbairn experienced some relief and moved on to have a family of his own, to whom he was devoted.

Building a family supported a sense of masculinity that underwent stress, however, when he lost the support of his wife, who became furious at his preoccupation with work instead of social life, and at the same time his mentors at the University of Edinburgh withdrew their backing for his psychoanalytic interests. In the face of the enraged woman and the absent men, his masculinity foundered and he developed a fear of urinating in the presence of others, a symptom that had troubled his father even at home and once led to such a full bladder that his father had to void in a train compartment with members of his family present, which was traumatic to the young Fairbairn. When the symptom arose in Fairbairn, it may have contributed to his avoiding train travel and isolating himself in Scotland, an overnight journey from London, the location of Britain's only analytic community—which accounts for his theories not being given full recognition but, on the other hand, may have protected him from political constraints that could have affected his creativity. Ellinor Fairbairn Birtles told me that, with proper medical treatment, this symptom would not have become significant, but Sutherland felt that the urinary phobia was psychologically determined. He thought that Fairbairn became like his father through this shared symptom in order to bring him back to life inside himself. Identified both with his stay-at-home father and his intellectually ambitious mother, Fairbairn reunited both parents inside himself and experienced a tremendous surge of creative energy that came to fruition with the writing of his papers in the late 1930s in which he was respectfully able to confront inadequacies in the instinct theory of Freud, the father of psychoanalysis.

In writing Fairbairn's biography, Sutherland felt that Fairbairn had taken possession of him. He was aware of a profound process going on inside himself, in parallel to Fairbairn's struggle to unite male and female elements to provide an integrated self. Sutherland had written expository texts and edited creative theoretical papers of others, but he always found himself to be hopeless at abstract thinking and yet had not brought this to the attention of an analyst. Stimulated by Fairbairn's insights, he concentrated on his self-analysis and especially his tendency to discount his father. He analyzed the negative influence on his self-functioning of his attitudes toward his parents as an internal couple. Through this self-analysis, he found that he had been keeping his mother and father separate as different individuals. He concluded that much of his work life had been a way of keeping busy to gratify his mother's ambition and push aside his father, who liked to take it easy—a collusion rather like the one that Sutherland (1994) described as a destructive force in Fairbairn's personality. Even though he was effective as Fairbairn's expositor, Sutherland did not really let himself pursue the implications of Fairbairn's ideas for the development of the self until late in his life.

By allowing himself to slacken his pace and identify more with his father's leisure-time interests—including the wearing of the kilt—Sutherland paradoxically found himself able to devote himself to the serious, creative work and original, abstract, theoretical thinking that he had avoided while fostering its expression in others. He recreated his parents in a harmonious union inside himself and freed himself from inhibitions resulting from his envious way of separating the internal couple. Thus, he became able to deal effectively with hatred and envy, responses that he did not usually evoke or, perhaps, had avoided by his self-effacing manner and personal modesty— and now, we have to add, by his work inhibition, strange as that sounds, given all his accomplishments and productivity. It was not until he did self-analysis that Sutherland was able to pay attention to what Fairbairn was saying about selves and subselves and apply it to healing himself. His late-life paper "The

Autonomous Self" (Sutherland, 1993) is evidence of his capacity to use Fairbairn's ideas to lead him into his own contemporary theory.

His later-life achievements of building the Scottish Institute in a nonanalytic climate and writing—at the age of 83— *Fairbairn's Journey to the Interior* (Sutherland, 1989) mark the emergence of Sutherland's own autonomous self after effective self-analysis. The success of his self-analysis led him to encourage all of us to practice self-analysis, with the emphasis on "the self"—analysis *by* the self *of* the self. If we could count on getting such a wonderful response, surely we would all be doing it! By self-analysis he did not mean the kind of associative stream of dream deconstruction that went on in the Fleiss correspondence. Sutherland recommended simply that you look at yourself in personal, work, and social situations and add insights from art and literature. Then, with his characteristic impish humor, he would tease, "Anyone can do self-analysis once they get the hang of it—the perpetual problem is the countertransference!"

The Challenge to Freud's Classical Drive/Structural Theory

Sutherland had tremendous respect for Fairbairn's intellectual strength, his scholarly, critical argument based on sound philosophical training, and his systematic theory building. He saw that Fairbairn's concept of the endopsychic situation as a dynamic structure challenged the theoretical assumptions of Freud's classical analysis based on drive theory (Freud, 1905, 1915, 1916–1917; Harrow et al., 1994). Like Fairbairn, Sutherland did not agree that the ego evolved to cope with the id's constant press to action and gratification. Not that they denied the instincts; he and Sutherland simply insisted that instincts are not external to the structures of the self or of subselves but are inherent in them (Padel, 1995). Although he welcomed the advances of the structural theory that made analysis of more conditions possible, Sutherland still found Fairbairn's theory superior because, even though the Freudian tripartite structural model now took into account the social reality of the family in the oedipal phase, the new Freudian theory was still built on a scheme of development starting from the drives of the impersonal biological instincts, much as the ego was thought to emerge out of the id (Freud, 1923). Although he appreciated Freud's genius in seeing so far beyond his contemporaries, Sutherland nevertheless thought that Freud's perceptions and ideas were inevitably somewhat constrained by the influence of concepts of scientific materialism, duality, and the preference for permanence, heirarchical control, and predictability current during the times in which he lived (Jantsch, 1976, 1980).

Sutherland appreciated Greenberg and Mitchell's (1983) review of diversity and incompatibility in psychoanalytic theories; and, although he agreed with Wallerstein (1988) that psychoanalysis is not one monolithic theory but a collection of theories, he retained the view that object relations theory is the overarching one. He agreed with Greenberg and Mitchell (1983) that object relations theory is now offering a credible alternative to drive/structural theory, permeating the analytic culture and influencing technique in the field in general. He thought that object relations theory would have more explanatory power if it could focus more on the self and its subselves and less on the ego and its objects. So it was in this direction that he developed Fairbairn's theory by looking into other studies from psychoanalysis and social science that illuminated the development of the self.

Related Theories Pertaining to the Self

Klein, Kohut, and the Independents

Like Fairbairn, Klein (1955) thought of the ego as a unity; she too described, in her own empathic and colorful way, the terrifying force of aggressive wishes threatening the ego; and she noted defensive splitting of the ego. Unlike Fairbairn, Klein attributed the potential or actual disintegration of the ego to the power of the death instinct. Fairbairn was influenced by Klein's thinking, especially by her 1935 paper on manic-depressive states, which propelled him to consider the issue of urinary-sadistic attacks on the parental couple—an issue that we now recognize as personally relevant to him. Sutherland thought that Klein's (1946) brilliant paper on schizoid states, which introduced the clinically helpful concept of projective identification, was influenced by Fairbairn's (1944) earlier paper on endopsychic structure based on his work with schizoid patients. Even though she emphasized the importance of object relations, she did not agree that the need to be in a relationship was primary, and she retained her adherence to the instinctual basis for psychic development, which did not impress Sutherland. Klein, in Sutherland's opinion, did not give enough theoretical attention to the real structuring of the self compared with the infant's fantasied object relationships, which she had described so thoroughly.

Sutherland thought that Kohut (1971) seemed to have borrowed ideas from Fairbairn to conceptualize the self, but his theory disappointed Sutherland in that it failed to account for aggression, was oversimplified, and problematically regarded the self at birth as largely a potential that must merge with the undifferentiated mother to become organized as a self with a selfobject.

For Sutherland (1980) the combined contributions of Guntrip (1961), Balint (1968), and Winnicott (1958, 1965), object relations theorists of the British Independent group, offered a more satisfactory approach to the concept of the self. Fairbairn had clearly put the ego, not the id, at the center of the personality (Sutherland, 1985). Guntrip (1961; Hazell, 1994) translated Fairbairn's theory of the ego and its internal objects into a more accessible theory of personal relations and focused attention on the experience of the self, rather than adhering to the mechanistic term ego, which Fairbairn had used in deference to the Freudian tradition. Balint

(1968) described the regressed patient's universal need for a sense of recognition as a whole person. Winnicott (Winnicott and Khan, 1953) disagreed with Fairbairn's radical revision of Freud, which he found disrespectful, but his own ideas were equally unable to fit the Freudian schema, a problem that he preferred to ignore. Winnicott (1960) addressed himself to the function of the false self, a structure that arises to preserve a level of fit between the infant's actual needs and the mother's unempathic or intrusive perception of them, to protect the true self from the dreaded loss of self in madness. This group of theoretical contributions supported the view that what is important to us at birth is to be recognized and loved for ourself. What the theories lacked was the capacity to account for growth over time. Here is where Sutherland had to invoke his understanding of social and evolutionary process.

Modern Evolutionary Biology and the Open Systems Framework

The Organism as an Open System

What appealed to Sutherland about Fairbairn's theory of the endopsychic situation was not only the complex structure that Fairbairn described, but also the dynamic relation between the structures. The term dynamic structure signifies the inherent power of the instinctual forces being governed within the ego and its interactive object relationships. Sutherland, informed by open systems theory not available to Fairbairn, modernized the theory. He replaced the term structures with the words processes and systems, better suited to describing the internal and external object relationships that the self engaged in over time (Padel, 1995).

Sutherland viewed the personality as being in a state of constant flux and interaction with the environment. He wanted a theory to go beyond the Freudian idea of tension discharge of energy and negative feedback leading to homeostasis. He was interested in positive feedback from the environment leading to disequilibrium and unpredictability (Prigogine, 1976). Out of chaos comes new forms. He was interested in self-regulation, self-organization, self-renewal, and self-transformation as life-determining processes that could account for behavioral changes, neural development, and ultimately genetic transmission of changes in the phenotype. Sutherland's is a fantastically proactive view of the human potential.

The Holistic Organizing Principle from Embryo to Ego to Adult Self

According to Sutherland, the holistic ego of the newborn that Fairbairn hypothesized is the direct successor of the organizing principle of the embryo. The infant's ego already has the shape of a person and is strongly motivated to encounter this shape in the outer world and also is encouraged to grow into the adult shape (Tustin, 1972) or image (Chein, 1972) by the model provided by its parents, by their expectations of the child, and by holistic fields of force in the infant organism. The infant ego functions with an inherited gestalt that seeks to become a person by finding expected encounters with important others whose personalities will shape the infant's development.

Infant research now confirms the competence of the infant self for invoking attachment responses from the adult, for self-regulation, and boundary setting (Stern, 1985). Sutherland used these observational research findings as evidence for his contention that, from the start, the ego exerts a powerful assertion and maintenance of autonomy and integrity. From infancy and throughout the life cycle, a person has to be, do, and relate. More than that, a person is always both being and becoming (Sutherland, 1990a). Particularly human is our capacity to conceive of ourselves as having a self, a continuity of self-feeling that we can take for granted, an inner space for reflection and for planning.

Aggression and the Autonomous Self

I close with an idea in Sutherland's (1993) last paper, which summarizes his objection to Freud, reaffirms his stance on Fairbairn, and takes us beyond into his own theory of the autonomous self. He wrote, "Far from being undifferentiated, the self is being formed steadily, and any interference with this self-determined dynamic elicits intense aggression" (Sutherland, cited in Scharff, 1994, p. 330).

This is Sutherland's most important idea, one that is independent of Fairbairn and yet is an extension of his views of the central ego and its freedom to operate in consciousness. For Sutherland, aggression is not the product of an instinct (as Freud thought), not the desperate attempt to protect the self from the death instinct (as Klein thought), not the reaction to frustrated attachment (as Bowlby thought), nor even the frustration of the need to be in a satisfying relationship (as Fairbairn thought). Sutherland now postulates that aggression results from the self's struggle for its autonomy, which it is competent to pursue, but which is inevitably frustrated by the facts of infantile dependence—even when these are met in an entirely satisfactory manner.

Sutherland's theory moves away from a classical base in defense against instinctual tension or structural conflict and out to the biopsychosocial nature of the self having to contain anxiety, conflict, hatred, and envy; maintain its integrity; sustain its life-giving relationships; be of service to others; and even make its mark on the future expression of the phenotype.

References

Balint, M. (1968), *The Basic Fault*. London: Tavistock.

Bertalanffy, L. Von (1950), The theory of open systems in physics and biology. *Science*, 111:23–29.

Bowlby, J. (1969), *Attachment and Loss*. New York: Basic Books.

——— (1973), *Separation*. New York: Basic Books.

Chein, I. (1972), *The Science of Behavior and the Image of Man*. New York: Basic Books.

Dicks, H. V. (1967), *Marital Tensions*. London: Routledge & Kegan Paul.

Fairbairn, W. R. D. (1944), Endopsychic structure considered in terms of object relationships. In: *An Object Relations Theory of the Personality*. New York: Basic Books, 1954, pp. 82–132.

—— (1963), Synopsis of an object-relations theory of the personality. *Internat. J. Psycho-Anal.* 44:224–226.

Freud, S. (1905), Three essays on the theory of sexuality. *Standard Edition*, 7:135–243. London: Hogarth Press, 1953.

—— (1915), Instincts and their vicissitudes. In *Standard Edition*, 14:109–140. London: Hogarth Press, 1957.

—— (1916–17), Introductory lectures on psycho-analysis. *Standard Edition*, 16:243–463. London: Hogarth Press, 1963.

—— (1923), The ego and the id. *Standard Edition*, 19:12–66. London: Hogarth Press, 1961.

Greenberg, J. R. & Mitchell, S. A. (1983), *Object Relations in Psychoanalytic Theory*. Cambridge, MA: Harvard University Press.

Guntrip, H. S. (1961), *Personality and Human Interaction*. London: Hogarth Press.

Harrow, A., Leishman, M., MacDonald, M. & Scott, D. (1994), Introduction. In: *The Autonomous Self*, ed. J. S. Scharff. Northvale, NJ: Aronson, pp. xv–xxv.

Hazell, J., ed. (1994), *Personal Relations Therapy*. Northvale, NJ: Aronson.

Jantsch, E. (1976), Introduction and summary. In: *Evolution and Consciousness*, ed. C. H. Waddington & E. Jantsch. Reading, MA: Addison-Wesley, pp. 1–8.

—— (1980), *The Self-Organizing Universe*. New York: Pergamon Press.

Klein, M. (1935), A contribution to the psychogenesis of manic depressive states. In: *Love, Guilt and Reparation & Other Works, 1921–1945*. New York: Delacorte Press, 1975, pp. 262–289.

—— (1946), Notes on some schizoid mechanisms. In: *Envy and Gratitude*, New York: Delacorte Press, 1975, pp. 1–24.

—— (1955), *New Directions in Psycho-Analysis, 1921–1945*. London: Tavistock.

Kohon, G. (1996), Review of *The Autonomous Self*, ed. J. S. Scharff. In: *J. Amer. Psychoanal. Assn.*, 44:1261–1262.

Kohut, H. (1971), *The Analysis of the Self*. New York: International Universities Press.

Miller, J. G. (l965), Living systems, basic concepts. *Behav. Sci.*, 10:337–379.

Padel, J. (1995), Review of *The Autonomous Self*, ed. J. S. Scharff. *Internat. J. Psycho-Anal.*, 76:177–179.

Prigogine, I. (1976), Order through fluctuation: Self-organization and social system. In: *Evolution and Consciousness*, ed. C. H. Waddington & E. Jantsch. Reading, MA: Addison-Wesley, pp. 93–126, 130–33.

Savege, J. (1973), Psychodynamic understanding in community psychiatry. *Psychother. & Psychosom.*, 25:272–278.

Scharff, D. E. & Birtles, E. F., eds. (1994), *From Instinct to Self, Vol. 1.* Northvale, NJ: Aronson.

—— & Scharff, J. S. (1987), *Object Relations Family Therapy.* Northvale, NJ: Aronson.

Scharff, J. S., ed. (1994), *The Autonomous Self.* Northvale, NJ: Aronson.

Stern, D. N. (1985), *The Interpersonal World of the Infant.* New York: Basic Books.

Sutherland, J. D. (1963), Object relations theory and the conceptual model of psychoanalysis. In: *The Autonomous Self*, ed. J. S. Scharff. Northvale, NJ: Aronson, 1994, pp. 3–24.

—— (1980), The British object relations theorists: Balint, Winnicott, Fairbairn, Guntrip. In: *The Autonomous Self*, ed. J. S. Scharff. Northvale, NJ: Aronson, 1994, pp. 25–44.

—— (1989), *Fairbairn's Journey into the Interior.* London: Free Association Press.

—— (1990a), On becoming and being a person. In: *The Autonomous Self*, ed. J. S. Scharff. Northvale, NJ: Aronson, 1994, pp. 372–391.

—— (1990b), Reminiscences. In: *The Autonomous Self*, ed. J. S. Scharff. Northvale, NJ: Aronson, 1994, pp. 392–423.

—— (1993), The autonomous self. In: *The Autonomous Self*, ed. J. S. Scharff. Northvale, NJ: Aronson, 1994, pp. 303–330.

—— (1994), Fairbairn and the self. In: *The Autonomous Self*, ed. J. S. Scharff. Northvale, NJ: Aronson, 1994, pp. 331–349.

Tustin, F. (1972), *Autism and Childhood Psychosis.* London: Hogarth Press.

Wallerstein, R. S. (1988), One psychoanalysis or many? *Internat. J. Psycho-Anal.*, 69:5–21.

Winnicott, D. W. (1958), *Collected Papers.* New York: Basic Books.

—— (1960), Ego distortion in terms of true and false self. In: *The Maturational Processes and the Facilitating Environment.* New York: International Universities Press, 1965, pp. 140–152.

—— (1965), *The Maturational Processes and the Facilitating Environment.* New York: International Universities Press.

—— & Khan, M. J. (1953), Review of *Psychoanalytic Studies of the Personality*, by W. R. D. Fairbairn. *Internat. J. Psycho-Anal.*, 34:329–333.

◆ Part 4 ◆

Artistic Connections

10

Alter Egos—Close Encounters of the Paranoid Kind
W. R. D. Fairbairn, Salvador Dali, and Me

Steven Z. Levine

As an art historian writing for psychoanalysts, I confess to a certain measure of paranoia in projecting before you my quite possibly delirious images of the encounter—indeed, the vexed or symptomatic encounter—between the studiedly outrageous objects of Surrealism and the outwardly staid object relations theorist W. R. D. Fairbairn. This incongruous encounter between Parisian panache and Scottish reserve is quietly enacted for us across the seemingly sage pages of two articles on artistic expression and aesthetic response published in 1938 by Fairbairn in the *British Journal of Psychology*—"Prolegomena to a Psychology of Art" and "The Ultimate Basis of Aesthetic Experience"—both now deservedly rescued from oblivion by Ellinor Fairbairn Birtles and David E. Scharff (1994) in their edited volume of Fairbairn's papers.

In my remarks here the troubled encounter of Fairbairn and Surrealism will be seen to implicate, directly or indirectly, a long series of personifications or provocateurs of paranoia, whether in the form of Freud's (1911) famous depiction of the disavowed homosexuality of Judge Schreber and his transgendered delusion of having been impregnated by God; or in the form of Klein's (1935) fearsomely bad-breasted mother of infantile persecutory fantasy; or in the form of the hallucinatory crimes and dissociative writings of the mad women of France celebrated by

179

the Surrealists under the leadership of André Breton and contemporaneously analyzed in the doctoral thesis, *On Paranoid Psychosis in Its Relations to the Personality*, by Lacan (1932); or in the form of the self-styled "paranoiac-critical activity" of Lacan's friend, Salvador Dali, wherein the painter externalizes in lurid visual imagery the destructive rage and unassuageable desire incited by external events, such as his mother's death and his father's remarriage; or, finally, in the form of Fairbairn's own urinary-retention symptom, his transcriptions and drawings of dreams, and his carefully preserved self-analytic notes, all regarding, in the words of his former analysand and colleague, John Sutherland (1989), both an ambivalent identification with his father, whose "phobia of urinating in the presence of others" Fairbairn's own symptom reproduces, and "a sharp splitting off in his self of a deep sadistic rage against his internal bad mother" (p. 36).

The definitive crystalization of the urinary symptom and the concerted effort to clarify its meanings relative to his mother, father, colleagues, and wife was taking place just at the time Fairbairn was writing both in his clinical papers and in his papers on art about the need of the artist and analysand—and analyst, too, it seems right to add—"to restore [in his dreams] the object destroyed by his urinary sadism" (Fairbairn, 1936, p. 226), and to make creative restitution in art for his "destructive phantasies regarding love objects" (Fairbairn, 1938a, p. 394). The nursery-names Fairbairn gave these intimate objects of love and hate in his first paper on art are "'Mummy,' 'Daddy,' and 'Nanny'" (p. 395). These are the figures, with the destroyed-and-restored-image of the mother very much to the fore, in whose disturbing presence Fairbairn suddenly found himself at the International Surrealist Exhibition he attended, in London in 1936.

A 1936 photograph (Figure 1) of the Surrealists of Paris and their English supporters provides me with an opportunity to slow the pace of my narrative so far and begin my story once more by setting out a theoretical frame within which to view Fairbairn's overdetermined foray into the psychoanalytic interpretation of Surrealist art. In the photograph of the London exhibition we can make out the mustachioed likeness of the

Fig. 1. International Surrealist Exhibition, London, 1936, with Salvador Dali (first from left) and Herbert Read (fourth from left). From *La Vie Publique de Salvador Dali* (Paris: Centre Georges Pompidou, 1979).

notorious Catalonian-Parisian painter, filmmaker, exhibitionist, and all-round *agent provocateur*, Salvador Dali. Next to Dali is his English patron, Edward James, with whom the painter would later visit Freud in London in 1938; next to James is the Surrealist poet, Paul Eluard, husband of Dali's mistress and later wife, Gala; and directly next to Eluard, all but obscured from view by the woman standing in front, is Herbert (later Sir Herbert) Read, poet, critic, champion of Surrealism, and, most important for our purposes, Fairbairn's friend. A lecture given by Read at the International Surrealist Exhibition, "Art and the Unconscious," bears the same title as a chapter in his book *Art and Society*. Fairbairn (1938a, b) quotes from this and other writings by Read in his own papers on art, and we can assess something of the creative, as well as possibly defensive, nature of Fairbairn's contribution to aesthetics and psychoanalytic art theory by looking closely at what he accepted and what he rejected in the work of his friend.

According to Sutherland (1989), Fairbairn admired Read's writings on art and enjoyed conversations with him during the time Read was a professor of fine art at Edinburgh University between 1931 and 1933. Fairbairn shared with Read a strong grounding in the philosophy of mind of Kant and Hegel, although he did not share Read's enthusiasm for the revolutionary social philosophy of Marx. Fairbairn had earned an M.A. degree with honors in philosophy at Edinburgh University in 1911, and we may think to hear in the title of his essay, "Prolegomena to a Psychology of Art" (Fairbairn, 1938a), the modest or immodest echo either of Kant's (1783) *Prolegomena to Any Future Metaphysics That Will Be Able to Present Itself as Science* or perhaps William Wallace's (1894) *Prolegomena to the Study of Hegel's Philosophy and Especially of His Logic*. Read thought Hegel's (1835) *Lectures on Aesthetics* to be the chief treatment of the subject in its understanding of art's indivisibility of idea and material embodiment. Fairbairn (1938b), too, was positively Hegelian not only in the rather grandiose title of his second paper on art, "The Ultimate Basis of Aesthetic Experience," but more significantly in the presentation of this "ultimate" claim in explicitly dialectical terms, namely, that "the highest unity is to be reached only through the full development and reconciliation of the deepest and widest antagonism" (pp. 407–408). Fairbairn is here quoting a summary statement by Edward Caird (1901), and we will see that Fairbairn's adamant and repeated stress on reconciliation in his papers on art—and not only on art—will ultimately distinguish his philosophy and politics from the more revolutionary inflections of the Hegelian dialectic in the art of the Surrealists and in the criticism of Herbert Read.

Beginning his chapter on "Art and the Unconscious" not with Hegel but with Freud, Read asserts that he takes it for granted that it is no longer necessary to justify a psychoanalytic approach to artistic expression. Providing paragraph-long excerpts from Freud's *Introductory Lectures on Psychoanalysis*, Read (1937) reproduces Freud's contention that the artist, like the neurotic, is first a man of unsatisfied libidinal and practical longings for "honour, power, riches, fame, and the love of women." Unable to obtain these coveted rewards in actuality, the artist and the neurotic both turn away from the dissatisfactions of reality in order to enter the more satisfying world of fantasy; but it is precisely at this point that the artist, unlike the neurotic, manages to avoid the illness of introversion and symptom formation and finds his way back to reality. The artist does this by means of the formal elaboration of his fantasies in a material medium and by their subsequent presentation to an audience, thus achieving secondarily, by way of what Freud calls sublimation, what he has wanted from the first, namely "honour, power, riches, fame, and the love of women" (pp. 85–87). (Obviously it is of male artists that Freud and Read are speaking; we may ask ourselves whether their accounts fully pertain to women as well.)

As a limitation of the theory of sublimation Read notes Freud's acknowledgment of the mysterious nature of this transformational process whereby the forbidden impulses and raw fantasies of the individual are given a disguised and hence socially acceptable form. To solve the mystery of sublimation Read turns to Freud's *New Introductory Lectures* and finds in the structural theory of ego, id, and superego the dynamic ratio he needs in order to explain the invaluable and multivalent achievements of art. Read (1937) writes:

> For obviously the work of art has correspondences with each region of the mind. It derives its energy, its irrationality and its mysterious power from the id, which is to be regarded as the source of what we usually call inspiration. It is given formal synthesis and unity by the ego; and finally it may be assimilated to those ideologies or spiritual aspirations which are the peculiar creation of the super-ego [pp. 91–92].

Too much id, and the "bare truth" of the work of art will "repel us"; too much superego, and the work of art will suffer from a deadening subordination to "religion or morality or social ideology." Like the mystics to whom Freud referred, for

Read the ego of the artist has the flexible capacity to make contact with those "deeper layers" of the mind that for most people remain inaccessible to normal consciousness; and, by investing the id-inspired work of art with the "superficial charms" of "wholeness or perfection," the artist enables at least a portion of his "deeper intuitions" to be shared by the public (pp. 94–95). As Read pithily put it, "The ego intermediates between the primal force and the ultimate ideal" (p. 92). For Fairbairn (1938a), too, "art is seen to be not only a sublimated expression of repressed urges, but also a means whereby *positive values* are created in the service of an ideal" (p. 394).

Many of Read's formulations anticipated Fairbairn's very closely, but Fairbairn (1938a) cited Read only to the effect that "art begins as a solitary activity" (p. 382) and made no further mention of Read's articulation of a theory of the work of art as effectuating a formal compromise on the part of the ego between the disturbing impulses and private fantasies of the id and the superego's socially ordained constraints of collective norms and ideals. Fairbairn initially turned away from an emphasis on the social function of the artist in order to stress the individualistic scenario of pleasurable discharge. He summarized this view with the formula that art is "making something for fun" (p. 383). With his emphasis on pleasure Fairbairn may have been covertly defying the stern Calvinist attitudes of his deceased father by pointedly observing that "the essence of puritanism lies in an extreme intolerance of all forms of activity inspired by pleasure-seeking motives" (p. 385). Despite this seemingly emancipatory pronouncement against the puritanical reproach of pleasure as sin, Fairbairn's own tastes in art remained conservative, just as his somewhat later theory of internalized libidinal objects saw the pleasure to be pursued in solitary fantasy as a poor second-order simulacrum of the pleasure to be achieved in so-called real or actual relationships with others.

Fairbairn exemplified his thesis of the essential pleasure or fun of art by way of a reference to a *Poème-objet* of 1935 by André Breton (Figure 2). It and other works of art to which

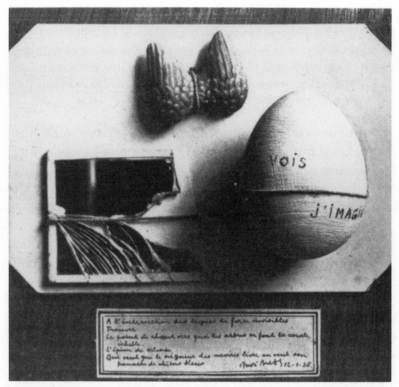

Fig. 2. André Breton, *Poème-objet*, 1935. From *Surrealism*, ed. H. Read (London: Faber and Faber, 1936).

Fairbairn referred are illustrated in Read (1936). There Read, comparing the work of art with Freud's dream-work, insisted that both arise from "an unconscious impulse" and both feature the irrationality of regression as well as the disguises of repression (p. 77). Read referred principally to the parallel formal processes in what he called dream-formation and poem-formation (p. 70); without acknowledging Read's discussion, Fairbairn (1938a) developed a similar analogy between visual art and the dream:

Like dream-work, art-work must be regarded as essentially unconscious. . . . It is through the agency of art-work that the repressed phantasies of the artist, in the form of "manifest

content," are placed at his conscious disposal for embodiment in
works of art. . . . Art-work thus provides the means of reducing
psychical tension in the artist's mind by enabling his repressed
urges to obtain some outlet and satisfaction without unduly disturbing his equanimity [p. 387].

Fairbairn wrote very similarly about the compromise formation of his symptom. Forbidden by his mother to touch himself
for pleasure as a boy, as a man he wrote in his self-analytic notes
that "the situation favored a regression to the position of treating my penis as an essentially urinary organ and extorting what
pleasure I could get out of it in a urinary capacity" (Sutherland,
1989, p. 75). We might remember here that Freud (1913) equated
the corporeal conversion of hysteria with the materiality and
mimeticism of the work of art (p. 73).

For Fairbairn (1938a), a painting of the Madonna and Child
by Leonardo da Vinci clearly manifested a suitable ratio
between "the repressed urges and the factors responsible for
repression," whereas the same theme treated by the Surrealist
Joan Miró in his painting *Maternity* (Figure 3) is seen to exhibit
only a "comparative poverty of the art-work which . . . is
directly related to pressure of unconscious phantasy combined
with weakness of repression" (p. 387). Unfortunately, Fairbairn
made this pat diagnostic assessment without adducing any of
the unique circumstances in the very different lives and careers
of these 16th-century and 20th-century artists. Rejecting the
Surrealist project supported by his friend Read "to break down
the barriers existing between the world of the unconscious and
the world of outer reality," Fairbairn here placed himself
squarely on the side of the very same "tyrannical superego" of
puritanism that just paragraphs earlier he had roundly condemned (p. 385). "Without repression no high achievement in
art is possible," he concluded (p. 388), thus repeating Freud's
(1938) contemporaneous view on Surrealism as expressed in a
letter to Stefan Zweig after a visit from Salvador Dali. Impressed
by the "undeniable technical mastery" of the artist—who made
a number of portrait drawings showing Freud's skull as the spi-

ral shell of a snail (Figure 4) or already as the death's head it would soon become—Freud conceded that he had been forced to reevaluate his opinion of the Surrealists as "absolute . . . cranks" yet nonetheless maintained "that the notion of art defies expansion as long as the quantitative proportion of unconscious

Fig. 3. Joan Miró, *Maternity*, 1924, From *Surrealism*, ed. H. Read (London: Faber and Faber, 1936).

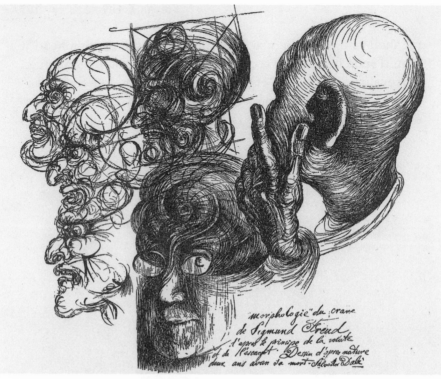

Fig. 4. Salvador Dali, *Morphology of the Skull of Sigmund Freud According to the Principle of a Snail's Shell*, 1938. From *The Secret Life of Salvador Dali*, by S. Dali (New York: Dial, 1942).

material and preconscious treatment does not remain within definite limits" (pp. 448–449). In the face of Surrealism Fairbairn also came up against the limits of what he found acceptable in art.

What are the unruly urges and impulses that Fairbairn found so transgressive in Surrealist art? If Read principally understood these desires to be sexual in nature, Fairbairn (1938a) registered his chief difference from Read by insisting on the role of the "aggressive and destructive impulses, which represent a denial of the life principle" (p. 388). What was here still understood as an inborn impulse or drive in line with the theories of Freud and Klein would later be understood by Fairbairn as the second-order internalization of an unsatisfying object relation that includes the splitting off of those portions of the ego that are bound up with the falsely enticing or cruelly rejecting maternal and paternal imagos. Paranoid fantasies of persecution at the hands of these love objects reactively occasion sadistic fantasies of their destruction; the destruction in fantasy of these ambivalently loved-and-hated objects further occasion depressive guilt about their fate as well as depressive anxiety about one's own; and, finally, as first proposed by Klein (1929), Fairbairn concluded that the destructive dialectic of paranoia and sadism gave rise to "compensatory phantasies of restitution" (p. 389).

Combining the Hegelian reconciliation of opposites with the Kleinian resolution of paranoid fears and depressive guilt, Fairbairn concluded that "the principle of restitution is the governing principle in art," more specifically, "that the work of art represents a tribute of restitution paid by the artist's ego to his superego" (Fairbairn, 1938a, p. 390; 1938b, p. 398). In keeping with his conservative tastes in art, it is easy enough for Fairbairn to allege that an ancient Aphrodite "conveys the impression of 'the integrity of the object'" in spite of its fragmentary condition. On the other hand, Fairbairn exhibited his greatest and most dangerously personal creativity by acknowledging that even in Salvador Dali's work "the sadistic, 'tearing in pieces' tendency'" (a phrase he adopted from Klein) is accompanied by evidence of formal restitution. As examples Fairbairn chose Dali's Aphrodite-like nude drawing, *City of Drawers* (Figure 5), and *Specter of Sex-Appeal* (Figure 6), a painting not illustrated in Read's (1936) *Surrealism* but taken from Dali's (1935) own small volume, *La Conquête de l'Irrationnel* (*The Conquest of the Irrational*). Fairbairn (1938a) wrote:

> Here we see the minute figure of a boy contemplating a colossal female figure, whose head merges into a rugged mountain mass in the background. The figure is deformed, contorted and mutilated; and various parts of the body are missing. Yet, apart from the unifying effect of the composition, evidences of restitution are not wholly lacking from the subject itself; for the figure is propped up by crutches and the missing parts of the trunk are at any rate replaced by sacks [pp. 390–391].

Fig. 5. Salvador Dali, *City of Drawers*, 1936. From *Surrealism*, ed. H. Read (London: Faber and Faber, 1936).

Once again Fairbairn rendered his interpretation without adducing any information about the personal or professional circumstances of the artist, but in the case of Dali there may be reason to think that Fairbairn looked upon him as a veritable alter ego.

In his description of the painting by Dali, Fairbairn barely mentioned "the minute figure of a boy" at the lower right of the composition. In a later commentary, Dali claimed of this figure that "it represents me at the age of six, holding a fossil specter. I see the biological cataclysm dripping from the eternal female, deluded and hyper-terrifying" (quoted in Morse, 1958, p. 38). The fossilized bone that the boy holds between his legs is the rigid, mortified member of his compulsive masturbatory practices in the conjured-up presence of the colossal earth-mother of simultaneously exciting and annihilating allure. In the face of such paranoid and schizoid fantasies of solitary isolation and

Fig. 6. Salvador Dali, *Specter of Sex-Appeal*, 1934. From *La Conquête de l'Irrationnel*, by S. Dali (Paris: Editions Surréalistes, 1935).

dyadic engulfment, Fairbairn chose to look away—though as a young boy he too was once photographed in just such a cap and suit (see Birtles and Scharff, 1994, p. 463). Thus Fairbairn the "fair child" became father to the man, who now found himself still anxiously living out as adult analyst the torments of sexual inhibition and urinary dysfunction ordained in his personal history by the violent maternal intrusions and pathetic paternal phobias of his first youth. With no analyst in Edinburgh to go to for help, Fairbairn must have been terribly alone with his pain, as Sutherland (1989) suggests. On the other hand, writing about the destructions and restitutions he found in the art of Dali may have provided Fairbairn with a cracked mirror of self-recognition with which to view his own inner world. Moreover, if he chanced to read Dali's description of the "paranoiac-critical method" in the little book in which he saw the plate of *Specter of Sex-Appeal*, Fairbairn would have discovered there a dreamlike series of images, a paranoid process of self-reference, and a concrete symptomatology uncannily like his own.

Here is a long passage from Dali (1935) in which he provocatively exemplifies his "spontaneous method of irrational knowledge based on the interpretive-critical association of delirious phenomena." Unlike the dream narratives, free associations, and paranoia-inducing regressions of the analytic process, Dali's manifestations of subjective reality are purposefully projected into the externalized form of a revolutionary public gift of hallucinatory images and delirious texts; their purpose is to transform the world:

> It is a question of the systematic-interpretive organization of the material experimental surrealist dispersed and narcissistic sensation. In effect, the surrealist events of the day: nocturnal emission, false memory, dream, daydream, the concrete transformation of the nocturnal firefly into an hypnagogic image or of the morning firefly into an objective image, nutritional caprice, intrauterine protests, anamorphic hysteria, the voluntary retention of urine, the involuntary retention of insomnia, the fortuitous image of an exclusive exhibitionism, the failed act, the delirious feat, regional sneezing, the anal wheel-barrow, the minimal error, the Lilliputian malaise, the super-normal physiological state, the picture one stops painting, the one one paints, the territorial telephone call, "the deranging image," etc., etc., all

these, I say, and a thousand other instantaneous or successive solicitations, revealing a minimum of irrational intentionality or, on the contrary, a minimum of suspect phenomenal nullity, are associated, by the mechanisms of the precision apparatus of paranoiac-critical activity, in an indestructible delirious-interpretive system of political problems, paralytic images, more or less mammalian questions, playing the role of the obsessional idea [pp. 17–18].

Converted into somatic symptom, the obsessional idea becomes Fairbairn's or Dali's protest against outer reality in the "paranoiac-critical" form of a "voluntary retention of urine." Itself an "anamorphic hysteria," a distention of the language of the bladder and of blather, the symptom, like the work of art, is a Surrealist event, a delirious projection of an untenable position in the everyday world. The only difference is that Fairbairn suffered in Edinburgh in silence and Dali cavorted beneath the whole world's gaze.

What might it have meant to Fairbairn to read the words "voluntary retention of urine" in Dali's text? Would they have loosened or perhaps only strengthened his defenses? Despite the fascination exerted on him by the "art-work" of Dali, Fairbairn (1938a) insisted that it "cannot be regarded as representing a very high level of artistic achievement" (p. 392). This alleged failure of art is due to a supposed failure of repression, "to an inadequacy of disguise," which Fairbairn labeled "under-symbolization" and "which leaves the requirements of the superego unsatisfied." The converse case of "over-symbolization" would involve "an over-elaboration of disguise, which precludes any appeal to the repressed urges." The trick, then, for each artist and beholder, for each analyst and analysand, will be somehow to contrive a work—whether a painting, a paper on art, or the psychoanalytic story of a life—that "enables both his repressed urges and the demands of his superego to obtain a maximum of satisfaction" (Fairbairn 1938b, pp. 406–407).

Dali said that the only difference between himself and the mad was that he was not mad. Dali said that the only difference between himself and the other Surrealists was that he was a Surrealist. Dali, of course, never had the occasion to say that the only difference between himself and Fairbairn was that he was the real psychoanalyst, publicly living out the implications of unconscious paranoia that still kept a huge portion of Fairbairn's life imprisoned in a symptomatic crypt. It would be too harsh to conclude that Fairbairn's theory of art and life remains wholly hostage to the tyrannical superego whose rigorous prohibitions his body and mind both reviled and revered. Nevertheless, his most Dalian gift to an art historian like me, to a man like me, is not his puritan and patriarchal theory of the ego's "atonement to his superego for the destruction implied in the presence of repressed destructive impulses" (Fairbairn, 1938b, p. 407). No, for me Fairbairn at his most heroic is not the author of the theory of the central ego's victory over the combined forces of dissolution of the libidinal and antilibidinal subsidiary egos and objects. For me Fairbairn the Surrealist is the one who makes something "for fun" even in his pain after Fairbairn the analyst has failed. Through Sutherland's (1989) editorial efforts, the Surrealist art of Fairbairn's transcriptions of memories and dreams and his astonishing self-analytic notes have come down to us; we know nothing quite like them, I think, in the entire analytic literature:

> The anxiety when my bladder is over-full and I am unable to pass water is quite capable of giving rise to suicidal thoughts. . . . I fancy that, when my bladder is over-full and I can't pass urine, I identify myself with my Mother and identify my bladder with her breast bursting with bad milk. This, I think, must partly account for the suicidal ideas, because my bladder is something alien and hostile on these occasions [p. 76].

For Fairbairn to write of his vexed maternal identification in such delirious and hallucinatory images and words—and for Sutherland to transmit them to us—is a work of emancipatory Surrealist paranoia at its critical and nutritional best. From this master theoretician of the eternally internalized parental object we are bequeathed a gift of great insight into what Lacan calls the "paranoiac alienation of the ego" (Lacan, 1953, p. 12). Freud (1913), you remember, called paranoia "a caricature of a philosophical system" (p. 73); the work of Dali reminds us that, in its projection of systematic knowledge, a unitary philosophy of life is already a delusional paranoia as well.

References

Birtles, E. F. & Scharff, D. E., eds. (1994), *From Instinct to Self: Selected Papers of W. R. D. Fairbairn, Vol. 2.* Northvale, NJ: Aronson.

Caird, E. (1901), *Hegel.* Edinburgh: Blackwood.

Dali, S. (1935), *La Conquête de l'Irrationnel.* Paris: Editions Surréalistes.

Fairbairn, W. R. D. (1936), The effect of a king's death upon patients under analysis. In: *Psychoanalytic Studies of the Personality.* London: Routledge & Kegan Paul, 1952, pp. 223–229.

——— (1938a), Prolegomena to a psychology of art. In: *From Instinct to Self*, ed. E. F. Birtles & D. E. Scharff. Northvale, NJ: Aronson, 1994, pp. 381–396.

——— (1938b), The ultimate basis of aesthetic experience. In: *From Instinct to Self*, ed. E. F. Birtles & D. E. Scharff. Northvale, NJ: Aronson, 1994, pp. 397–409.

Freud, S. (1911), Psycho-analytic notes on an autobiographical account of a case of paranoia (dementia paranoides). *Standard Edition*, 12:3–79. London: Hogarth Press, 1955.

——— (1913), Totem and taboo. *Standard Edition*, 13:1–161. London: Hogarth Press, 1955.

——— (1917), Introductory lectures on psycho-analysis. *Standard Edition*, 15–16. London: Hogarth Press, 1963.

——— (1933), New introductory lectures on psycho-analysis. *Standard Edition*, 22:3–182. London: Hogarth Press, 1964.

——— (1938), Letter to S. Zweig, July 20. In: *The Letters of Sigmund Freud*, ed. E. L. Freud (trans. T. Stern & J. Stern). New York: Basic Books, 1960, pp. 448–449.

Hegel, G. W. F. (1835), Lectures on aesthetics. In: *The Philosophy of Fine Art*, 4 vols., trans. F. P. B. Osmaston. London: Bell, 1920.

Kant, I. (1783), *Prolegomena to Any Metaphysics That Will Be Able to Present Itself as a Science*, trans. P. G. Lucas. Manchester: Manchester University Press, 1953.

Klein, M. (1929), Infantile anxiety situations reflected in a work of art and in the creative impulse. In: *The Selected Melanie Klein*, ed. J. Mitchell. New York: Free Press, 1987, pp. 84–111.

———— (1935), A contribution to the psychogenesis of manic-depressive states. In: *The Selected Melanie Klein*, ed. J. Mitchell. New York: Free Press, 1987, pp. 115–145.

Lacan, J. (1932), *De la Psychose Paranoïaque dans ses Rapports avec la Personnalité, Suivi de Premiers Ecrits sur la Paranoïa*. Paris: Seuil, 1975.

———— (1953), Some reflections on the ego. *Internat. J. Psycho-Anal.*, 34:11–17.

Morse, A. R. (1958), *Dali: A Study of His Life and Work*. Greenwich, CT: New York Graphic Society.

Read, H. (1936), Introduction. In: *Surrealism*, ed. H. Read. London: Faber & Faber, pp. 17–91.

———— (1937), *Art and Society*, 2nd ed. New York: Pantheon Books, 1945.

Sutherland, J. (1989), *Fairbairn's Journey into the Interior*. London: Free Association Books.

Wallace, W. (1894), *Prolegomena to the Study of Hegel's Philosophy and Especially of His Logic*. Oxford: Clarendon Press.

11

A Fairbairnian Analysis of Robert Louis Stevenson's *Strange Case of Dr. Jekyll and Mr. Hyde*

Robert Louis Stevenson and Ronald Fairbairn were born almost 40 years apart, the former in 1850 and the latter in 1889, in the same city and into a culture of middle-class respectability and dour Scots Calvinism that had remained essentially unchanged in the interim. The parallels between their early lives are striking. Both were only children who had pious, possessive, hypochondriacal mothers, devoted nannies, and conventionally Presbyterian fathers who failed to provide a sufficient counterweight to the female presences in their sons' lives. Both had difficulty in escaping home and the stifling weight of parental expectations, and both made detours toward conventional professions (Stevenson was forced to study first engineering and then law, and Fairbairn at first intended to become a clergyman) before devoting themselves to their true métiers. Both showed keen psychological acumen and were vividly aware from early on of the conflict between social respectability and hidden passion, between what Stevenson (1894), toward the end of his short life, was to describe, despairingly, as "the prim obliterated polite face of life, and the broad, bawdy, and orgiastic—or maenadic—foundations" (p. 362).

This conflict was to form one of the principal themes of Stevenson's work, and it is therefore fitting that we examine the most famous of all his stories about the duality of good and evil in the light of the psychological theories of his distinguished countryman. It should be recalled that the full title of this story (the best-known "double" story in the English language, perhaps in any language) is *Strange Case of Dr. Jekyll and Mr. Hyde* (Stevenson, 1886). In other words, it was conceived of not just as a "penny . . . dreadful" (Stevenson, vol. 5, p. 128) but as, in effect, a case study in abnormal psychology (a field with which Stevenson may have been acquainted through the work of French writers of the 1870s and 80s: Swearingen, 1980, p. 101).

The story, first published in January 1886, is presented by the unseen narrator through the eyes of Utterson, a middle-aged, celibate bachelor who is both lawyer and friend to the respected Dr. Henry Jekyll. Utterson, with the inadvertent help of his kinsman, Enfield, gradually pursues and uncovers the story of Dr. Jekyll's sinister and mysterious young friend and heir, Edward Hyde, whom he suspects of persecuting or blackmailing Jekyll. Eventually, after he has brutally murdered a distinguished older man, Sir Danvers Carew, Hyde is revealed to be none other than the evil alter ego of Jekyll himself, produced through the ingestion of powders developed by Jekyll in the course of his ambitious researches into the divided nature of man and the "perennial war among [his] members" (Stevenson, 1886, p. 60). The dramatic dénouement is explained not by the narrator but in two, posthumous, written statements left for Utterson; one is by Hastie Lanyon, an estranged friend and colleague of Jekyll, who sickens and dies after witnessing Jekyll's transformation from the state of Hyde back to his own form; the other is by Jekyll himself, just before his suicide, when he finds himself finally trapped forever in the persona of Hyde, giving his own "full statement of the case."

The tale is a variant on the classic 19th-century double story, in which morality and sensuous or ambitious impulse are at war in the divided person of the hero. On the surface it might be, and has been, taken as a case illustration for "Civilization and Its Discontents" (Freud, 1930 [1929]) in that the ego of the hypocritical Henry Jekyll succumbs in the war between his sanctimonious and self-righteous superego and his lustful, aggressive id, with its illicit and implicitly sexual desires. I hope to show, however, that analyzing the story in the light of Fairbairn's revisions of Freudian theory can deepen significantly our reading of it and illuminate certain of its features in a way that a more straightforward Freudian interpretation cannot.

To begin with, a closer look at *Jekyll and Hyde* reveals that the doubles consist not merely of the two eponymous protagonists but comprise also the third principal character, Utterson, whose perspective initially frames the story. He is both a counterpart to Jekyll (minus the ambition) and a sibling rival to Hyde, whom he destroys and disinherits ("'If he be Mr Hyde' . . . 'I shall be Mr Seek',"" p. 17). He is further doubled in the person of his livelier kinsman, Enfield, just as Jekyll is doubled with his skeptical and eventually defeated colleague and rival, Lanyon, and with the esteemed M.P., Sir Danvers Carew, whom Hyde murders. In short, all these male protagonists can be shown to be in certain respects contrasting counterparts of each other, linked in shifting relationships of affection and, not always so obviously, of aggression (they are, in effect, the different "members" whose warfare the tale describes). Equally confusing and disconcerting is the fractured narrative technique, with its multiplicity of perspectives and time frames, and dissociated jumps in chronology, such that the reader is left in uncertainty until Henry Jekyll's "full statement" at last provides some cohesion.

Structurally, in fact, *Jekyll and Hyde* must be one of the most complex double stories ever written (equaled in this respect only by its Scottish predecessor, James Hogg's [1824] *The Private Memoirs and Confessions of a Justified Sinner*, which certainly must have influenced it). In *Jekyll and Hyde* we have not just a doubling, but a case of multiple splits in the ego, to use Fairbairns's concept. Stevenson himself makes this clear when he puts into Jekyll's mouth the words: "Man is not truly one but truly two. I say two, because the state of my knowledge does not pass beyond that point. . . . I hazard the guess that man will be ultimately known for a mere polity of multifarious, incongruous and independent denizens" (p. 61). These dissociated and independent-seeming denizens in *Jekyll and Hyde* can, however, be shown to have an intimate and organic connection to one another.

Another question then becomes, whose ego is it that is thus multiply split? A clue is afforded here not only by the disconcerting shifts and abrupt scene changes of the narrative, but by its equally strange and abrupt juxtapositions of the comfortingly ordinary and domestic with the nightmarish and the uncanny. This split is typified by Dr. Jekyll's dwelling, whose handsome, opulent living quarters, fronting on a formerly fine square, seem to have no outward connection with his sinister, dreary, windowless laboratory, giving on to a commercial street, in the back. The atmosphere of the story, from first to last, has the quality of a dream, something that draws our attention to the putative dreamer, the unnamed witness and narrator of the entire action, the only one who can encompass all the other perspectives, namely, its creator (and, with him, the reader, who endlessly recreates the creator's view).

At this point we may recall that the story has its origins in an actual dream or, rather, a nightmare, that woke Stevenson up, screaming, one autumn night in 1885. We know this from an 1888 essay ("A Chapter on Dreams"), in which he described his use of dream material in his creative work. He noted that he had long been wanting to write a story on the theme of duality, "to find a body, a vehicle, for that strong sense of man's double being which must at times . . . overwhelm the mind of every thinking creature" (p. 208). He was also at the time under considerable financial pressure to publish something, and thus, after racking his brains for two days for a plot, on the second night he dreamed "the scene at the window, and a scene, afterwards split in two, in which Hyde, pursued for some crime, took the powder and underwent the change [i.e., back into Dr. Jekyll] in the presence of his pursuers" (p. 208). These three scenes, along with the "central idea of a voluntary change becoming involuntary" and the notion of the powders as the material agent of change, were all that was "given"; "the rest was made awake, and consciously, though I think I can trace in it much of the manner of my Brownies" (p. 208).

To explain this last allusion, it is necessary to review briefly Stevenson's (1888) account in this essay of the role of his dream life in his creative endeavors. He had been tormented from childhood on by nightmares that plucked him "strangling and screaming from his sleep," nightmares that all too often had to do with his terror of Hell and damnation, and of being struck dumb and blank in his frantic efforts to exculpate himself. In adolescence he was plagued by a recurrent nightmare so vivid that he actually had the sense of leading a "double life"; in his dream life, which seemed as real as his normal one, he played the role of a medical student condemned to watch "monstrous malformations and the abhorred dexterity of surgeons" by day and endlessly to climb stairs, brushing past a dreary procession of men and women coming down, at night. He remained unable to master the overwhelming anxiety aroused by dreams like these, or to find words adequate to describe them, until he entered on his vocation of writer. Then, instead of making up tales simply to amuse himself as he fell asleep (something that his father had in fact done to distract him from his childhood night terrors), he began quite deliberately to utilize the stories and scenes presented nightly by the "little people" on the stage of the "internal theatre" of his mind. These "little people" were now benign, like the "Brownies" of Scottish legend who do the work of the household at night in exchange for food; and the spectator/author up "in his box-seat" would awake no longer in doubt or terror but amid "growing applause" and "growing exultation at his own cleverness" (pp. 202–203). At the same time, he could, so he said, disclaim all responsibility for the frequently immoral content of the Brownies' productions, since his role was limited to that of the editor and censor who has to take into consideration the requirements of social propriety and the literary marketplace (pp. 207–208).

This seems to me to anticipate rather strikingly Fairbairn's

(1944) notion of dreams not so much as wish fulfillments but as dramatizations or cinematographic "shorts" of situations existing in inner reality, in which the personages represent parts of the ego or internalized objects (p. 99). Elsewhere in the same paper Fairbairn noted that it is all too easy for the ego—by which he meant the central ego—to defend against the impact of fantasies released by the traditional kind of analytic drive interpretation, through precisely the kind of spectatoring described by Stevenson. As Fairbairn put it, the central ego merely

> sits back in the dress circle and describes the dramas enacted upon the stage of inner reality without any effective participation in them. At the same time, it derives considerable narcissistic satisfaction from being the recorder of remarkable events [as well as from] furnishing the material for observation [p. 85].

If we take "fantasies" as applying equally to sleep generated fantasies, we may surmise that, for Stevenson, the writing of fiction became one means of mastering or, at least, keeping at bay the terrifying conflicts within his own split ego and among his inner objects or "members."

This is not to say that we should attempt to read *Jekyll and Hyde* simplistically as autobiography. Although it can be shown to have its roots in the circumstances of its author's life, it remains an extraordinarily complex literary creation that can be deconstructed in any number of ways. Fairbairn, however, gives us one powerful key to the structure of the story, in particular to the possible meanings of its multiple characters in their relationships to each other; his theories also afford insight into the uncanny, menacing nature of the tale by pointing to what remains repressed, although alluded to, even after the shattering dénouement.

If the original dreamer, then, represents the central ego, to what or whom do the personages of his dream-tale correspond? The only person named by Stevenson (1888) in the original dream scenes (p. 208) is Hyde, although Jekyll is implied as the person into whom Hyde changes after taking the powder. There is, however, a third party, who is represented not just by Hyde's anonymous "pursuers" but by the unnamed Other who is present in the "scene at the window." This brief, pivotal scene, titled in the book "Incident at the Window," takes place after the murder of Carew, the mysterious death of Lanyon, and Dr. Jekyll's renewed disappearance from public life. Dr. Jekyll, sitting at the upstairs window of his laboratory, declines, with a sad smile, the invitation of the lawyer, Utterson, standing in the inner courtyard below, to accompany him on a walk. As he speaks, "the smile was struck out of his face and succeeded by an expression of such abject terror and despair, as froze the very blood [of his interlocutor]"; he then abruptly disappears (pp. 39–40). Only at the very end, in Jekyll's own "statement of the case," do we learn that the "terror and despair" must have been occasioned not only by the sight of Utterson but also by a simultaneous inner vision or awareness of the "indescribable sensations that heralded" the by now involuntary change into the person of Hyde. This scene immediately precedes that of "The Last Night" where Utterson, in his misguided zeal to help Jekyll and learn the truth, inadvertently brings about the death(s) of Jekyll-Hyde.

In short, the crucial third party of the tale is the pursuer/persecutor, Utterson, who precipitates and unmasks Jekyll's hitherto secret transformations, but who at the same time stands as a kind of protective, unambitious counterpart to Jekyll and an aggressive, confrontative sibling rival to Hyde. It appears that Utterson too can be taken as representing the central or ideal ego, which defends against the secretive activities of the other two protagonists, who represent the libidinal and the antilibidinal egos. As such, Utterson also constitutes a projection of the authorial persona into the story; he is the one who "utters" the tale, whose consciousness encompasses those of the other two and finally merges, as he reads the explanatory statements of Lanyon and of Jekyll, with that of the unseen narrator/reader at the end. He is also, if we take the other meaning of his name, the ultimate, perfect son, asexual and ascetic, "lovable" yet never seeking love, tolerant of other men's high-spirited misdeeds yet submerging his own avowed envy and secret hostility ("Cain's heresy") in outward helpfulness in their time of ruin. He is rewarded not only with the gift of wealth and of victory over his rival (for it is revealed at the end that Jekyll has disinherited Hyde in Utterson's favor) but also with that of sheer survival at the expense of his twin counterparts.

As regards these two counterparts, the most obvious doubles of the story, one might, on a superficial reading, take Jekyll to represent the good, virtuous one, and Hyde to be his purely evil, depraved alter ego who gets out of control. In Fairbairnian terms, however, one might see it differently. Stevenson, in his first written version of the tale, may have made Jekyll into the villain, who used Hyde simply as a disguise (Swearingen, 1980, p. 100), and even in the final version Jekyll is ambivalently presented as a sly, respectable hypocrite who wishes to enjoy his illicit pleasures secretly and irresponsibly in another body, whose actions he can distance himself from until they court society's wrath and possible discovery, at which point Jekyll tries to kill off his other self and is persecuted by it in turn. Thus, in Jekyll, we have a representation of the antilibidinal ego, whose "morbid sense of shame" and desperate desire for "position in the world," as well as his schizoid-seeming overvaluation of his intellectual accomplishments and ambitions, lead him to repudiate entirely his pleasure-loving self. Although he tries to depict this self, when he makes it materialize as Hyde, as inherently evil and depraved, he makes it clear that his initial fault was nothing worse than "a certain impatient gaiety of disposition, such as has made the happiness of many" (p. 60).

Hyde, then, represents the hopeful, libidinal ego and is at first far from being the merely bestial and inhuman creature that Jekyll would make him out to be. On the contrary, Jekyll at first greets him, in the mirror, not with "repugnance, rather with a leap of welcome. This, too, was myself. It seemed natural and human. . . . it bore a livelier image of the spirit . . . than the imperfect and divided countenance, I had been hitherto accustomed to call mine" (p. 61). Hyde is also emphatically young, masculine, and virile; small, swarthy, and hairy, in contrast to the middle-aged, large, smooth-faced Jekyll, with his "white and comely" hands. When Jekyll splits off this libidinal self and sends it secretly out of his back door, his escapades are at first merely "merry" and "undignified," like those of a schoolboy plunging "headlong into the sea of liberty" (p. 65). As time goes on, Jekyll becomes dismayed at his "vicarious depravity" and increasingly licentious acts, but it is only when he he is terrified to find the transformation happening involuntarily and becoming harder to reverse that he makes sporadic and ultimately futile efforts to curb or do away with Hyde entirely. And it is only when he is thus repeatedly frustrated, repudiated, and demonized, that the aggressive, "hellish" aspects of Hyde's nature are fully released, leading him to commit, in effect, two vengeful murders (much as Frankenstein's monster becomes vengeful and murderous only when his frightened creator persistently persecutes him and thwarts his need for love). Ultimately the split between the two warring egos cannot be maintained, and they are driven to destroy each other while the bland, central ego, in the person of Utterson, exposes them and triumphs.

It is at this point in our attempt at a Fairbairnian analysis of *Jekyll and Hyde* that we have to confront one of the most puzzling aspects of the story, namely, what are the internalized objects to which these split off egos correspond? One of the most striking aspects of the tale is in fact the absence of significant object ties. None of these male characters (except for Jekyll, in a schematic, conventional way) has a past, and none has any passionate relationships in the present. These men form a group of seemingly asexual, celibate, childless bachelors, whose pleasures are limited to companionable talk, eating, drinking, intellectual pursuits, and conventional entertainment (although Utterson, who enjoys the theater, has not set foot in one for 20 years!). The only passions that break the surface of their bland detachment are negative ones, whether they take the form of rivalry and contempt (Lanyon's ultimately deadly quarrel with

Jekyll over his "transcendental" researches) or outright violence (e.g., the trampling of the little girl or the murder of Carew). Aside from these violent incidents, we have no idea what Mr Hyde does with his time or what his increasingly "monstrous" debaucheries consist of, other than that they sound sadistic, perverse, and anonymous, rather than related to other people.

What we seem to see here are differing levels of repression of bad objects. Since the story is told exclusively in terms of male relationships, both positive and negative, though never overtly homosexual, it appears that male objects are much less threatening, or more protective, than female. (We may recall, parenthetically, that it was from his father that Stevenson learned his technique of soothing his night terrors with storytelling.) Insofar as we can glimpse formative object relations in the tale, they are between father and son. Henry Jekyll's father is evidently an ideal object, whose memory, coupled with that of God, helps recall him from his frenzy of delight at Hyde's murder of Carew ("I saw my life . . . from the days of childhood, when I had walked with my father's hand," p. 70). At the same time, Carew, the "aged and beautiful" white-haired gentleman who arouses Hyde's fury by politely inquiring directions of him and is smashed by him as "a sick child may break a plaything," must surely represent the same father as the enticing/exciting libidinal object who disappoints once too often. This episode, the telling of which is toned down by being split between two different chapters, is the most passionate, and the most obviously sexual, in the whole book. Carew, with his innocence, "kindness," and "well-founded self-content," is said to "accost" Hyde "with a very pretty manner"; Hyde, on this "pitiful . . . provocation," using a stick originally given to Jekyll by Utterson, attacks and mauls his victim, "tasting delight from every blow," until the "unresisting body" (p. 69) "jumps upon the roadway" (p. 26) and his own "lust of evil" is "gratified and stimulated" (p. 70).

This attack on the sanctimonious and ultimately withholding patriarch also represents an attack on Jekyll himself, who is portrayed as sympathetic father to his phallic son, Hyde ("Jekyll had more than a father's interest; Hyde had more than a son's indifference," p. 68), but who tries to put an end to the son's pleasures when they threaten to expose him. The conflict is dramatized again in the final encounter between Hyde and Lanyon, Jekyll's disapproving rival (another white-haired, patriarchal figure). By inducing Lanyon to witness the phallically portrayed physical transformation, and thereby the triumph of his own "transcendental medicine" over Lanyon's "narrow and material views" (p. 58), Hyde/Jekyll effectively commits another father-murder, for Lanyon is so literally sickened by what he sees and hears that he suddenly ages and dies.

At first sight, all this might be taken for straightforward oedipal conflict between father and son, but what is missing, on closer examination, is any sign of rivalry for the (female) Other as object of desire. Rather, what is desired is the father's love, in the form of acceptance and approval of the powerfully sexual and intellectual self, as reflected in Jekyll's all-seeing mirror. The withholding of this love engenders rage, but also a continuing, desperate struggle against the return, or the emergence to consciousness, of the father as a bad object. The failure of this struggle is seen at the end, in Jekyll's failure to prevent Hyde from scrawling, in his own hand, "startling blasphemies" in the pages of his own "pious books" and from "burning the letters and destroying the portrait of [his] father" (pp. 50, 75).

The central enigma of the tale then becomes, in Fairbairnian terms, what has happened to the mother, the more thoroughly repressed, female object? The first critic to draw attention to this problem was Stevenson's extremely perceptive friend, Henry James (1888), who put it thus:

> Mr Stevenson achieves his best effects without the aid of the ladies, and *Doctor Jekyll* is a capital example of his heartless independence. . . . in the drama of Mr Hyde's fatal ascendancy they remain altogether in the wing. It is very obvious—I do not say it cynically—that they must have played an important part in his development. The gruesome tone of the tale is, no doubt, deepened by their absence [p. 1252].

Women are indeed excluded from the tale, other than as marginal and accessory characters. These are further split into two sorts: the young, innocent, and victimized (such as the little girl whom Hyde tramples; the romantic maid servant who witnesses his murder of Carew; and Jekyll's whimpering housemaid); and the older, evil, and vindictive (the "harpies" who try to attack Hyde after he tramples the girl, and Hyde's evil, hypocritical landlady). One might say that the first category represents the ideal object, who has to be shielded from sexual knowledge and contact (but may be brutally exposed to it); the second represents the nominally protective but essentially antilibidinal object, who punishes such knowledge and contact. The only possible exciting female object is the adult woman (by implication, a prostitute) who encounters Hyde in his frantic nighttime wanderings before his meeting with Lanyon and offers him a "box of lights." Rather than kindling any flame in him, she evokes the usual aggressive response: he smites her in the face, and she flees (p. 73).

Although these females are thus kept as far as possible from the protagonists and are repelled by force, if necessary, there are indeed hints of a shadowy, less conscious female presence, that is alluded to by way of the other central element in the story that was part of Stevenson's original dream, and which he resolutely refused to alter despite the complaints of some of his first readers. I refer here to the mysterious powders, the white salt that, when dissolved in a pungent, "blood-red liquor," shakes "the very fortress of identity" and effects the bodily transformation from Jekyll to Hyde and back again. This concoction has to be taken orally, and instantly produces intense reactions that are suggestive of an orgasmic, anal birth fantasy; first, "racking pangs," "deadly nausea," and "a horror of the spirit that cannot be exceeded at the hour of birth or death"; followed by lightness, relief, and voluptuous-seeming sensations that are "indescribably new" and "incredibly sweet," although definitely not "innocent" (p. 62). These powders, we learn toward the end of the story, were originally supplied by a firm of chemists named Messrs. Maw. This is a name with unmistakeable oral and maternal connotations. "Maw," after all, means mouth or gullet and, in an older sense, stomach. It is also not very far from "Ma," and in modern, lowland Scots the child's word for mother can be written this way. Yet it is Maw who proves to hold the key to Jekyll/Hyde's fate, for when the original salt runs out, what the firm later supplies turns out not to have the crucial effect. When Jekyll, suspecting the original to have been "impure," sends desperate requests for "some of the old," he is angrily rebuffed by "the man at Maw's" (pp. 44–45). Surely it is not far-fetched to see here hints of a shadowy, archaic, maternal exciting object, who first "impurely" stimulates desire to uncontrollable levels and then abruptly and arbitrarily withholds the means both for gratification and for self-control. The male figures who screen her are ultimately powerless to prevent the return of this terrifying bad object, and all that is left is for the ego to self-destruct sooner than face exposure of the rejected libidinal self that is identified with it.

Were there space, I could cite much other internal evidence to support this reading of *Jekyll and Hyde* as depicting a struggle against the internalized exciting and controlling maternal object. For example, Jekyll himself embodies feminine qualities (he is described as "smooth-faced" with "white and comely" hands) against which the swarthy, hairy, apelike Hyde represents an exaggeratedly masculine defense. Jekyll attempts in vain to castrate and banish this phallic, libidinal ego when, after the murder of Carew, he locks his back door and breaks the key (p. 70). Yet Hyde himself ultimately succumbs to the return of the feminine. When terrified that Lanyon will withhold the means for him to turn safely back into Jekyll, he wrestles "against the approaches of . . . hysteria" (p. 57) and when trapped, on the last night, he is heard to weep "like a woman or a lost soul" in a way that excites pity even in Dr. Jekyll's old servant (p. 48).

In the end, however, both the exciting and the rejecting maternal objects are too terrifying to be admitted to consciousness. After their corresponding egos merge and perish, it is the desexualized, ideal maternal object that prevails and triumphs, in the strangest scene of the book. After Utterson, with the help of Dr. Jekyll's servant, breaks down the door of the doctor's cabinet to find the still twitching, poisoned corpse of Edward Hyde in Henry Jekyll's clothing, he is struck by the uncanny tranquillity of the surroundings:

> There lay the cabinet . . . in the quiet lamplight, a good fire glowing and chattering on the hearth, the kettle singing its thin strain, . . . the things laid out for tea; the quietest room, you would have said and, but for the glazed presses full of chemicals, the most commonplace that night in London [pp. 48–49].

Here, surely, we are back in the idealized nursery of childhood. Cozy, feminine domesticity has won out, and the rebellious, incompatible, sexual, and aggressive selves have been annihilated. They are represented only by the mysterious, empty, upturned mirror, which once revealed to Jekyll/Hyde their multiple transformations but which now shows only the rosy firelight playing on the ceiling.

Much more could be said about the conflicts represented in *Jekyll and Hyde*, about their origins in Stevenson's conventional yet tormented and lonely childhood, and about how they were progressively played out and elaborated in the rest of his work. That will have to wait for another paper. What his fellow Scot, Fairbairn, helps us see more clearly is the primitive fears of maternal—and paternal—rejection and loss, the complex layering of internal objects, and the ego splitting and hysterical dissociation of genital and oral needs that underlie the fractured surface of the story and that ultimately unite its "multifarious denizens" and "warring members."

References

Fairbairn, W. R. D. (1944), Endopsychic structure considered in terms of object relationships. In: *Psychoanalytic Studies of the Personality*. London: Routledge & Kegan Paul, 1952, pp. 82–132.

Freud, S. (1930 [1929]), Civilization and its discontents. *Standard Edition,* 21:64–145. London: Hogarth Press, 1961.

James, H. (1888), Robert Louis Stevenson. In: *Essays on Literature, American and English Writers.* New York: Library of America, 1984, pp. 1231–1255.

Stevenson, R. L. (1885), Letter. In: *The Letters of Robert Louis Stevenson, Vol. 5,* ed. B. A. Booth & E. Mehew. New Haven, CT: Yale University Press, 1995.

——— (1886), *Strange Case of Dr. Jekyll and Mr. Hyde and Weir of Hermiston.* Oxford: Oxford University Press, 1987.

——— (1888). A chapter on dreams. Appendix B. In: *Dr. Jekyll and Mr. Hyde.*

——— (1894), Letter. In: *The Letters of Robert Louis Stevenson, Vol. 8,* ed. B. A. Booth & E. Mehew. New Haven, CT: Yale University Press, 1995.

Swearingen, R. G. (1980), *The Prose Writings of Robert Louis Stevenson.* Hamden, CT: Archon Books.

◆ Part 5 ◆

Clinical Connections

12

Fairbairn's Theory of Depression

Richard L. Rubens

Fairbairn developed a theory of endopsychic structure that turned all of psychoanalytic theory on its head: instead of seeing relationships as the result of drive discharge, his theory saw self-expression in relationship as the foundation of all psychic functioning; instead of seeing growth as synonymous with progressive structuralization, it understood the structuring of the self as being a process of splitting and repression that was fundamentally pathological; and, most crucially, instead of a biological theory of the vicissitudes of the instincts, his theory provided a way of understanding both healthy development and psychopathology in terms of the history of attachments. On the basis of this radically different theory, Fairbairn developed strikingly original and brilliant ways to understand the nature of schizophrenia and schizoid states and the clinical phenomena of hysteria, obsession, phobias, and paranoia. Curiously, however, Fairbairn had very little to say about depression.

What Fairbairn did have to say about depression he adopted directly from Melanie Klein. He never articulated a theory of depression distinctively his own; and it is for this reason that what he had directly to say on the subject is not nearly so compelling as the rest of his theory. As we shall see, he himself became noticeably disinterested in depression as a concept, and it all but disappeared from his later writings. Nevertheless, depression is an extremely important and ubiquitous issue; and, what is more, Fairbairn *indirectly* has a great deal to offer to our understanding of it. I summarize what Fairbairn wrote about depression and I examine what his other contributions offer by way of an implicit "Fairbairnian" theory of this most significant clinical entity.

In the two instances in which Fairbairn took up the question of depression before the emergence of his pivotal object relations based theories in the 1940s—a case study (Fairbairn, 1936) and the paper on aggression (Fairbairn, 1939)—he basically adopted the existing view that aggression and oral sadism were the main issues in the condition.

As I have discussed elsewhere (Rubens, 1996), Melanie Klein's notion of "positions" had a profound effect on Fairbairn's object relations theory. Klein (1935) had posited the existence of two positions, the paranoid and the depressive. These two developmental stages defined the two earliest phases of an infant's object relations. Fairbairn quite predictably had difficulty with Klein's paranoid position, predicated as it was on the death instinct; but he developed in its stead his own pivotal concept of the schizoid position. The depressive position he adopted intact from Klein. He was profoundly influenced by the metapsychological nature of these positions: they were not biologically determined, zonally characterized stages of instinctual discharge; rather, they were fundamental patterns of interaction that characterized a person's relation to an other. Fairbairn clearly felt the potential in this notion of positions for a developmental theory based on object relations rather than on drives. It is also true that Klein's idea allowed him to shift the exploration of the origins of personality and psychopathology away from the Oedipus complex and back into the infant's first year of life. Most importantly, of course, the concept of the schizoid position, which Fairbairn developed on the basis of this theoretical departure of Klein, became the central factor in his understanding of later human development.

While in the early 1940s Fairbairn quickly abandoned the drive-based epigenetic developmental schema of Freud and Abraham, he retained a notion of the oral stage, since this stage, at least, was based on a relationship between a person and a real or "natural" object and could be directly construed as referring to actual relationship between the infant and its mother. He also accepted the division of the oral stage into "the early oral phase and . . . the late oral phase, when the biting tendency emerges and takes its place side by side with the sucking tendency. In the late oral phase there occurs a differentiation between oral love, associated with sucking, and oral hate, associated with biting" (Fairbairn, 1940, p. 24).

About these phases he wrote:

> The emotional conflict which arises in relation to object relationships during the early oral phase takes the form of the alternative, "to suck or not to suck," i.e., "to love or not to love." This is the conflict underlying the schizoid state. On the other hand, the conflict which characterizes the late oral phase resolves itself into the alternative, "to suck or to bite," i.e., "to love or to hate." This is the conflict underlying the depressive state. It will be seen, accordingly, that the great problem of the schizoid individual is how to love without destroying by love, whereas the great problem of the depressive individual is how to love without destroying by hate [Fairbairn, 1941, p. 49].

Fairbairn noted that, in the late oral phase, "The object may be bitten in so far as it presents itself as bad. This means that differentiated aggression, as well as libido, may be directed towards the object. Hence the appearance of the ambivalence which characterizes the late oral phase" (p. 49). And, further,

> the great problem which confronts the individual in the late oral phase is how to love the object without destroying it by hate. Accordingly, since the depressive reaction has its roots in the late oral phase, it is the disposal of his hate, rather than the disposal of his love, that constitutes the great difficulty of the depressive individual. Formidable as this difficulty is, the depressive is at any rate spared the devastating experience of feeling that his love is bad. Since his love at any rate seems good, he remains inherently capable of a libidinal relationship with outer objects in a sense in which the schizoid is not. His difficulty in maintaining such a relationship arises out of his ambivalence. This ambivalence in turn arises out of the fact that, during the late

oral phase, he was more successful than the schizoid in substituting direct aggression (biting) for simple rejection of the object. ... the depressive individual readily establishes libidinal contacts with others; and, if his libidinal contacts are satisfactory to him, his progress through life may appear fairly smooth. Nevertheless the inner situation is always present; and it is readily reactivated if his libidinal relationships become disturbed. Any such disturbance immediately calls into operation the hating element in his ambivalent attitude; and, when his hate becomes directed towards the internalized object, a depressive reaction supervenes [pp. 54–55].

And he concluded in that paper that

no one ever becomes completely emancipated from the state of infantile dependence, or from some proportionate degree of oral fixation; and there is no one who has completely escaped the necessity of incorporating his early objects. It may be consequently inferred that there is present in everyone an underlying schizoid or an underlying depressive tendency, according as it was in the early or in the late oral phase that difficulties—chiefly attended infantile object-relationships. We are thus introduced to the concept that every individual may be classified as falling into one of two basic psychological types—the schizoid and the depressive [p. 56].

The foregoing quotations, from two papers Fairbairn wrote in 1940 and 1941, are all basically he had to say about depression. He reiterated this basic view of the depressive position as late as 1951 (p. 163); but he never had anything further to add to these ideas about depression. So depression was viewed by him as a reaction in which hate and aggression are turned inward against the self when circumstances disturb the object relations of individuals of the depressive type. And this depressive type refers to someone whose basic endopsychic structure is founded on the ambivalence of the late oral phase of development, as opposed to being founded on a schizoid endopsychic structure.

Although Fairbairn never retracted this theory, there was precious little he had to say at all about depression as his theory matured. In his final, succinct summary of his theory in 1963, his only mention of depression is in his statement that the structure of the human psyche "represents a basic schizoid position which is more fundamental than the depressive position described by Melanie Klein" (p. 156), which certainly does nothing positively to embrace the theory.

While the notion of two positions representing, as Klein had believed, two basic underlying organizations of the psyche sounded reasonable, it *never* seemed to Fairbairn that the positions were of equal importance. From the beginning, he saw the schizoid position as far more basic and universal. Eventually he concluded that the schizoid position, representing as it did the fundamental state of the existence of split-off subsystems within the self, was the position that underlay *all* of human psychopathology. And if everyone was schizoid with respect to his underlying endopsychic structure, to whom then would be applied the label depressive? Consequently, Fairbairn began progressively to lose interest in the depressive position, until it all but disappeared from his theory. Moreover, the drive emphasis in the theory of depression, as he inherited it from Klein and Freud, led him to begin to distance himself from the concept of depression all together.

Fairbairn (1944) began to express the opinion that the theory of psychic structure "had suffered from too great a preoccupation with the problem of melancholic depression" (p. 84). He correctly understood that "Freud's theory of mental structure is based in no small measure upon a consideration of the phenomenon of melancholia" (p. 90), but he mistakenly decided that it was this basis that had led Freud away from a more object relations theory and toward a more Oedipus-centered and drive-based notion of psychopathology.

It is true that the observations Freud (1917) made did lead to his developing his theory of the superego and ultimately to his tripartite structural theory. Fairbairn acknowledged that it was with the theory of the superego that Freud came closest to the idea of experience with real people in the world resulting in the formation of an active, functioning structure within the psyche

(1943, pp. 60, 80; 1949, pp. 153–154) and therefore represented the *most* object related arena of Freud's theory. It is also clearly the jumping off point for all later object relations theories. Nevertheless, Fairbairn disagreed about its being the motive for repression, as he had developed a far more compelling explanation based on attachment in the schizoid phase. Thus Fairbairn (1944) took issue with the way "Freud's theory of the superego . . . represents an attempt to trace the genesis of guilt and the instigation of repression to a common source in the Oedipus situation" (p. 93). He was led to conclude that "Freud's theory of the mental apparatus was, of course, developed upon a basis of the depressive position; and it is on a similar basis that Melanie Klein has developed her views. By contrast, it is the schizoid position that constitutes the basis of the theory of mental structure that I now advance" (p. 107).

While I agree that Fairbairn was completely correct to insist on the schizoid position as the basis of psychopathology, and that he was correct in asserting that the depressive position ought not be accorded a similar status in the theory of psychic structure, it is my contention that it is unfortunate that these factors subsequently led Fairbairn to lose interest in the dynamics of depression as they relate to psychic structure. It led to such conclusions as the following about "individuals suffering from true depression or . . . individuals of a depressive type. So far as my experience goes . . . such individuals do not constitute any appreciable part of the analyst's clientele" (1944, p. 91). Such a statement could be made only because Fairbairn was *excluding* "patients suffering from anxiety states, psychoneurotic symptoms and character difficulties" (1944, p. 91) from those to which depression was applicable.

Fairbairn had taken Klein's notion of a paranoid position, separated it from its original foundation in instinct theory, and transformed it into his own notion of a schizoid position. This schizoid position, representing as it did the fundamental pathological outcome of the unavoidable ego splitting that was engendered by intolerably bad experience of the infant with its absolutely important attachments, became the cornerstone of his entire theory of development and of endopsychic structure, as well as of his theory of psychopathology.

In the case of the depressive position, Fairbairn simply left the concept as he had originally inherited it from Klein. He accorded it equal metapsychological status with the schizoid position; and he then lost interest in it because it could not support such a status in his theory. He accepted as fundamental the connection of depression to the aggressive drives and its association with oedipal guilt; and he then proceeded to reject it *because* it was drive based and Oedipus centered. It is understandable that Fairbairn took exception to Freud's explanation of repression in terms of this constellation; but, instead of examining the issue of depression separate from this metapsychological notion, he simply maintained the association and became progressively disinterested.

Had Fairbairn separated depression from this drive-oedipal constellation, he might have recognized the enormous role it plays in his object relations theory. Had he been able to drop Klein's notion of a depressive position and think about depression free from these theoretical underpinnings, Fairbairn would not have viewed it as a relatively uncommon or insignificant factor. Rather he would have viewed it as the ubiquitous and important element it really is in psychopathology.

I am proposing that, in a Fairbairnian theoretical context, it is not necessary or useful to understand depression as a position in the developmental organization of the psyche. Fairbairn's theory of endopsychic structure is entirely adequate without any such addition—which is, of course, precisely why he became uninterested in depression viewed in this way. Nor is it necessary to link depression with oedipal guilt or with internalization conceived of in terms of aggressive instincts. These are the connections that led Fairbairn to become actively antagonistic about the theory of depression. Rather, it is my contention that *depression should be viewed as a very general mechanism of conservation of the endopsychic situation and stasis in the closed system of experiencing the world.*

In this view, depression is a technique for avoiding, or at least denying, the existence of change. As I have written elsewhere (Rubens, 1992), the desire to deny change, and thereby to deny the experience of loss, is one of the deepest of human resistances. This resistance is readily understandable from a Fairbairnian perspective, as it represents the ultimate, closed-system attempt to maintain the existing endopsychic situation.

Fairbairn himself provided some hints in this direction. While he insisted that depression was not an important psychoanalytic phenomenon, he did go on to write that "the familiar term 'depressed' is frequently applied in clinical practice to patients who properly should be described as suffering from a sense of futility" (1944, p. 91). He saw in the schizoid dilemma a threat of loss of the object (and of the self) regardless of whether the individual attempted to love the object or attempted to withhold that love, and thus "the result is a complete *impasse*, which reduces the ego to a state of utter impotence. The ego becomes quite incapable of expressing itself; and, in so far as this is so, its very existence becomes compromised. . . . *the characteristic affect of the schizoid state is undoubtedly a sense of futility*" (1941, p. 51).

It is obvious that the sense of futility Fairbairn was describing *is* what we know as depression. It is not based on a redirection of aggression or on oedipal guilt. It is that state of hopelessness, powerlessness, and immobilization that derives from the individual's inability to relinquish his absolute and immutable hold on his internal objects in the face of events that press for him to do so. On another level, it represents the general attempt to deny any change in the internal state of affairs. Because Fairbairn had assigned depression to a separate stage of development, he had to devise another name for it as it operated on the schizoid level. But his calling it by another name does not alter the fact that it is precisely what I am here defining as depression. And, once the metapsychological supposition that depression be viewed as a distinct and separate developmental position is abandoned, there is no reason why depressive reactions cannot apply directly to schizoid situations.

It is clear that this expanded Fairbairnian understanding of depression allows the view that, like his transitional techniques, depression can function across a broad spectrum of developmental levels. Also like the transitional techniques, the actual manifestations of depression will, of course, be different depending on the level on which they are occurring. Fairbairn was correct to notice a distinct quality in the schizoid sense of futility that was unlike the manifestations of depression on later developmental levels; but he was wrong not to notice its underlying continuity with those other manifestations. Just as he insisted in his 1941 paper that it was an error to assign obsessive and hysterical techniques to specific developmental levels and that instead they could be viewed as existing at varying levels of development, so, too, can his work incorporate a notion of depression across varying levels of development.[1]

Despite the similarities between the process of mourning and that of depression, Freud had understood that there was a fundamental difference between the two. He saw the work of mourning as that of the recognition, acceptance, and ultimate transcendence of loss: "mourning impels the ego to give up the object by declaring the object to be dead and by offering the ego the inducement of continuing to live" (Freud, 1917, p. 257). In depression, however, Freud saw an ambivalence as to whether the work was attempting to sever the tie to the object or to maintain it: "Countless separate struggles are carried on over the object, in which hate and love contend with each other; the

---

[1] It is my belief that what Fairbairn called transitional techniques (which included paranoid and phobic mechanisms, as well as hysterical and obsessive ones) should be understood as styles existing across the entire developmental spectrum of possible self and object configurations—from the schizoid (and even schizophrenic) right through to the highest levels of relationship, in which both parties are recognized and treated as subjects in their own right (i.e., as ends in themselves; cf., Kant, 1785). Although Fairbairn precisely laid the foundation for such an understanding, he did not quite go far enough, in that he viewed these techniques as operating only in the transitional phase. While he made ample provision for seeing this "phase" as covering the great majority of human experience, he still overly limited the theory in this way.

one seeks to detach the libido from the object, the other to maintain this position of the libido against the assault" (p. 256).

If we leave behind the drive-based emphasis on the aggression in this ambivalence, we are left with a distinction that is far more profound: sadness represents the healthy affective recognition and acceptance of loss, whereas depression represents the neurotic attempt to deny loss.

The phenomenological reality of loss in human experience is one of the most centrally defining facts of our finite lives. To be alive means eventually to die. To make an attachment always opens one to the possibility of having to mourn the loss of that attachment. Moreover, as I have written in a paper on tragedy, "the very process of living, that of growth and change, implies continuous loss. To move on to a new stage of life always involves abandoning some prior developmental level; to formulate a higher integration of one's experience always involves relinquishing an earlier integration" (Rubens, 1992, p. 356).

This growing, changing process is what Fairbairn called living in an open-system way.

It was Fairbairn's basic notion that psychopathology represented an attempt to live in a closed system. He wrote, "the maintenance of such a closed system involves the perpetuation of the relationships prevailing between the various ego-structures and their respective internal objects, as well as between one another" (Fairbairn, 1958, p. 380).

His entire theory of endopsychic structure, about which I have written at length elsewhere (Rubens, 1984, 1994), was predicated on the formation of subsystems of the self which attempt simultaneously both to isolate and to preserve certain aspects of experience.

> Fairbairn arrived at the notion that existence as a structure within the self means existence as a split-off subsystem of the self, created and maintained by repression, and owing its existence to the self's inability to deal with some important aspect of its experience that it found intolerable. He termed the process of

establishing such structures "schizoid," because the splitting and repression by which it is constituted invariably diminish the self's capacity for growth and expression, and are therefore pathological [Rubens, 1994, p. 162].

These subsystems of the self are preserved within the psyche as crystallized, closed systems that strive for expression, but always in accordance with the same, unchanging pattern as the template upon which they were based.

Thus Fairbairn's theory potentially provides an understanding of depression exactly along the lines that are here being proposed. To understand that depression has as its *purpose* the maintenance of an attachment not supportable in reality is precisely an idea that would fit with Fairbairn's whole notion of closed systems. And Fairbairn's notion of the nature of attachment in unconscious functioning provides a compelling basis for understanding the resistance to recognizing and dealing with the reality of loss.

Thus depression becomes something that one experiences in response to a loss—or a change—that threatens to affect the shape of one's inner world. The loss may be real or imagined, external or internal, concrete or symbolic. *Any* change that does not fit with the expectations of one's closed system can precipitate depression. It does not matter if the change is in a positive direction. In fact, it is *precisely* changes in the direction of growth that often trigger a depression, because they most directly threaten the internal status quo.

Fairbairn's theory specifically explained how new experience in a deeply important, affectively engaged relationship had the effect of loosening the attachment to the patterns embodied in the subsystems we hold split-off within our psyches; and he knew that *"the maintenance of the patient's internal world as a closed system . . .* [was] *the greatest of all sources of resistance"* (1958, p. 380). The defensive reaction to avoid or deny such change is best dynamically understood as depression in the sense here being discussed, since it not only describes the affective reaction to the threat of the loss of internal objects (and the accompanying fear of the loss of self involved with those objects), but it also explains the active resistive motive of that reaction. In this view, depression is a defense that actively attempts to maintain the stasis of this closed system.

If we examine the clinical manifestations of depression, its nature as a defense of conservation becomes more clear. To be depressed is to feel hopeless, helpless, and powerless in a way that insists *precisely* that nothing can be changed. The experience is that one is powerless to effect any change, helpless in the face of what is happening, and, therefore, without any hope of being able to deal with—or even survive—the loss that is occurring or threatening to occur. And thus depression leads progressively to a complete psychic (and often physical) immobilization, in which any meaningful action—or even continued living—becomes unimaginable. (It is not difficult to see why Fairbairn emphasized the sense of futility in this phenomenon.) Nevertheless, to the psychoanalytic mind such a configuration must suggest the wish that is contained therein: if nothing *can* be changed, then nothing *will* change. If I simply cannot tolerate what is happening to me, it will not happen. And, on perhaps the deepest level, if I refuse to live this new experience as new (Fairbairn would say in an open-system way), I can continue to live the old, closed-system experience of my inner object world.

Loss is an irreducible fact of the external world, however. It occurs despite all efforts to avoid it, and it is a reality despite all manner of attempts to deny it. Thus it is that the depressive is forced to retreat into the closed system of the inner object world. There he can cling to the belief that relationships, objects, and self-states can be maintained in an unchanging, eternal way. Like Freud's (1907) artifacts buried at Pompeii, they are "at once made inaccessible and preserved" (p. 40) by their entombment. Like the lovers frozen in the world of Keats's (1819) "Ode on a Grecian Urn," they are held perfect and undying for all eternity. In this inner world there is no death or loss, but neither is there any growth or change. Pompeii is a dead city; the lovers on the urn never consummate their kiss. The price of this eternity is the absence of vitality and life.

Although depression is a denial of change, the depressed person feels so overwhelmed by the "loss" he is experiencing that he becomes trapped in the experience in a way that refuses to resolve itself. I place the word "loss" in quotes because, while the depressed person is virtually completely immersed in a pre-occupation with "loss," he simply does not experience it as true loss. The reaction does not in any way accept the change of internal state that would of necessity eventuate from the acceptance of the reality of an actual loss. In fact, the depressed reaction actively strives to deny the reality so as to preserve that prior internal state. From Freud on it has been clear that while mourning (or sadness, as I am using the term here) involves an acceptance of loss that results in the person's eventually moving on with the business of living, depression works against a resolution that enables one to go on with one's life.

From this viewpoint, an inverse relationship exists between sadness and depression. Insofar as one is able to experience sadness, one is not depressed; and insofar as one is depressed, one cannot experience sadness. This is true because sadness is a reaction to the acceptance of loss, whereas depression is always a denial of loss. Clinically it is of the utmost importance to differentiate between these two similar-looking but diametrically different states.

The theory of depression being proposed here sheds some light on the old analytic saw that the emergence of depression in a patient in treatment is a positive development. From this view, it is clear that when an analysis has reached a point where some structural change may be in the process of occurring—or "threatening" to occur—it is quite likely that the patient may resort to the defense of depression to forestall or deny that change. Since it is unlikely that such a defense would be mounted were no change "threatening," it is therefore reasonable to view depression as a positive sign in the course of a treatment. Clinically, it is extremely useful to be aware of this mechanism of depression as a defense against some specific progress in treatment, or other area of the patient's life, because it enables one not to be dissuaded from pursuing the direction against which the defense is reacting. Whereas the depression makes the claim that things are going dangerously wrong in the patient's life, it may be crucial to remain aware that this is true *only* from the perspective of the unhealthy desire to maintain the closed system. Such an awareness ultimately may enable analyst and patient alike to find the courage to endure at such moments.

Nevertheless, the truly most positive treatment development is not the emergence of depression—which, after all, represents a resistance to an impending change—but rather that of sadness, which marks the actual acceptance of change. This fact may underlie in a more positive way Freud's rather pessimistic assertion that the end result of analysis is the replacement of neurotic misery by everyday unhappiness (Breuer and Freud, 1893–95, p. 305). Although depression is analyzable, sadness is not. This conclusion is in no way pessimistic, since sadness as we are here understanding it contains within itself the ultimate possibility of resolution, whereas depression specifically struggles to defy resolution.

It is interesting to note that the very thing that makes Fairbairn's theory so conducive to this formulation of depression is partially hinted at in Freud's original theory. Fairbairn insisted that it is the attachment to the internal bad objects—begun in the state of absolute dependence at the stage of primary identification—that is responsible for our reluctance to live life in a more open and healthy way. Freud (1917) concluded that it is the narcissistic element in object choices that predisposes one to depression (p. 249). Recalling Fairbairn's (1941) definition of primary identification as "the cathexis of an object which has not yet been differentiated from the cathecting subject" (p. 34n) it is clear that both men recognized that the inability to experience sadness and loss is based on a primitive level of connection to one's internal objects. Such connections do not permit loss without the threat of an accompanying loss of that portion of the self which is bound up with the object. And both men consequently knew that it is to avoid such loss of self that the depressed person retreats into his inner world, where he can deny the possibility of such loss.

Of course, Freud's theory of narcissism was based on an instinct theory in a way that Fairbairn's notion of primary identification pointedly was not. Nevertheless, it is a fascinating question why Fairbairn did not seize more directly on the object relations orientation inherent in this area of Freud's thinking. It was, after all, in "Mourning and Melancholia" that Freud (1917) developed his famous notion of "the shadow of the object" falling on the ego (p. 249), and the resulting idea of the formation within the self of a subsystem that he was eventually to call the superego. Certainly this notion of such a subsystem of the self having its genesis in an individual's experience with people in the world and then proceeding to have an ongoing, albeit repressed, life within the psyche was an idea that profoundly affected Fairbairn. Although he was to reject the instinctual underpinnings of this concept, shift away from aggression and guilt in the explanation of its origin and substitute instead an emphasis on relationship and positive attachment, and move its timing from the time of the triadic Oedipus complex back to the dyadic relationship of the infant's earliest experience, still, the compelling notion of endopsychic structuring therein contained was pivotal for Fairbairn. He did have to struggle mightily to differentiate his structural theory from that of Freud, and so he had to draw careful distinctions when it came to comparisons with Freud's structural model. Nevertheless, here is one area where I believe his real need carried him in an unfortunate and misguided direction.

Instead of connecting to that object relations oriented thinking apparent in Freud's theory of depression, Fairbairn chose to emphasize his differences from the drive theory and the oedipal orientation that was also linked to it. Unfortunately, because he never successfully separated these aspects from the theory of depression, he never made the connection to the possibilities that are herein being discussed.

It would be a mistake, however, to overlook the contribution Fairbairn did make to the theory of depression as conceived on the level of "superego guilt" and aggression. Fairbairn was quite aware of the way anger at the object was turned inward as aggression against the self in depression. His theory accounted for this phenomenon on two levels. On the deepest level, it explained how a child would identify with and "take on" the intolerable badness of his objects in order to preserve their "goodness" and availability to him (Fairbairn, 1951, p. 164). Using his observations of sexually abused children, Fairbairn described how they would direct their anger and negative accusations against themselves, rather than against the more appropriate objects, on whom, unfortunately, they were absolutely dependent. In this arena he implicitly understood the conservative role of depression in the attempt to avoid and deny loss. That this operation occurred on the schizoid level precluded his recognition that it was depressive, however, owing to his insistence that the term depression applied only to operations at a later stage of development And, at the later stage of development where he could understand this operation to be more directly associated with depression, Fairbairn developed his notion of the moral defense.

The moral defense reworks this maneuver of feeling "bad" rather than "sad" on a level once farther removed. In doing so, it increases the distance from the dangers of intolerable badness by introducing the concept of conditional badness. Instead of dealing with unconditional badness (that state in which the loving attachment itself is seen as destructive), the child develops the notion of conditional badness, or moral badness, which allows him to operate on a less terrifying level (p. 165). It then becomes possible for the child to avoid the loss of his parents' goodness by treating himself as morally bad—an unpleasant situation, but in no way as horrifying as having to see himself as unconditionally, and therefore irredeemably, bad. This state of affairs is how Fairbairn understood guilt and the self-directed aggression of Freud's superego-based notion of depression.

On the level of the moral defensive, Fairbairn clearly understood the sort of defensive and conservative explanation of depression that I am more generally propounding. Depression on this level was understood by him precisely as being a technique for preserving the inner endopsychic situation and insulating the individual against having to deal more directly with its shortcomings. The particular manner in which depression manifests itself on these varying levels is different, but the underlying defensive purpose is the same.

Clinically it is worth a digression at this point to take up the consideration of neurotic guilt from the standpoint of our emerging theory of depression. Authentic, moral guilt is an extremely mature and healthy aspect of human functioning. The ability to feel deep remorse for transgressions one commits against one's understanding of what is morally right and wrong is a developmental achievement of the highest order. This ability is quite distinct, however, from the neurotic expressions of guilt that so plague the discourse of depressed individuals. The Fairbairnian notion of depression that is being elucidated here gives immediate explanation to this phenomenon. The expression of neurotic guilt always represents a measure of self-flagellation (i.e., aggression directed at the self) that clearly is intended to allow a person to maintain the status quo unchanged in the face of some input or awareness that pushes in the direction of change. To wit, the patient who goes on about how guilty he is about his smoking/drug taking/infidelity/overeating is not likely to be expressing the kind of real remorse that leads to changing the prevailing state of affairs. On the contrary, this self-flagellation is actually offered up as some form of penance to allow him to continue in precisely in the same fashion as before. Once again we see that, because the reaction is based on a depressive dynamic, the intent is to preserve the existing situation; were it not so based, there would be far more hope that it could eventuate in the real action and change that depression is a defense against.

In conclusion, let me say that it was most unfortunate that Fairbairn accepted the metapsychological assumptions that placed depression in a competing role with the fundamental schizoid mechanisms that he had come to understand as underlying all psychopathology. This stance resulted in his viewing depression as separate from his basic explanatory paradigm of object-seeking and active attachment and thereby deprived us of what he might have contributed directly to our understanding of depression in this light.

Summary

I have attempted here to develop a theory of depression based on Fairbairn's general approach to psychic functioning. It is a theory that sees depression as a reaction against the awareness of loss or change. In this view, depression works at all times to maintain the closed system of the inner world, protecting the attachments therein at all costs. While, as Fairbairn demonstrated, the structure of this inner world is created and maintained by a process of ego splitting and repression, depression functions to insulate the closed world that was thus created from the loss and change that is a part of lived experience in the external world. Depression attacks a person's sense of vitality, efficacy, and even will to live in order to enforce a sense of stasis and a feeling of inertia designed to reassure one that the inner world need not change because it feels as if it cannot change.

Just as Fairbairn's basic theory has enabled us to work directly with the active attachments that underlie other forms of psychopathology, so too does this Fairbairnian view of depression allow us to work with depression as it represents an active attempt to defend these attachments. Therein lies the tremendous power of this understanding as a clinical tool: it provides a way to penetrate beneath the defensive mechanism of depression to the neurotic closed systems that it defends. If depression is understood as the denial of loss in order to maintain the integrity of a closed system, it loses its ability to resist the process of opening up such systems. If the self-denigration and self-punishment of depression are seen as mechanisms designed to protect the relationships with bad internal objects, they cease to obscure the process of confronting the true nature of these attachments. If the helplessness, hopelessness, and powerlessness of the depressed person are recognized as attacks on that person's positive capacity for growth at just those moments when growth is a possibility, it makes it less likely that they will succeed in undermining that process.

Such an understanding of depression is also in accordance with the more phenomenological realities of this clinical entity, for it explains how it can exist at every level of development and within any character style. I think it is an understanding Fairbairn would have liked.

References

Breuer, J. & Freud, S. (1893–95), Studies on hysteria. *Standard Edition*, 2. London: Hogarth Press, 1955.

Fairbairn, W. R. D. (1936), The effect of a king's death upon patients under analysis. In: *Psychoanalytic Studies of the Personality*. London: Routledge & Kegan Paul, 1952, pp. 223–229.

——— (1939), Is aggression an irreducible factor? In: *From Instinct to Self, Vol. 2*, ed. E. F. Birtles & D. E. Scharff. Northvale, NJ: Aronson, 1994, pp. 253–263.

——— (1940), Schizoid factors in the personality. In: *Psychoanalytic Studies of the Personality*. London: Routledge & Kegan Paul, 1952, pp. 3–27.

——— (1941), A revised psychopathology of the psychoses and psychoneuroses. In: *Psychoanalytic Studies of the Personality*. London: Routledge & Kegan Paul, 1952, pp. 28–58.

——— (1943), The repression and the return of bad objects (with a special reference to the "war neuroses"). In: *Psychoanalytic Studies of the Personality*. London: Routledge & Kegan Paul, 1952, pp. 59–81.

——— (1944), Endopsychic structure considered in terms of object-relationship. In: *Psychoanalytic Studies of the Personality*. London: Routledge & Kegan Paul, 1952, pp. 82–136.

———— (1949), Steps in the development of an object-relations theory of the personality. In: *Psychoanalytic Studies of the Personality*. London: Routledge & Kegan Paul, 1952, pp. 152–161.

———— (1951), A synopsis of the development of the author's views regarding the structure of the personality. In: *Psychoanalytic Studies of the Personality*. London: Routledge & Kegan Paul, 1952, pp. 162–179.

———— (1952), *Psychoanalytic Studies of the Personality*. London: Routledge & Kegan Paul.

———— (1958), On the nature and aims of psychoanalytic treatment. *Internat. J. Psycho-Anal.*, 39:374–385.

———— (1963), Synopsis of an object-relations theory of the personality. In: *From Instinct to Self, Vol. 1*, ed. E. F. Birtles & D. E. Scharff. Northvale, NJ: Aronson, 1994, pp. 155–156.

Freud, S. (1907), Delusions and dreams in Jensen's *Gradiva*. *Standard Edition*, 9:7–95. London: Hogarth Press, 1959.

———— (1917), Mourning and melancholia. *Standard Edition*, 14:243–258. London: Hogarth Press, 1957.

Kant, I. (1785), *Foundations of the Metaphysics of Morals*, trans. L. W. Beck. New York: Liberal Arts Press, 1959.

Keats, J. (1819), "Ode on a Grecian Urn." In: *Selected Poems and Letters*, ed. D. Bush. Cambridge, MA: Riverside Press, 1959.

Klein, M. (1935), A contribution to the psychogenesis of manic-depressive states. In: *Love, Guilt and Reparation & Other Works 1921–1945*. London: Hogarth Press, 1975.

Rubens, R. L. (1984), The meaning of structure in Fairbairn. *Internat. Rev. Psychoanal.*, 11:429–440.

———— (1992), Psychoanalysis and the tragic sense of life. *New Issues in Psychology*, 10:347–362.

———— (1994), Fairbairn's structural theory. In: *Fairbairn and the Origins of Object Relations*, ed. J. S. Grotstein & D. B. Rinsley. New York: Guilford, pp. 151–173.

———— (1996), Review essay: The unique origins of Fairbairn's theories. *Psychoanal. Dial.*, 6:413–435.

Scharff, D. E. & Birtles, E. F., eds. (1994a), *From Instinct to Self, Vol. 1*. Northvale, NJ: Aronson.

———— (1994b), *From Instinct to Self, Vol. 2*. Northvale, NJ: Aronson.

13

Structural Sources of Resistance in Battered Women
A Fairbairnian Analysis

David P. Celani

Fairbairn theorized that all resistance was a consequence of "obstinate" and often self-destructive attachments to internal objects that are both intolerably frustrating and equally intolerably exciting. As Ogden (1983) has noted, Fairbairn (1943) was the first to conceptualize resistance in terms of attachments to internalized objects, and his radical view represents a complete paradigm shift when compared with the classical model of resistance that he was challenging. Resistance to change (and to the therapist's interventions) becomes a critical issue when working with repeatedly battered women because this patient population displays the most extreme form of attachment to bad objects, one that leads to at least two million serious physical assaults every year (Browne, 1992).

When taken as a whole, Fairbairn's model is a theory of repetition compulsion. According to Fairbairn (1944), the basic developmental situation that leads to eventual repetitions is the child in relationship to an unsatisfying object, one that frustrates his legitimate needs by depriving him of essential gratification and then exciting him intolerably with the promise of future gratification. The extremely frustrating experiences (temptation followed by rejection) that the child endures at the hands of his objects cannot be avoided because of his absolute dependency on them as well as his inability either to reject or to change them. The frustration of his legitimate needs causes an ever-increasing internal deficit, and the child compensates by grasping on to whatever objects that enter into his experience:

> Fairbairn's thinking stems from the idea that a human being's sanity and survival depend on object-relatedness, and a person experiences the terror of impending annihilation when he feels that all external and internal object ties are being severed. Therefore, he clings desperately to any object tie (external or internal), even ones that are experienced as bad, when that is all that is available [Ogden, 1983, p. 104].

The neglected child internalizes his object in an atmosphere of desperation. His whole sense of security depends on how tightly he holds on to these objects in his inner world. His inner objects are more controllable than are objects in the unpredictable external world, so these object relationships are depended on almost completely.

The absoluteness of the child's dependency needs impel him to erect powerful defenses that help him remain attached to an unsatisfying object, one who is in reality abusing or neglecting him. The fundamental defense mechanism that protects the child from experiencing painful rejections as being directed toward him is the splitting defense, which Fairbairn (1944) defined as a specific and selective use of repression. Splitting is essentially forced disintegration, based on the child's need to remain consciously unaware of how severely he is being rejected. The split inner structure helps the child to minimize the relationship-destroying negative pole of ambivalence by allowing him to relate to the rejecting parent as if he were an entirely separate person from the gratifying parent. This lack of awareness of the single identity of his frustrating/exciting parent then preserves his dependency relationship on his objects.

The structure that is created by the splitting of the two aspects of the unsatisfying object relationship produces two mutually exclusive part-self and part-object constellations. The part-self of the child, which relates only to the rejecting aspects of the object, was originally called the internal saboteur (and later changed to antilibidinal ego) by Fairbairn (1944). The second part-self, which relates to the exciting and promising aspects of the object, was called the libidinal ego. Each part-self/part-object constellation remains isolated from its opposite. Thus, the libidinal ego is completely unaware of the rejecting aspects of the object, and it can remain securely attached to the exciting object as long as the rejecting object–antilibidinal ego remain split off. Conversely, the antilibidinal ego can passionately hate and despise the rejecting object without disturbing the libidinal ego's unrealistic hope.

Applying Fairbairn's Model to the Analysis of the Dynamics of Battered Women

The most common personality organization of battered women is the borderline personality disorder (Celani, 1994). Splitting in this population is so severe, and the central ego so weak, that one or the other of the subegos can emerge and displace the attenuated central ego and dominate the patient's consciousness. This clinical observation is in contrast to Fairbairn's (1944) view of the dynamics of splitting; he believed that the central ego, which develops in relation to an appropriately gratifying object (the ideal object), keeps both subegos and their related objects under repression. Work with battered women suggests that many extremely disturbed patients have less central ego than Fairbairn observed in his, perhaps healthier, patients. Patients with severely attenuated central egos have enormous difficulty keeping the two powerful subegos under repression. Extremely frustrating developmental experiences increase the strength of the two subegos (while simultaneously decreasing the size and power of the central ego) because the child has experienced great numbers of interactions with her objects that were either excessively tempting or exceedingly frustrating. The two subegos must develop in parallel because the more deprived the child is, the more she must exaggerate the alluring aspects of the object. Ultimately, extremely poor histories of appropriate parenting produce borderline adults who appear to operate with one or the other subegos as the conscious ego (Celani, 1993), while the tenuous and debilitated central ego exerts almost no influence of its own. The rapid repression and derepression of the two sub-egos (unmodulated by the central ego) produce the characteristic extreme and opposite feeling states that dominate the borderline patient's experience of the world.

Fairbairn often emphasized his patients' inner worlds and paid less attention to the ways that they were transformed into external reality. This is a second difference that becomes evident when working with a battered woman because she is actively engaged in a relational struggle with an external object that exactly fits the template in her internal structure. So accurate is this translation that the terrors, monsters, and devils of childhood that Fairbairn was so fond of describing are reencountered in the patient's external world.

Most battered women come from families in which there is no more violence than in normal controls (Hotaling and Sugarman, 1990). However, the hurts, disappointments, and, conversely, the excitements were so extreme during childhood that many women unconsciously choose men who will bring the acute and exaggerated emotionality of their inner world to life in their relational world. This model accounts for the legions of battered women who far exceed their male partners in level of education and social skills.

A primitive and violent batterer produces an immediate reality that matches the inner world of the abused woman patient. Typically, the batterer stimulates excessive hope in his partner by exaggerating his love for her. This causes her libidinal ego to become the dominant (conscious) part-self. That is, his behavior matches her expectation of an exciting object, and this provokes her libidinal ego to become the dominant ego. Then, in rapid succession, he abuses her and becomes an unambivalently experienced rejecting object. The battering provokes the repression of her libidinal ego and the derepression of her enraged antilibidinal ego (Celani, 1994). This continuous and rapid alternation of one split part-self/part-object and the opposite part-self/part-object constellation was characteristic of her childhood relational world.

The size and power of the two subegos in a battered woman take up territory normally occupied by the central ego. The absence of a strong central ego results in a dilemma for the patient. Simply put, the central ego is not strong enough to act as the mediator of reality for any length of time, and one or another of the subegos is pressed into the role of conscious ego by default. The central ego is weak because it has experienced too few appropriate, gratifying interactions with a good object and therefore has few (if any) positive introjects. Without supportive introjects, it is vulnerable to constant abandonment and collapse the moment the negative pole of ambivalence is experienced. This lack of a central sense of self provides a great technical problem for the therapist, who is frequently under pressure to keep the patient from being further abused. The only way that the patient can effectively escape from her abuser is to develop a strong central ego through internalizations of the therapist. Yet most of the positive introjects offered by the therapist are initially resisted, split, and destroyed by the patient's internal structure.

Two Categories of Resistance: Relational Resistances and Self-Resistances

Rubens (1984) was specific when he cited the two categories of loss experienced by patients when they successfully give up their long-standing relational patterns. These two fundamental sources of loss will be encountered by an analyst when working with the abused woman patient:

> The loss is twofold: most obviously, it involves the loss of the object component, which is felt as having made possible the

particular internal relationship; and, perhaps more importantly, albeit less obviously, it involves a sense of loss of self, in so far as part of the self had been defined in the crystallization around the particular paradigm [p. 434].

I have categorized these two different types of resistance into relational resistances and self-resistances. Relational resistances involve the loss of the relationship between a part-self and its specific object, and these resistances are obvious when one is working with battered women. It is the hopeful relationship between the libidinal ego and the exciting object that is at risk if the exciting object is lost. Conversely, it is the reforming, or revenging, relationship between the antilibidinal ego and the rejecting object that will be lost if the rejecting object is lost.

The second class of resistances involve loss of the self, or, more accurately, loss of part-selves, and these resistances show up in more subtle ways in the transference. Each of the four substructures is a relatively complete dynamic self that has the capacity to feel, think, plan, and react to external events; and each resists giving up its individual identity. Second, the two organic selves (the libidinal and antilibidinal egos) have a deeply embedded, meaning-sustaining role. Each of these subegos is absolutely rigid to the point that it resists all feedback from external objects that does not match its expectations. These subegos will create, through transference, an external relational world that mirrors the inner structure even in the absence of an exciting or rejecting object. Their ability to construct reality prevents change by distorting external objects and thus convincing the person that she is always in the identical relationship to others as she experienced in her development.

Relational Resistances Based on Fear of Loss of the Object

Resistance to change based on the fear of loss of the object can originate from either the libidinal or the antilibidinal subego.

The libidinal subego fears loss of hope in the exciting part of the bad object. This is more often the obvious source of resistance to change than of the resistance from the antilibidinal ego's attachment (by way of attempts to reform, conquer, or punish the rejecting part-object) in the battered woman patient. In practice, both attachments contribute in equal proportion to the resistance to change.

The abused woman patient who is in the grip of her libidinal ego is impossible to dissuade from the obviously destructive attachment to her abusive object. Most commonly, the desire of these patients to return to their abusers is based on a libidinal ego fantasy. Often, they will see the potential for love and gratification from an intimate connection with their unambivalently perceived exciting object. The patient may misperceive a moment of contrition on her partner's part as evidence of a hidden loving nature. The libidinal ego is often so powerful and unrealistic that the therapist will only create hostility and increased resistance if he points out the history of the relationship, which contradicts the patient's fantastic views when her libidinal ego is dominant (Celani, 1994).

If a patient dominated by her libidinal ego is prevented from returning to her abuser, she will risk the collapse of her entire internal structure. This is particularly true in the early stages of therapy, before she has been able to internalize the therapist as a good object to support her when she is separated from her desperately needed abuser. Armstrong-Perlman (1991) noted that many hospitalizations are the result of the collapse of the hopeful relationship between the libidinal subego and its exciting object. When hope breaks down, the patient is often overwhelmed with fear, anguish, and the loss of her sense of self.

The second category of loss of an object that is resisted by a battered woman patient is based on the attachment of her antilibidinal ego to the rejecting part of the bad object. In general, the attachment to this part of the batterer is less apparent than is the libidinal ego's attachment to his exciting part. Fairbairn (1944) recognized the importance of and strength of attachments through hate: "The individual is extremely reluctant to abandon his original hate, no less than his original need, of his original objects in childhood" (p. 117).

The antilibidinal ego is suffused with rage, a desire to reform the rejecting object, and vengeance. It is not only hurt, but also fascinated by and attracted to the rejection that it experiences. Many battered women are engaged in intense, hate-filled struggles that appear more serious than the women's childhood histories would suggest. As Fairbairn (1944) noted, however, the child has to hold back her expressions of rage in order not to make the object on whom she is dependent love her even less. In adulthood, the rejecting object is externalized and experienced as unambivalently bad, and so the rage can emerge without restraint.

Many abused women express incredulity that their batterers are not being stopped from battering them by the formal sources of authority in the culture. Often, when the authorities are indifferent or slow to come to her aid, a battered woman will take it upon herself to punish the man who has repeatedly jeopardized her life. The antilibidinal ego is so determined to reform the rejecting object (as opposed to avoiding or fleeing) that the reality that the batterer is far beyond the victim's power to reform is lost on her. This lack of realism is based on the infantile nature of the antilibidinal ego as well as the defensive notion of a just and orderly universe (Kopp, 1978; Stark, 1994). It is also related to the ancient hope of this part-ego that she could reform her parents and somehow force them to love her.

Levenson (1972) has described a milder, but psychologically identical, antilibidinal attachment to a rejecting object in his analysis of Alexander Portnoy, protagonist of Philip Roth's (1967) *Portnoy's Complaint*. Levenson (1972) notes that Portnoy is extremely resistant to interpretations; in fact, they seem to be incorporated and become part of his resistance:

> He is the psychoanalytic Anti-Christ. He has total recall of every traumatic childhood incident. . . . He is aware of the incestuous hate love relationship with his mother Sophie, knows all about his ambivalent feelings toward his up-tight, and compulsive,

tortured father, and still he suffers. . . . Poor Portnoy is the whole
man manqué. He is not artist enough to make a new environment for himself, a new world. He can only long, like fallen
Lucifer, for a lost paradise [p. 105].

If we were to apply Fairbairn's model to Levenson's example,
Portnoy would be seen as too attached to his antilibidinal relationship with his rejecting object mother and, to a lesser extent,
his libidinal hopes for a good and gratifying father. His central
ego is not potent enough to give up the comforting inner struggle between these psychic structures and is completely unable
to create a new life for him, free of his bad objects.

The patient's early deprivation requires that the relationship
between the rejecting object and the antilibidinal ego continue
on uninterrupted, or she will be plunged into emptiness and
possible ego disintegration. This loss would destroy her understanding of herself in relation to the universe, which is a a completely intolerable consequence. The actual goal of her struggle
with the batterer is to keep her inner object relationships
unchanged, thus allowing her to remain grounded in the only
objects that she could internalize in childhood. There is no victory sought or desired in this struggle. If the antilibidinal ego
reforms the rejecting object, then this aspect of the early ego
(invested in and identified with the original frustrating parent)
will be destroyed along with the comforting and sanity-support-
ing struggle. Conversely, if the rejecting object destroys the
antilibidinal ego, then this crucial and massive part of the self
will be lost. The batterer is a psychologically perfect representation of the internalized rejecting object, one that the patient's
antilibidinal ego can hate with ferocity and vengeance and one
that appears to be absolutely immune to change.

The following example of a patient in once-a-week treatment
illustrates relational resistance to change. This particular patient
was selected because she was simultaneously struggling with
her family of origin as well as with her current batterer.

Caroline was a 51-year-old mother of two adult children who
came to therapy in order to resolve her relationship with a

batterer as well as cope with an immediate crisis with her family of origin. The topic that most occupied her mind was an upcoming family gathering to celebrate her sister's wedding, from which her outspoken and independent daughter had been banned. Her daughter had spent a summer with her grandparents (Caroline's parents) at their beach-front home, helping them do chores around their house and enjoying the beach atmosphere. She was an idealistic and outspoken young woman who soon came into conflict with her apparently benign but covertly overbearing and tyrannical grandmother. Her grandmother ran the extended family with a combination of techniques that included bribes and special favors, actual neediness that provoked rescue by one or the other of her four adult children, and threats of banishment for those who challenged her version of reality. Her success was based on a long history of family dysfunction that had left her four children internally empty and vulnerable to her control.

This was not the case for her granddaughter, who had not been raised with the same combination of deprivation and indulgence. She and her granddaughter became embroiled in open conflict as the summer wore on, owing to the granddaughter's increasingly direct challenges to the way her grandmother treated her oldest son, who was a chronic alcoholic and who lived in a basement apartment. This middle-aged man (brother to my patient) was spectacularly dependent and unable to care for himself, and he provided a needed service to the family system by serving as the target of his mother's negative projections. My patient's daughter brought her grandmother's rage down on her by writing an open letter to all the family members detailing her perceptions of her grandmother's abuse of her uncle and describing her grandmother's techniques for intimidating the family members.

My patient was covertly delighted at her daughter's exposure of the family corruption. It, however, placed her in an impossible dilemma, as she could not tolerate the feelings of abandonment that would result if she did not attend the all-important wedding. The wedding acted as a potent exciting object in Caroline's inner world, as it tempted her with the promise that she would feel cared for and be a part of a loving family. Like Fairbairn's (1943) patient who dreamed that he was starving and saw a bowl of chocolate pudding next to his mother (pudding that he realized was filled with poison), my patient went to the wedding and felt sickened as a result. She reported that, during the first two days of the family gathering, she had almost called me to demand to know why I was trying to force her to believe that her family was "bad." This libidinal view of her object world was replaced by its antilibidinal reciprocal when her inebriated mother went on a tirade about her oldest son's absence from the wedding rehearsal. The mother was physically restrained by a family friend, who prevented her from going downstairs to confront and punish her adult son. This family friend, who was nearly 70, had engaged in an exploitative covert sexual relationship with Caroline 20 years earlier, and he suggested that they resume their liaison. These two events, both typical of her years at home, occurring in rapid succession, provoked the repression of her libidinal ego and the derepression of her antilibidinal ego, and she remained in that ego state during the duration of her visit. During the wedding itself, she felt enraged and repulsed by her mother, who seemed to be getting away with another enormous deception, as she presented herself to the world as a model matriarch, despite the fact that she had threatened to kill her son the night before.

Caroline's relationship with her abuser was also characterized by extreme splitting, as well as primitive emotionality, which mirrored her rage and excitement from childhood. Her abuser was an uneducated wallpaper hanger, 20 years her junior, in contrast to my patient, who worked as the registrar of a junior college. He had a long history of petty drug offenses and, not surprisingly, still lived with his parents, after failing to earn enough to live on his own. Caroline's relationship with him, which lasted for two years, jeopardized her position as registrar, and so it was carried on covertly, much as her earlier sexual liaison with the older friend of her parents had been. There was no evidence, direct or indirect, of inappropriate sexual boundary violations with her father. Rather, her covert affairs were an unconscious imitation of him, and thus a way of getting closer to her father, who had consistently ignored her. Her father's affairs were known to all the children, as they each worked for him in his insurance agency during their college years, and each was pressed into the conspiracy to keep his affairs a "secret" from their mother.

Caroline's relationship with her battering partner consisted of heavy drinking and intense, excessive sexuality during those periods when they both saw each other as exciting objects. This mutuality of perception was, however, often short lived and would shift unpredictably when her partner would suddenly fear losing her to an imagined rival. His perception of her would suddenly shift from an exciting to a rejecting object. He would then accuse her of infidelity, and this accusation would often deteriorate into battering and imprisonment. The longest incident of imprisonment lasted two days and was known to her two similarly battered female friends. These two friends negotiated a one-hour release for her during which Caroline was allowed to visit with them in a coffee shop. She could have easily escaped, but she refused. These imprisonments were not characterized by constant battering; rather there was an alternation between libidinal ego dominance in both partners, which was expressed by frenzied sexuality, followed by an antilibidinal perception (originating in the batterer) that transformed my patient into a rejecting object, which provoked violence toward her. The batterings included punching, choking, and slapping. This externalized frenzy of fast-shifting, highly charged perceptions was a recreation of the hope and despair that pervaded much of her childhood. Even when the patient broke free from her frustrating and exciting batterer, she continued to engage in "drive-bys" for two years. These were searches of the neighborhoods where her now ex-boyfriend typically worked. If she found his truck in front of a particular house, she would alter her route in order to pass by the house in the hope of catching a glimpse of him. This behavior continues sporadically at the present time and indicates that her libidinal ego is still active.

This patient's fascination with, and attachment to, her bad object allowed both of her part-selves to emerge in relation to promising and rejecting behaviors from her batterer. This alternation of intolerable longing with absolute despair was, for Fairbairn, the essential aspect of the repetition compulsion. Interestingly, the primitiveness of her behavior and the emergence of sex and aggression as the two fundamental categories of behavior superficially supports a more classical view of the basis of the human personality. As Rubens (1996) has noted, however, Fairbairn did not deny the importance of sex and aggression, but rather he put them in a relational context: "Rejecting Freud's drive theory did not mean ignoring the deep, primitive forces that operate within the personality, but rather creating a more relationally determined structure for understanding their presence in the psyche" (p. 428).

The example of Caroline illustrates this point exactly. Her failed relationships with her parents forced her to use the splitting defense in order to remain attached to them. This split structure, suffused with inordinate (and primitive) hope and enormous despair, guided the recreation of her inner relational world with her batterer. Her behavior is not a window into or a model of the interior world of well-functioning people. Rather, it represents the remnants of human relating after all vestiges of whole-object relationships have been abandoned. As Bromberg (1996) has noted, "We do not treat patients . . . to cure them of something that was done to them in the past; rather, we are trying to cure them of what they still do to themselves and to others in order to cope with what was done to them in the past" (p. 70). Thus, the major thrust of treatment in therapy with battered women is to focus on reducing their splitting by gradually introducing whole-object relationships into the therapeutic dyad.

Resistance to Change from the Self-Structures

I have divided this second category of resistances into two parts. The first category of self-resistance results from each of the structures fighting against annihilation as a response to the growth of the central ego as a consequence of psychotherapy. The second group of self-resistances manifest themselves as transferences, and these are the result of rigid role enactments by the two principal part-selves, regardless of the actions of the objects.

Each of the split structures individually resists losing its separate identity. The following quote by Ogden (1983) illustrates the struggle of the internalized rejecting object to remain "alive"; however each of the four structures can similarly resist the loss of its separate identity:

> The suborganization of ego identified with the object experiences as much need for object relatedness as the self component of the internal object relationship. . . . The object component may taunt, shame, threaten, lord-over, or induce guilt in its object (the self component of the internal relationship) in order to maintain connectedness with the self component. These efforts at control over the self-component become greatly intensified when there is a danger of the bond being threatened, e.g., by a more mature form of relatedness to the therapist [p. 106].

This is a perfect example of a unilaterally generated self-resistance. The internalized rejecting object will redouble its efforts to remain in a relationship with the antilibidinal ego when the patient begins to lose interest in the rejecting voice of her original objects. The internalized rejecting object comprises remnants of the frustrating original parents that have coalesced into a structure in the patient's interior world. This subego is invested in, and identified with, the role and outlook on life of one or both of the original parents. Paradoxically, a piece of the patient's own ego becomes completely allied with the once external parents and after internalization it attacks the host.

Because the internalized rejecting object is actually part of the patient's (now split) ego structure, it has a distinct identity, and it resists loss of significance in the interior world.

Typically, a therapist will encounter this type of resistance after considerable time, when most traces of the antilibidinal, ego-rejecting object struggle are no longer apparent. The patient's central ego-ideal object relationship with the therapist challenges and reduces the bitterness of the antilibidinal ego, and it becomes less responsive to the taunts of the rejecting object. Simply put, the therapist's opinion of the patient has become more important than the internalized relationship.

This waning interest on the part of the antilibidinal ego in the rejecting object will provoke this structure into a frenzy of activity. The sudden struggle for survival of this subself will appear in the transference as an unprovoked regression. It can take two forms, either as a sudden antilibidinal reaction to previously ignored internal criticism or, as a patient enactment of the role of her punitive and rejecting internalized object. The patient's sudden aggressive attack can force the therapist into the position once occupied by her antilibidinal ego. This transference pattern (and the therapist's countertransference) can be the major source of subjective information about the patient's early relational experiences.

The second source of self-resistances in abused women patients are generated by the existence, activities, and rigid roles of the two part-selves, which may constitute almost all of her conscious personality. Each subego derives meaning from a task that was critical to it as it related to either the exciting or the rejecting aspect of the bad object. The libidinal subego's task is to win the love of an object who promises to gratify its needs but is maddeningly out of reach. The antilibidinal subego is motivated by a revenge-driven desire to reform or punish the rejecting aspect of the bad object for not fulfilling the implied promise of the parent–child relationship. The loss of these self-defining tasks, which are always expressed in object relationships, is equivalent to the loss of almost the entirety of the patient's self. Once again, the importance of these two subselves is based on the lack of a strong and coherent central ego. Rubens (1984) notes that each of the subegos has a rigid pattern of behavior when it is in the dominant position, and each derives meaning from the struggle to be loved by the tantalizing exciting object, or to defeat the rejecting object:

> There exists, at the very structural foundation of these subsidiary selves, an attachment to some negative aspect of experience which is felt as vital to the definition of the self. . . . The raison d'être of these endopsychic structures is to continue living out these "bad" relationships [p. 434].

Fairbairn (1958) outlined this same principle, but in general terms: "I have now come to regard as *the greatest of all sources of resistance—viz. the maintenance of the patient's internal world—as a closed system*" (p. 380). This is possible only if the subegos distort reality to the extent that the established relationships between the internalized part-selves and their respective objects are recreated in the external world. Fairbairn was more concerned with internalized relationships, but clinical experience clearly indicates that the internalized relationships are projected into actual external objects, and these powerful projections allow the entire inner structure to remain intact. Thus, the subegos distort reality so that the patient sees certain objects as containing the possibility of love and gratification where none was offered, and small, even unintentional rejections from others will be reacted to in an intense and personal way.

These ferocious and rigid roles, either libidinally based pursuits of exciting objects or antilibidinally based battles with rejecting objects, give patients a sense of vitality, purposefulness, and meaning that has often been ignored, perhaps because Freud (1920) saw repetitions as motivated by the death instinct. In reality, an abused woman is energized while she is either pursuing inappropriate exciting objects for love or attempting to reform or destroy her rejecting object with aggression. These passionately enacted roles will emerge in the transference when one is working with an abused woman patient, and she will transform the therapeutic endeavor into yet another version of her inner world. The therapist is not only misidentified, but pressured and set up to respond in the reciprocal role to the part-self in the patient that is dominant. It is simply impossible to resist being transformed by the patient's intense pressure, as Levenson (1972) has noted: "In any engagement with another person, one enters a series of isomorphic transformations of great significance. The therapist and patient become each other's creations" (p. 185). For example, the most obvious and often most intense transformation of the therapist who is working with a battered woman patient is for the therapist to become an actual rescuer. But the patient who has been battered repeatedly has also been rescued repeatedly by others, and this transformation defeats the Fairbairnian therapist's fundamental goal of increased ego strength and a shift in the patient's attachments from bad to good objects.

In terms of Fairbairn's inner structures, an abused woman patient will transform the therapist into an exciting object by seeing him through the eyes of her libidinal ego, regardless of his actual behavior. Her transformation of the therapist's role is based on her covert fantasy (assuming a male therapist) of him as a rescuer, protector, possible mate, father to her children, and benevolent parent, all of which thoroughly obscures and negates his actual role. Extreme transformations of the therapist serve as a major resistance because the patient misinterprets and is disappointed by nearly everything the therapist does. Mitchell (1993) discusses this point, which was originally made by Sass and Wolfolk: "The value of a good interpretation is not a correspondence with some external, objective truth but rather in a correspondence of coherences, the tendency of analyst and analyzand to organize experience in similar ways" (p. 241).

The actions and roles of the two subegos can keep the patient on a completely different plane of reality from that of the therapist, and therefore the therapist's actions and intentions will be completely negated. An example of this distortion is a patient who noticed my bicycle behind the office building and asked where I rode. She then bought bicycles for herself and her two children and frequented the public bike path where I mentioned that I occasionally rode. Several months later she bitterly complained that she never saw me riding there. This patient switched from a libidinal ego view of me during her search to an antilibidinal view when she could no longer tolerate the frustration of not finding me. This extreme lack of correspondence is common in the treatment of battered women. More sophisticated patients will accept the therapist's interpretative stance, but their extreme libidinal view will exaggerate his or her professional skills. A battered woman patient has to cling to an extreme libidinal ego view of the therapist because she cannot bear any hint of negative information that might provoke a sudden split into an antilibidinal view of the therapist and see him as a completely rejecting object.

To describe the battered woman patient's antilibidinal view of the therapist (despite his or her appropriate interventions) as a source of resistance is a major understatement. Therapeutic work with this population is always threatened by the sudden splitting of the therapist into a rejecting object. The patient's central ego is so attenuated that minute levels of negative ambivalence can overwhelm it (or, alternatively, the libidinal ego if it is in the dominant position) and provoke the antilibidinal ego to become dominant. Generally, the patient senses that, if she were to experience the therapist as a completely rejecting object, then therapy would cease and never resume, which does occasionally happen. As a protection against this eventuality, the patient's antilibidinal ego will shift its focus onto the badness of her batterer (to whom she still may return between sessions), or to battles with social service agencies over custody of her children, or toward the authorities for their poor and unresponsive treatment of her problems. An initial strategy that can help the patient remain in therapy is to keep her antilibidinal ego focused outside the therapy dyad until a large number of positive introjects are internalized and stabilize the patient's central ego (Celani, 1993). When this has been accomplished, the central ego can remain dominant in the face of normal ambivalence, which both diminishes the chance of a sudden split into the antilibidinal ego and increases the probability of a psychic reorganization based on good internalized objects.

References

Armstrong-Perlman, E. (1991), The allure of the bad object. *Free Association*, 2:343–356.

Bromberg, P. M. (1996), Hysteria, dissociation, and cure: Emmy von N revisited. *Psychoanal. Dial.*, 6:55–71.

Browne, A. (1992), Violence against women: Relevance for medical practitioners. *J. Amer. Med. Assn.*, 267:184–189.

Celani, D. P. (1993), *The Treatment of the Borderline Patient*. Madison, CT: International Universities Press.

——— (1994), *The Illusion of Love*. New York: Columbia University Press.

Fairbairn, W. R. D. (1943), The repression and the return of bad objects (with special reference to the "war neuroses"). In: *Psychoanalytic Studies of the Personality*. London: Routledge & Kegan Paul, 1952, pp. 59–81.

——— (1944), Endopsychic structure considered in terms of object-relationships. In: *Psychoanalytic Studies of the Personality*. London: Routledge & Kegan Paul, 1952, pp. 82–136.

——— (1958), On the nature and aims of psychoanalytical treatment. *Internat. J. Psycho-Anal.*, 19:374–385.

Freud, S. (1920), Beyond the pleasure principle. *Standard Edition*, 18:7–64. London: Hogarth Press, 1955.

Hotaling, G. T. & Sugarman, D. B. (1990), A risk marker analysis of assaulted wives. *J. Family Violence*, 5:1–13.

Kopp, S. (1978), *An End to Innocence*. New York: Macmillan.

Levenson, E. (1972), *The Fallacy of Understanding*. New York: Basic Books.

Mitchell, S. (1993), *Hope and Dread in Psychoanalysis*. New York: Basic Books.

Ogden, T. (1983), The concept of internal object relations. In: *Fairbairn and the Origins of Object Relations*, ed. J. Grotstein & D. Rinsley. New York: Guilford, 1994, pp. 88–111.

Roth, P. (1969), *Portnoy's Complaint*. New York: Random House.

Rubens, R. (1984), The meaning of structure in Fairbairn. *Internat. Rev. Psycho-Anal.*, 11:429–440.

——— (1996), The unique origins of Fairbairn's theories. *Psychoanal. Dial.*, 6:413–435.

Sass, I. & Wolfolk, R. (1988), Psychoanalysis and the hermeneutic turn: A critique of narrative truth and historical truth. *J. Amer. Psychoanal. Assn.*, 36:429–454.

Stark, M. (1994), *Working with Resistance*. Northvale, NJ: Aronson.

14

Object Construction, Object Sorting, and Object Exclusion
Implications of Family and Marital Therapy for Object Relations Theory

David E. Scharff

Fairbairn put the need for relationships throughout life at the center of development. He wrote that infants, in the face of the intrinsic need for relationships and of inevitable disappointment with them, take in the experience with the object and then split off and repress the intolerable parts of painful or bad aspects. Sorting of experience leads to the structuring of mind. Thus, introjection is the hallmark of Fairbairn's (1944, 1956) model, in contrast to Klein's (1975a, b) model, which emphasizes projective processes, on ridding the self of the excesses of drive derivatives. In Fairbairn's (1951, 1963) model, however, the introjection of good experience comes as a kind of afterthought: good objects are introjected only to compensate for bad. Klein (1946) disagreed with Fairbairn about the primacy of the introjection of good experience. She thought that, under the influence of the life instinct, good experience is also taken in from the beginning. Infant research has demonstrated that she was right that infants, and all of us, take in good and bad experience, not because of the life and death instincts, but simply because we are built to take in all kinds of experience as we relate in order to provide the building blocks for psychic structure, which must always be fully informed by a sense of the realities of all aspects of external experience. Fairbairn's student J. D. Sutherland (1994) wrote that it is loving and being loved which are primary and that the human organism grows naturally through the construction of progressively integrated and complex organizations of the self in relation to others. In the service of this growth, children and adults do more than simply introject or project; they take in experience, which they use as material to construct an inner world, and they then actively seek to realize that inner world in the outer world both through interaction and through internal modification of their selves. In this process, each individual constructs relations with the outer world in a way that will give realization to the developing self and to the inner relations between object and self.

Henry Dicks (1967) was the first to apply Fairbairn's work systematically to marriage, much as Bion had applied Klein and Freud to nonfamily groups in the 1950s. Using his original amalgam of Fairbairn's system of endopsychic organization and Klein's concept of projective identification as his explanatory vehicle, Dicks described the reciprocity of object relations in marital partners. He detailed the way couples find their repressed libidinal and antilibidinal objects in each other, recover lost parts of themselves through the return of the repressed in the marital relationship, and share in the creation of a new "joint marital personality" belonging to the relationship the couple shared rather than to either partner individually. Dicks synthesized the contributions of Fairbairn and Klein to yield a psychology of human interaction, an endeavor still continued at a few places, including the Tavistock Marital Studies Institute, the Tavistock Clinic, and the Scottish Institute of Human Relations in Great Britain, the relational track of the New York University Postdoctoral Program in Psychotherapy and Psychoanalysis, and the International Institute of Object Relations Therapy in Washington, DC. Family studies and family therapy enlarged the laboratory both for the study of intimate human interaction and the effect it has on the growth of the individual throughout life and for the study of the model that Dicks's work began.

Despite his discovery of the importance of relationships throughout life, Fairbairn focused on the intrapsychic level, in particular on the return of the repressed bad object (Fairbairn, 1943), which is split off and repressed early in life and is reorganized in the oedipal phase (Fairbairn, 1944). And he went much further. The superego, Fairbairn (1956) thought, is a function rather than a specific structure. It consists of suborganizations of ego and object coming together—the internal saboteur, the antilibidinal object, and the ideal object, which work together as combined internal critic and guide. He continued to develop this concept until he got it the way he wanted it late in his life (Fairbairn, 1963).

In describing this set of combined functions, he was describing more than the working together of subunits of the self. The functioning unit also has new qualities, formed by what I call object construction, a process that is intrinsic to the continuing process of self-modification that is central to emotional growth. The concept of object construction calls for us to take more into account than the return of repressed bad objects: It is a concept built first on the internalization of new *external* objects, the continual capacity to blend them with old internal objects to make new *internal* objects, and finally the reconfiguring of the self in relationship to these new internal objects. It is a process that goes on throughout life.

The Importance of Introjection

Fairbairn taught that introjection was central in individual development from the beginning of life. With the contribution of Dicks and others, we can now explore its role later in the life cycle, where we can see that introjection is fundamental to adult development, too. Internal object development continues in mate selection, marital adjustment, the birth of children, and their development through various stages including leaving home, divorce, illness, and death.

We can now see from Dicks's (1967) work on marriage, from study of the family (Scharff and Scharff, 1987), from experience in group therapy (Bion, 1961; Pines, 1983), from the study of introjective identification (Scharff, 1992), and from the accumulated experience of psychoanalysis and psychoanalytic therapy that the internalization of new experience and the building of new internal objects occur throughout life. Object construction is fundamental to the process through which the self develops cohesion and vitality, maintains its sense of self, and grows in complexity over time.

In this paper I explore the role of new internal objects throughout life, and I offer an illustration of how the conjoint therapies teach us about that. I hope to show that the findings of this exploration fundamentally alter basic analytic theory in ways that Fairbairn partly foresaw but that we can now articulate more fully.

Let us return to Dicks's starting point, the study of marriage. Whether to get married and whom to marry are usually the defining decisions of adult development. The choice not to have a partner is as defining as the choice of a particular mate, for each road determines the kind of object the self will meet in intimate encounters and the subsequent path of maturation. I am including here the choice of partner and patterns of partnering for homosexual couples. Having children and the growth of those children are similarly intricately interwoven with a person's continued development. Spouse and children provide the material for new objects, whose internal shapes and contours change over time in concert with the changes in the external object. The internal objects also change in ways determined by internal forces, by the influence of already existing aspects of self and object.

One implication of this point is that oedipal development need not be viewed as the fulcrum of development, as ego psychology has taught. Oedipal delineation was important historically because it was the stage in which Freud (1923) first studied the internalization of new objects, where he also saw the implications for the reorganization of the ego or self. (In doing so, he contributed the first major study in the object relations literature, building on his earlier work on internalization and mourning [Freud, 1917].) The literature on oedipal development remains a prototype of the birth and reorganization of new objects.

Object relations theorists, on the other hand, have been imperfectly understood to focus on infancy as the center of development and of introjection of new objects. But neither the oedipal era nor infancy is uniquely a stage in which new objects are constructed out of a blend of introjection and internal modification, and neither stands alone as the theoretical center of development.

Rather, we can now say that emotional development always centers on the capacity of each person to keep making internal objects throughout life, beginning in infancy, where the capacity is first exercised and where the first "working models" of self and other are formed (Bowlby, 1969). The fundamental human propensity to keep at it, to keep internalizing experience, and therefore to keep taking in and building new internal objects—this is the central organizing principle. The taking in and constructing of new internal objects happens at every major developmental step. Each time the new object comes with a set of affects that are its emotional markers and that provide meaning to the relationship. We are all familiar with falling in love at the birth of a new internal object and grieving at the loss of an important object. These are affective markers for the transformation of external objects into internal objects and for the loss of the external person who has been taken in as an internal object. These affective events are subjectively experienced, and they can also be observed by outsiders.

But we have to move beyond noting the affective markers that help identify the quality of internal objects if we are going to understand this process. The birth of internal objects follows interactions between a person and his or her external objects, and it is this interaction—this relationship—that is internalized. Internalizing bad objects is characterized by such affects as fear, disappointment, anxiety, and anger, which accompany interactions of rejection, neglect, and persecution. But a principal condition for the internalization of good objects is that the process should be mutual. Fairbairn (1941) taught us that we all want to be loved by someone who loves us in return. This is the colloquial translation of Fairbairn's dictum: "The object in which the individual is incorporated is incorporated in the individual" (pp. 42–43). This is to say, we look for an object in which to be incorporated, as in Bion's (1967) model of container–contained, but we also take that very process back inside us as a mainstay of our own makeup. Throughout life we look for objects to introject that feel to us as though they also contain us through their regard for us. Only then can we feel understood, loved, and valued—or "held" in Winnicott's (1960) description of the mother holding the baby. Only then do we feel that life has meaning. And to the extent that we take in objects who seem to misunderstand us, we feel hurt and diminished. These are the objects that transform the meaning of both outer and inner life experience for better or for worse.

Developmental Stages of Object Formation

We take in new objects throughout life, but we do so with the various wrinkles we are used to seeing at differing stages of the life cycle.

In infancy, the baby introjects objects on the basis of experience with mother, father, and a handful of other caretakers and siblings. The first introjections are especially powerful because they are nonverbal; because, being first, they have no competition; and because they are there to influence the formation of all later ones. I want to emphasize that the mother is most often *not* the only person taken in. There is usually a father or someone who has a fatherlike presence. Whenever there are others, they are also extremely important, which leads to my next point about the internal couple.

Soon, and certainly by seven or eight months, children are cognizant of the relationship of their external objects to each other (Abelin, 1971, 1975). What we call the internal couple is an internalization of the experience with the two parents as they love, fight, cooperate, and form a tantalizing and reassuring combined object for the child. Whereas Klein (1945) described a sexualized parental internal couple, other "internal couples" are formed out of the unit between a parent and one of the child's siblings—say, a mother and older brother, when they are inter- acting to draw attention from the young child or when they are taking care of the toddler—or equally between the mother and a younger sibling in the case of two- or three-year-olds who can- not have their former ready access to the mother. Another cou- ple might comprise a parent and a grandparent who share care and concern for the child.

Fairbairn (1944) was the first to suggest that between three and five years of age, oedipal reorganization allows for the sort- ing and sifting of images, the reorganization of ambivalence about each individual object relationship through splitting and reassignment of good and bad, usually along sexual lines. But he did not take into account the influence of the external objects' relationships to each other, something Freud noticed in passing, Klein (1945) noted in infancy, and that information from family therapy (Scharff and Scharff, 1987) now emphasizes. We can now say that the actual treatment of the child by real external objects and, for this discussion, especially the quality of the par- ents' relationship to each other, are the major influences on chil- dren's oedipal reorganization of their internal objects and selves.

Object Sorting: The Internal Family and Internal Groups

The child's relating to the various internal couples leads to an internalization of a family group made up of all combinations of the internal couples, modified, reduced, and elaborated to yield an internal organization and representation that is more than the sum of its parts. The larger group—containing all the sub-groups and representations of all the important external objects individually and in relationship—cannot be represented by the relatively simple structures we call internal objects or even by internal couples. The internal family and the internal group is an exceedingly complex structure that requires us to conceive of internal object organization in a significantly modified way that goes beyond any current psychoanalytic conceptualization. It draws on Nelson and Greundel's (1981) concept of Generalized Event Structures—the way an infant represents a group of similar, repeated events so as to build cognitive and emotional expectations, and Stern's (1985) Representations of Interactions that have been Generalized (RIGs) from a series of interactions. For instance, Stern describes the way a baby uses many encounters with its mother's face to construct a generalized image that the mother may never have actually presented but that is the infant's guide to understanding the many expressions she does present.

Building an internal family and an internal group relies on an analogous generalizing process applied to object construction and object sorting. Requiring a barely tolerable complexity of thought, experience with a group of people seems to be beyond the conceptual organizing ability of individuals most of the time. To solve this conceptual difficulty, people—not only small children but the rest of us too—interpret experience as though it were located in individual internal objects. Instead of feeling loved or unloved by the group as a whole, the child, often *constructing* an internal object relationship that represents experience with the group, reads the experience as though it were located in one object. Then the child searches for an external object who best fits this relationship between self and object, usually distorting its experience with that external person by generalizing it and attempting to pin the experience with the group on one object. In the process, the child substitutes an individual object for a group object. Here the child uses splitting as

Fairbairn described it, combined with object sorting to reorder its experience. For instance, just as bad experience is split and sorted onto one parent and good experience onto another, so experience with a complex group is imposed on individual objects and split among them. But it is also important to recognize that through generalizing and sorting, the child is essentially constructing fundamentally new objects in its internal world. The child does not merely split actual experience but actually makes up new versions of experience, which it *imposes* on the outer world but then *experiences* them as coming from outside. This description of the child's process also gives us new ideas for projective identification as a mode for the solution of difficulty in constructing internal objects that adequately resonate with external experience.

This process involves active construction in the inner world and employs a series of operations including splitting, object relations sorting of experience, and putting together new constructions. It is more than a cut-and-paste operation; new bits are also taken in from the outside world, and perhaps new things are added with which the child has little actual experience but that come from such precursors as stories that speak to an inner need. The child cannot keep in mind the complexity of large-scale, complex, group-level experience and resorts to sorting and coding, understanding, and storing. I emphasize that these are not just children who cannot "understand" group level experience and who focus on individuals in groups as the source of meaning. In families, this process accounts for the assignment of a family scapegoat, hero, or dependency object. Developmentally, the process begins in the early years at home in the extension from individual to family group experience, and it takes a developmental leap when the child goes to school and experiences a radically widening group there.

Beyond the concept of processing group experience through assignment to individual inner objects, the point to keep in mind is this: as children move from family to school and the wider world, they are also making new objects, taking in experience with teachers and other children as friends, competitors, and foes. There are new individual objects and new levels of object construction, such as the group, that must be internalized and built. Although the new objects are built on the model of earlier objects, they are also radically different. The process of understanding the new objects involves new levels of complexity and new organizational principles which do not simply flow from early object experience. The new object relations can modify early experience fundamentally, making it seem better or worse retrospectively, or they may maintain and confirm early internal objects while adding to them. The new objects are built through new principles of organization, like the ones involved in internalizing the family group, ones that require new complexity in brain development and social understanding.

At each major developmental stage, new objects are introduced. Going to school means the acquisition of teachers and peers as new external and internal objects. Children now oscillate between relations with one or two friends and with groups. Adolescence means further developments in the youngster's capacity to relate to groups and new subtlety in the move from dyadic and triadic relationships to larger groups, as the adolescent attaches to new peers, separates from incestuous internal objects, experiences the gradual sexualization of relationship between self and others, and develops a sense of the future for the self in object relationships. The internalization of new kinds of objects is spurred by sexual and intellectual development and the capacity to conceptualize and choose among alternative paths that may shift in direction and meaning every few days. As all these changes occur, teenagers also develop a new and ever more subtle ability to move between pairing and peering, to being intimate with one or two others and yet a functioning part of the wider group and even the wider society. They develop the sense that the intimate relationships remain with them when they are in the group and that the group provides an outer and inner context for the dyads and triads.

Object Exclusion

Another principle of object construction is emphasized in adolescence: the process of object exclusion. The principle of keeping parents out of the adolescent's life and mind may overlap
with installing them as bad objects, but it is not synonymous
with it. The process of rejecting parents, of making it clear that
there is internal territory parents should not inhabit as internal
objects, is a fundamental part of object sorting and construction
which cannot be fully subsumed by the notion of bad-object
construction, for it has more to do with clearing out internal
space for the construction of new objects and new aspects of the
self when the parental objects are felt to be crowding the
teenager's internal world.

The same developmental principles apply to the acquisition
of new objects in adult partnerships, most importantly in marriage and in the birth of children, who become new objects with
an impact that dramatically reorganizes the parents' sense of
themselves. The growth and eventual attenuation of these relationships when children leave home, the advent of grandchil-
dren as additional new objects, are all events of the life cycle
which elaborate on the processes we have been discussing.

The following example illustrates the reorganization of an
adult's internal family at the birth of a child. Mr. C was in his
mid-40s when his second wife unexpectedly became pregnant.
Stricken with fear, he became significantly depressed. He had
been reluctant to have a child with his second wife and had
withdrawn from her sexually out of a sense of loyalty to the
daughters of his first marriage and out of guilt and loyalty for
the damage he had done in sexually betraying his first wife
when he left her for the second wife. After significant work that
highlighted the way he hung on to the old objects as painful
ghosts of lost opportunity, the birth of the new baby offered him
a new object and new opportunity. This son, his first, became a
new focus and source of joy, offered him a sense of repair, and
gave him a reason to let go of the guilty bond to the first wife

and finally attach to the second wife in a new way, which now, finally, came to include a sexual attachment. The acceptance of a new external object and the building of new aspects of the self around it spurred a major transformation of Mr. C's self and, in consequence, of several of his internal and external relationships.

The second and more extensive example focuses on the finding of a mate and the way this new object gives meaning to the world of previous internal objects while at the same time, it represents new possibilities for the self and its object relations. This example illustrates some of the processes involved in the birth of new objects: the resorting of old object experiences; the repair of trauma and loss; the continuation of what has been valued while keeping it safe from the damage of everyday life, from the return of repressed bad objects, and from the damage of the external object itself. It demonstrates the gamut of processes I have described: refinding of old objects, object sorting, object construction, object exclusion, and indirectly, the process of locating painful group experience in a single individual.

William and Janis, a young black couple, were living together when they sought therapy for sexual difficulties. They planned to be married when they graduated from college but postponed their wedding when Janis told William she was not enjoying sex. When I saw them for a consultation, they had seen a therapist six times. Janis told me, "The act itself was fine, but getting me to want to participate was the problem." William was upset not only because she did not enjoy sex, but also because he felt deceived that she had not told him before, since he felt that they should be able to work things out if he knew about them. She said, "I didn't want to hurt him. Something like that can really damage a male's perspective on himself, and I thought I could make things better on my own. But as we got closer to getting married, I got more frightened. After a year passed and we were having sex less, I felt I had to tell him."

Janis said that they didn't communicate well and that she felt no one, not even William, really understood her. So he would become mad at her and not tell her, for instance when she pushed him to buy a car they did not really need. On another occasion, William took her shopping for groceries when she had spent all her own money shopping. When she asked for a soda, he said no, considering that a luxury. She couldn't believe he would say no to her, while he felt he was being reasonable. "I wasn't being mean. I was only saying no because it needed to be said."

Janis was the middle of three children; both brothers had been murdered. Her older brother was an outstanding young man, full of good and like a father to her. He was gunned down without cause in a neighborhood shooting. Her younger brother was killed after dropping out of school and selling drugs in the wake of the older brother's death. The older brother had been "her only positive male role model." When she talked about this brother, she cried and looked at William to ask if he understood what her brother had meant to her. Perhaps she had never told him. He said quietly that he understood.

Janis's father was an alcoholic, and her mother left him, taking four-year-old Janis with her. Her grandmother, also an alcoholic, raised her while her mother worked. She never experienced any direct abuse, but there had been arguing and violence among many drunken adults in the household. Janis focused on the disappointment she had experienced from her father, who repeatedly promised to help but never showed up. On one occasion, after her older brother's death, he did come but was so drunk that her younger brother had said, "I wish he hadn't even come. He's such a disappointment." Janis said, "If he had been the man, my younger brother might not have been dead. But to say he'll help, and then show up like that! Get out'a here! I never want to see him again." While she said this, I could feel the contrast between the father who "was not the man" and William, who she knew would stand by her.

William's father was not an alcoholic, but he was a perfectionist and the son of an alcoholic. When William was young, his father left William with his alcoholic mother and two younger brothers. Later, when William and his brothers briefly lived with the father, there was some physical abuse, most of it directed at the brothers, whom he tried to protect. Mostly, he took care of his mother and, in his teen years, supported the family.

By now I had a sense of their relational pattern: William, offering to repair her traumatized family, was the older brother Janis had lost. She was the mother and brothers he longed to care for. Therefore, he could hardly tolerate saying no to her. Both Janis and William longed for him to be a better father than either had had, to repair old objects and damage to their selves, and they wanted to form a couple that would compensate for their devastated internal couples. Although we had not yet discussed sex beyond the initial statement of difficulty, I began to see why sex would be so threatening to Janis: penetration threatened the return of the repressed persecuting and abandoning object, which, in fantasy, she split into the genitals.

Now Janis said that she had never really liked sex. It had been easier to go along with it in the beginning, when she and William had made love as often as every day or two. All her previous sexual relationships had made her feel pressured and abused. The boyfriend immediately preceding William had forced sex on her and then tried to persuade her that he had not, thus leaving her confused and upset. From the beginning, William was different, gentle and caring. Even so, as in all her previous relationships, she soon became reluctant about sex, which decreased in frequency to about once a month. At this point, she felt that he had increased the sexual pressure on her, whereas William felt there was too little sex. Once they began a sexual encounter, however, Janis felt that it always went well. When they did make love, she enjoyed it. He was a good lover but had not understood why sex had become so infrequent until she finally told him her difficulty.

William had had no previous difficulty with sex, but he had never had a girlfriend he actually cared for before, so his pattern was sex without intimacy or commitment—a pattern that seemed to have stopped short of exploitation but had nevertheless split off caring from sex.

I now said that the pattern in sex was that Janis felt she had to say no to protect herself from damage and that men would not let her. In the relationship generally, however, she pressured William not to say "no" feeling that he would be denying her. But then she was afraid she had damaged him because she wanted him to stand up to her to rein her in. She agreed: "I need him to say no or I'll go broke. And the funny thing is, I can't say no to my mother. She used my credit card and ran up a lot of debt that I have to pay because I couldn't say, 'You can't do that, Ma.'" "That's right," said William. "She has the same thing with her mother that I have with Janis. I tell her, 'You just have to say no to her,' but she has a lot of trouble doing it."

As we closed the consultation, I asked about their progress in therapy. When their therapist had provided reassurance along with understanding of their situation, Janis had experienced a sexual warming toward William. Their description of the therapy and the sexual improvement led me to think it was principally the therapist's provision of a firm, benign holding that had allowed the growth of a new physical intimacy, new to both partners. Janis had never before experienced desire that could be satisfied without fear, and William had never experienced sexual intimacy integrated with a caring relationship.

Discussion

In this interview we can see most of the elements of object relating and its effect on the self which I have discussed. To begin with the well-tried concepts, we can see splitting and the return of the repressed as both Janis and William locate the bad object in fathers and try to contain and repair it there. We can see that they share the oedipal reorganization that locates badness in the father, although Janis also tries to find the image of her lost older brother in William, the brother who made up for her alcoholic and abandoning father. In locating badness in the fathers and in sexual penetration of genital interaction (through the mechanism of shared projective identification), they spare their mothers, who are seen as good even if damaged. I did not even learn about Janis's mother's invasion of her finances until close to the end of the interview.

But William is not merely a replacement and repair for the lost bad object, enhanced through sorting of old part-objects. He is also a new independent object for Janis. Rather than seeing him as a replacement whose image is grafted onto the lost internal object, we can see him as a new object, whose importance is enhanced and given meaning from the many connections to her group of inner objects, reviving some, repairing some, extending some, and helping to exclude others. He becomes a new object that moves to the center of her galaxy of internal objects, providing a new organizational center to her internal relationships. In the process of relating to him as a new external object, she seeks to redefine aspects of her self, to modulate her excessive spending and neediness, for instance. She wants to become a better, less impulsive, and less needy person, more easily satisfied, more giving instead of grasping. Janis has had painful experiences, not only with her father but with most of the people in her family group certainly including her mother. To deal with her experience, she has generalized the bad experience and located it in her father, whom she now consciously tries to exclude as an object while locating the good experience in her dead brother. When she finds a new object in William, she seeks also to solve the painful experience with her whole family group by locating good family experience in him individually and by building a new version of her internal couple, one she has never experienced before. Membership in an external couple which gives her a new internal object and new internal couple offers to let her grow new aspects of her self, ones that ambivalently support William's efforts to "say no because it needs to be said." Through all of this we can see the process of object sorting, object construction, and object exclusion along with their accompanying effects on the self.

William, in turn, is seeking an external object to whom he can offer repair in order to repair damaged inner objects and build esteem for a shaky self. He treats Janis as a reedition of his internal object, which was damaged by abuse and alcoholism in his family, and fears the return of the repressed bad father and alcoholic, irrepressible mother. But Janis has also become a new object for him, although one whose contours are less clearly sketched in this interview as he waits in the shadows behind her more dramatic presentation. Dealing with her weakness, he grapples with the defects he sees in his own personality: the tendency to cling to her, which compels him to give in to her demands when firm limit setting would serve them both better. He searches for an object that can be made ideal both through his caretaking and his limit setting. Janis is unlike any previous object he has had. He is searching for a new self and sorting out bits of himself in relation to the new internal object he is attempting to construct by relating to her. He shares an unconscious pattern with Janis in the wish to exclude his father as an object and wanting to build a new self to replace him and a new external and internal couple to replace the disasterous one he experienced and still carries inside. In this interview, we see him join with Janis to construct a self in relation to a newly constructed object and a new internal couple while sorting other aspects of internal objects and excluding a bad-object father and disappointing aspects of his alcoholic mother. In both partners, we can get a shadowy idea of the group issues through an understanding of the way they use each other as primary objects to repair their wider family group. The group situation is too complex to be held in mind or solved, so they each condense group matters into the relationship with each other where they hope to solve everything about their lives. In summary, as we examine the situation William and Janis present, we begin to see how self-definition and growth are intrinsically tied to object choice, object sorting, object exclusion, object construction, and object relating.

Conclusion

Focusing on the relatively well-explored areas of infancy, young childhood, and adolescence, we have undervalued the possibilities of new object relating throughout the life cycle. As psychoanalysts and individual therapists, we must take far greater account of the evolving processes of object relating, object sorting, object construction, and object exclusion and the way these are intrinsic to the continual remodeling of the self, a process that persists into adulthood and throughout life and that goes on at the time of any therapy, whether during adulthood or childhood. *Developmentally we can note that when the infant is first building its world of internal objects, it is fundamentally dependent on the mother and father to take the infant in as a new object for themselves. That they build a new object is a requirement for infants' feeling loved and building a positive inner object world themselves.*

The process of object and self-construction that I describe here is, of course, the same process that makes up the therapist–patient relationship. We therapists are also the material out of which our patients make their new objects, the new material of their internal worlds—as they are new material of ours. Henry Dicks's (1967) joint marital personality, Thomas Ogden's (1994) concept of the "analytic third," and Christopher Bollas's (1992) concept of genera—the new constructions jointly made by analyst and patient—refer to versions of a shared venture that has the power to offer new internal objects to both partners in the two intimate venues of marriage and the therapeutic relationship. As therapists, we offer ourselves as partners in a life-sustaining and life-changing process, one in which we cannot help being modified too. We cannot avoid taking our patients into ourselves—sometimes more, sometimes less—and in the process they take up residence as denizens of our own internal worlds.

The process of therapy begins, as Fairbairn (1958) said, with an object relationship. He wrote:

In my own opinion, the really decisive factor is the relationship of the patient to the analyst, and it is upon this relationship that the other factors. . . . depend not only for their effectiveness, but for their very existence, since in the absence of a therapeutic relationship with the analyst, they simply do not occur [pp. 82–83].

We can expand Fairbairn's statement with another of his ideas: that the therapeutic relationship is the central factor in treatment because it is internalized as a new internal object organization. As is always the case, the internalizing of one intimate relationship reorganizes the entire internal world. This fundamental process occurs at any age. We take advantage of it to offer something new to the patient. When the new external relationship becomes a new internal-object relationship, the patient is fundamentally changed. In any such encounter, we ourselves cannot remain as we were before. In that relationship of mutual influence lies the hope for our selves and our patients.

References

Abelin, E. (1971), The role of the father in the separation-individuation process. In: *Separation-Individuation*, ed. J. B. McDevitt & C. F. Settlage. New York: International Universities Press, pp. 229–252.

——— (1975), Some further observations and comments on the earliest role of the father. *Internat. J. Psycho-Anal.*, 56:293–302.

Bion, W. (1961), *Experiences in Groups*. London: Tavistock.

——— (1967), *Second Thoughts*. London: Heinemann.

Bollas, C. (1992), *Being a Character*. New York: Hill & Wang.

Bowlby, J. (1969), *Attachment and Loss, Vol. 1*. London: Hogarth Press.

Dicks, H. V. (1967), *Marital Tensions*. London: Routledge & Kegan Paul.

Fairbairn, W. R. D. (1941), A revised psychopathology of the psychoses and psychoneuroses. In: *Psychoanalytic Studies of the Personality*. London: Routledge & Kegan Paul, 1952, pp. 28–58.

——— (1943), The repression and return of bad objects (with special reference to the "war neuroses"). In: *Psychoanalytic Studies of the Personality*. London: Routledge & Kegan Paul, 1952, pp. 59–81.

——— (1944), Endopsychic structure considered in terms of object-relationships. In: *Psychoanalytic Studies of the Personality*. London: Routledge & Kegan Paul, 1952, pp. 82–136.

———— (1952), *Psychoanalytic Studies of the Personality*. London: Routledge & Kegan Paul, 1952.

———— (1956), Reevaluating some basic concepts. In: *From Instinct to Self, Vol. 1*, ed. D. E. Scharff & E. F. Birtles. Northvale, NJ: Aronson, 1994, pp. 129–138.

———— (1958), On the nature and aims of psychoanalysis. In: *From Instinct to Self, Vol. 1*, ed. D. E. Scharff & E. F. Birtles. Northvale, NJ: Aronson, 1994, pp. 74–92.

———— (1963), An object relations theory of the personality. In: *From Instinct to Self, Vol. 1*, ed. D. E. Scharff & E. F. Birtles. Northvale, NJ: Aronson, 1994, pp. 155–156.

Freud, S. (1917), Mourning and melancholia. *Standard Edition*, 14:243–258. London: Hogarth Press, 1957.

———— (1923), The ego and the id. *Standard Edition*, 19:12–59. London: Hogarth Press, 1961.

Klein, M. (1945), The Oedipus complex in the light of early anxieties. In: *Love, Guilt and Reparation and Other Works: 1921–1945*. London: Hogarth Press, 1975, pp. 370–419.

———— (1946), Notes on some schizoid mechanisms. In: *Envy and Gratitude and Other Works: 1946–1963*. London: Hogarth Press, 1975, pp. 1–24.

———— (1975a), *Love, Guilt and Reparation & Other Works: 1921–1945*. London: Hogarth Press.

———— (1975b), *Envy and Gratitude and Other Works: 1946–1963*. London: Hogarth Press.

Nelson, K. & Greundel, J. M. (1981), Generalized event representation: Basic building blocks of cognitive development. In: *Advances in Developmental Psychology, Vol. 1*, ed. M. E. Lamb & A. L. Brown Hillsdale, NJ: Lawrence Erlbaum Associates.

Ogden, T. (1994), *Subjects of Analysis*. Northvale, NJ: Aronson.

Pines, M., ed. (1983), *The Evolution of Group Analysis*. London: Routledge & Kegan Paul.

Scharff, D. E. & Scharff, J. S. (1987), *Object Relations Family Therapy*. Northvale, NJ: Aronson.

Scharff, J. S. (1992), *Projective and Introjective Identification and the Use of the Therapist's Self*. Northvale NJ: Aronson.

Stern, D. N. (1985), *The Interpersonal World of the Infant*. New York: Basic Books.

Sutherland, J. D. (1994), *The Autonomous Self*, ed. J. S. Scharff. Northvale, NJ: Aronson.

Winnicott, D. W. (1960), The theory of the parent–infant relationship. *Internat. J. Psycho-Anal.*, 41:585–595.

Index